1869 — The Government of Canada buys Rupert's Land from the Hudson's Bay Company. Later that year, Riel leads a Métis uprising in Manitoba.

The North West Mounted Police — 1873 swear in their first recruits.

1876 — Canada passes its first Indian Act.

The second Métis uprising is crushed — 1885 in Saskatchewan, and Riel is hung for treason. Later that year, the last spike is driven to complete the CPR across Canada.

1891 — Death of Sir John A. Macdonald, Canada's first Prime Minister.

Canada sends troops to help — 1899 Britain fight the Boers in South Africa.

1913 — 400 870 immigrants arrive, setting an all-time record for Canada.

Canada participates in World War I. — 1914-1918

1918 — Canadian women win the right to vote in federal elections.

The Balfour Report declares that — 1926 Canada is independent of Britain and no longer a colony.

1929-1939 — Canada is held in the grip of the Great Depression.

Canada fights in World War II. — 1939-1945

1947 — The Leduc oil fields are discovered near Edmonton, Alberta.

Newfoundland enters Confederation — 1949 as Canada's tenth province.

1958 — John Diefenbaker wins the biggest margin of victory ever recorded in a Canadian federal election.

Canada and the United States — 1959 complete the St. Lawrence Seaway project.

1965 — Canada adopts a new flag, featuring a Maple Leaf design.

Canada celebrates its Centennial — 1967 with ''Expo '67''.

1968 — René Lévesque forms the Parti Québécois, whose goal is to make Quebec an independant country.

The Official Languages Act makes — 1969 Canada officially bilingual.

1976 — Canada hosts the Summer Olympic Games.

CALL US CANADIANS

Canadian Studies Program

Call Us Canadians
I. L. Martinello
Project Consultant: Allan S. Evans

North American Neighbours
Allan S. Evans
Riley Moynes

Many Cultures Many Heritages
Norman Sheffe, General Editor

Canada: Towards Tomorrow
Allan S. Evans
Lawrence Diachun

Front and Back Covers: Indian Lazystitch beadwork horse decoration. Courtesy of the Royal Ontario Museum, Toronto

CALL US CANADIANS

I. L. MARTINELLO
Assistant Head of History
Emery Collegiate Institute
Toronto

Project Consultant
ALLAN S. EVANS
Head of History
Emery Collegiate Institute
Toronto

McGraw-Hill Ryerson Limited
Toronto, Montreal, New York, London, Sydney,
Johannesburg, Mexico, Panama, Auckland,
Düsseldorf, Kuala Lumpur, New Delhi, São Paulo

Call Us Canadians

ISBN 0-07-082296-4

Printed and bound in Canada

7 8 9 0 D 5 4 3 2

Table of Contents

Acknowledgements

Photographs
p. 17: Public Archives Canada—C 29396. p. 23: Public Archives Canada—C 69767. p. 24: Public Archives Canada—C 73635. p. 26: Public Archives Canada—C 73382. p. 29: Public Archives Canada—C 73660. p. 30: Public Archives of Ontario. p. 35: both photos, Public Archives of Ontario. p. 37: Public Archives Canada—PA 13110. p. 38: both photos Courtesy of Northway Survey Corporation Limited, Toronto. p. 39: Ontario Ministry of the Environment, Air Resources Branch. p. 40: Toronto Transit Commission. p. 41: Applied Photography Ltd. p. 43: National Film Board Photothèque. p. 45: Public Archives Canada—PA 29173. p. 58: Public Archives Canada. centre—C 70306; left—C 70305; bottom—C 70307. p. 59: Public Archives Canada. top—C 5749; bottom—C 5407. p. 63: Public Archives Canada. top left—PA 20000; centre—C 69769. p. 64: Public Archives Canada. top—C 69760; bottom—C 12235. p. 65: Public Archives Canada—C 70293. p. 67: Public Archives Canada. top—C 69757; left—C 69758; right—C 69759. p. 68: Public Archives Canada. top—C 69766; bottom—C 24277. p. 70: Public Archives Canada. top—C 69796; left—C 69795; right—C 69797. p. 71: Public Archives Canada. top—C 70301; bottom—C 69786. p. 72: Public Archives Canada—C 73662. p. 73: Public Archives Canada. top—C 69799. p. 80, bottom: Public Archives Canada—C 70295. p. 81: Public Archives Canada. top—C 30174; bottom—C 30923. p. 82: Public Archives Canada—C 3805. p. 83: Public Archives Canada—C 3806. p. 84: Public Archives Canada—C 70288. p. 86: Public Archives Canada. left—C 21949; right—C 21950. p. 87: Public Archives Canada—C 37121. p. 89: Public Archives Canada—PA 48236. p. 92: Public Archives Canada—C 37117. p. 95: Public Archives Canada—C 4462. pp. 111-12: all three photos Courtesy of the Ksan Association, Hazelton, B.C. p. 120: Ontario Ministry of Industry and Tourism. p. 127: Public Archives Canada—C 10489. p. 131: Public Archives Canada—C 73678. p. 133: Public Archives Canada. top—C 69780; bottom—C 69777. p. 137: Public Archives Canada—C 9711. p. 141: Gouvernement du Québec, gracieuseté de la Direction Générale du Tourisme. p. 143: Public Archives Canada—C 11232. p. 145: Public Archives Canada. left—C 73397; right—C 73398. p. 149, left: Archives Nationales du Québec, collection Initiale. p. 150: Public Archives Canada—C 69560. p. 154: Public Archives Canada—C 73648. p. 155: Public Archives Canada. top—C 69644; bottom—C 73394. p. 171: Courtesy Nova Scotia Museum. p. 174: Public Archives Canada—C 73449. p. 175: Public Archives Canada—C 11092. p. 181: Public Archives Canada—C 2381. top right—C 69139. p. 183: Public Archives Canada—C 73435. p. 185: Public Archives Canada—C 73549. p. 186: Courtesy of the Public Archives of Ontario. p. 189, top: Royal Ontario Museum, Toronto; bottom: Public Archives Canada—PA 40744. p. 191: Public Archives Canada: top left—C 73696; bottom left— C 73535; right—C 73536. p. 192: Public Archives Canada—C 73419. p. 194: Public Archives Canada—C 69849. p. 195: Public Archives of Ontario. p. 197: Public Archives Canada—C 44633. p. 198: Public Archives Canada—C 73650. p. 200: Public Archives Canada—C 8205. p. 202: Public Archives Canada—C 70258. p. 205: Public Archives Canada—C 73663. p. 207: Public Archives Canada—C 13969. p. 213: Public Archives Canada—C 13974. p. 214: Public Archives Canada—C 4743. p. 217: Public Archives Canada—PA 30820. p. 218: both photos, Public Archives of Ontario. p. 219: Public Archives Canada. p. 221: Public Archives Canada—C 52819. p. 226: Public Archives Canada, top—PA 10399; bottom—C 681. p. 227: Public Archives Canada, top—C 57175; bottom—PA 20914. p. 229: Public Archives Canada—C 24884. p. 240: Public Archives Canada—PA 17803. p. 251: National Film Board Photothèque. p. 258: Quebec Film Board. p. 271: Public Archives Canada—C 13369. p. 274: Public Archives Canada—C 4263. p. 275: Public Archives Canada—C 7761. p. 283: Public Archives Canada—C 73427. p. 291: Public Archives Canada—C 70238. p. 292: Public Archives Canada—C 70229. p. 297: Courtesy Ontario Ministry of Industry and Tourism. p. 300: Public Archives of Ontario. p. 302: Public Archives Canada—C 70234. p. 306: Courtesy Rous & Mann Press Ltd. p. 307: Public Archives of Ontario. p. 313: Public Archives Canada—C 70252. p. 314: Public Archives Canada—C 6440. p. 315: Public Archives Canada—C 18737. p. 319: Public Archives Canada. top—PA 26375; bottom—C 7299. p. 321: Public Archives of Ontario. p. 325: Public Archives Canada—C 2500. p. 331: Public Archives Canada—C 16408. p. 335: Public Archives Canada—C 1876. p. 336: Public Archives Canada. top—C 1875; bottom—C 2425. p. 337: Public Archives Canada—C 2424. p. 342: Public Archives Canada. top—C 15366; bottom—PA 1017. p. 344: Public Archives Canada—C 42420. p. 348: Public Archives of Ontario. p. 349: Public Archives Canada—C 9021. p. 354: Public Archives Canada—C 10687. p. 358: Public Archives Canada: C 69138. p. 361: Public Archives Canada—C 22884. p. 364: Public Archives Canada—PA 30212. p. 368: Public Archives Canada—C 22851. p. 370: Karen Kain, principal dancer, National Ballet of Canada. p. 372: top, Public Archives Canada—C 21562; bottom, Murray Mosher Photo Features Ltd. p. 373: bottom, Public Archives Canada—National Photography Collection.

Text
p. 48: Two stanzas of the poem "We and They" copyright 1926 by Rudyard Kipling from the book *Rudyard Kipling's Verse: Definitive Edition*. Reprinted by permission of Doubleday & Company, Inc., Macmillan Company of Canada Ltd. and Mrs. George Bambridge. p. 65: from Biggar, H. P., ed., *The Voyages of Jacques Cartier*, (Ottawa, King's Printer, 1924). Reproduced by permission of Information Canada. p. 82: from *The Story of Comock the Eskimo*, by Robert Carpenter, copyright Simon and Schuster, Inc., N.Y. p. 83-5: Maurice Metayers, trans., *I Nuligak* (Toronto: Peter Martin Associates, 1966). p. 89-91: reprinted by permission of The Canadian Publishers, McClelland and Stewart Limited, Toronto. p. 101: from *Indians of Canada*, by Diamond Jenness, National Museum of Canada, 1955, p. 253. Reproduced by permission of Information Canada. p. 105, bottom: from *Famous Indians*, by Ethel Brant Monture. © 1960 by Clarke, Irwin & Company Ltd. Used by permission. p. 108, top: Cardinal, Harold, *The Unjust Society*, Edmonton: Hurtig Publishers. p. 108, centre: The Pierre Berton Show (TV). p. 109, centre: *The Way of the Indian*, copyright Canadian Broadcasting Corporation 1963. CBC Learning Systems, P.O. Box 500, Station "A", Toronto, Ontario M5W 1E6. p. 109, bottom: Cardinal, Harold, *The Unjust Society*, Edmonton: Hurtig Publishers. Reproduced by permission of Information Canada. p. 131-2: Yves F. Zoltvany, ed., *The French Tradition in America* (New York; Harper and Row, 1969), pp. 104, 106. Reprinted by permission of the publisher. p. 140: RAPQ, 1930, pp. 143-148. pp. 151-2: From Census of Canada, vol. 4, p. 13. Reproduced by permission of Information Canada. pp. 187 & 197: from *A Gentlewoman in Upper Canada: The Journals of Anne Langton*, edited by H. H. Langton. © 1950 by Clarke, Irwin and Company Limited. Used by permission. pp. 177 & 193: from *The Diary of Captain John Thomson*, Public Archives of Ontario. p. 196: *Daily Life in Early Canada* by Raymond Douville and Jacques Casanova (Copyright ©1967 George Allen & Unwin Ltd) p. 206: Pritchett, J.P., *The Red River Valley 1811-1849*. (New Haven, Yale University Press, 1942.) p. 90. Reprinted by permission of the Carnegie Endowment for International Peace. p. 214: from *The Colonization of Western Canada*, by R. England, reprinted by permission of The Canadian Publishers, McClelland and Stewart Limited, Toronto. p. 217: from *Reminiscences of a Raconteur* by G. H. Ham, published by Musson Book Company, 1921. p. 219-220: *Maclean's* (April 1, 1922). pp. 222-225: *The Imperial Oil Review*. p. 231: excerpts from Dr. W. D. Reid's address entitled "Pre-Assembly Congress of the Presbyterian Church in Canada" (Toronto, 1913) pp. 119-126. pp. 233-236: By permission of the Stokoe Family and The Glenbow-Alberta Institute. p. 319: Wilson, Edmund, *O Canada*, Farrar, Straus & Giroux, Inc., N.Y., 1964. pp. 356, 357, 358, 359, 360, 362: selections from *The Backwoods of Canada* by Catherine Parr Traill reprinted by permission of The Canadian Publishers, McClelland & Stewart Limited, Toronto.

Preface

Call Us Canadians is a new kind of history text. It presents the diversity of the Canadian identity in four units recreating past societies, events and personalities. The text spans the story of our past from the time of our first immigrants, the Native People, to today's newcomers from every corner of the globe.

Each unit is self-contained, introduced by a short chapter which highlights the unit's theme. The themes basic to Canadian history—individualism, diversity, courage and compromise—are emphasized.

The first unit, "Social Sciences and the Community," introduces students to the skills of social scientists who piece together our picture of the past. As well, a lengthy chapter on an often ignored subject, local history, will provide students with the tools to study the history of their own community.

The Indians and Inuit are the subjects of Unit 2, "Canada's First People". The history of Canada's original people is discussed, beginning with early Indian cultures, through first contacts with European society, to their prospects and aspirations for the future.

Unit 3, "Patterns of Settlement," gives insight into the pioneering experiences of Canada's European settlers. Beginning with the first probings of the French explorers and settlers, the unit outlines Canada's social landscape. It retraces the steps of the Loyalists establishing the English foundations of Canada, and follows the Red River carts settling the West. The unit concludes with a chapter describing the patterns of immigration today.

The concluding unit, "Shaping the Canadian Character," examines great individuals, both men and women, and key events in the creation of Canada's social and political "personality".

Call us Canadians goes beyond a mere factual backdrop to Canada's history. It asks the students as involved Canadians to discover and participate in the richness of our past, brought to life through source materials, such as letters, diaries, stories and illustrations, which require each student to analyse, evaluate and interpret the information, and to make individual judgments. It is the author's hope that in this way the old myth that Canadian history is dull and boring will be laid to rest.

Call Us Canadians is a companion volume within the Canadian Studies Program to *North American Neighbours*. The two books are written in a similar style, and have the same reading level. Both are organized thematically, with each theme chronologically developed. The texts may be used interchangeably where desired.

In producing a book of this type, many people must give generously of their time and talent. The author is particularly indebted to the following individuals for their invaluable assistance: Penny Fine, Josefa Kropp, E Palmer Patterson, Maureen Radley-Walters, and Allan Evans.

I.L.M.

Unit 1
Social Science and the Community

1
Introduction

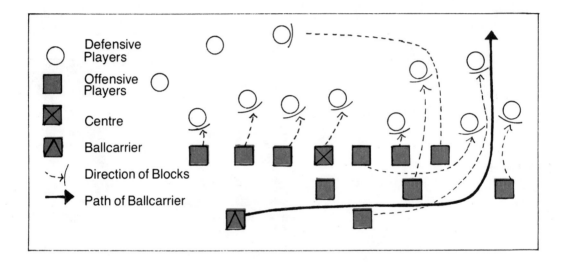

Symbol	Meaning
○	Defensive Players
■	Offensive Players
⊠	Centre
⊼	Ballcarrier
⇠→	Direction of Blocks
→	Path of Ballcarrier

The diagram you are looking at may be very confusing to you. Actually it is a play which might be used in a game of Canadian football. In the game of football, the aim of the offensive team is to have one player carry the ball across the opposition line. The aim of the defensive team is to stop the ballcarrier.

Very complicated plans are sometimes made up to help the offensive team reach its goal. The diagram above is an example of such a plan. If you look at it closely, you will see that each member of the offensive team has a role to play. If each player does his job well, the play will succeed. The player who scores the touchdown often gets most of the credit. Yet we can see that each member of the team has played a vital part in the results. This is the importance of teamwork.

You are probably asking yourself, "What does football have to do with history?" Of course, the important thing in this example is not the football play itself, but the idea of *teamwork*. The co-operation of other people is necessary for success in all walks of life. We see evidence of this every day. At the Ford Motors plant in Oakville, Ontario, hundreds of people work together to build cars. Each one's skill is needed if a good product is to result. If even one person failed to do a job properly, the work of all the others would be spoiled. Similarly, teamwork is needed in other occupations, whether the result is to be a skyscraper, a television show, or the book you are reading.

You may already have discovered that the co-operation of others is important to you. Can you make a list of the number of things you do every day both at school and at home which require co-operation?

Teamwork is also important to those people whose job it is to piece history together.

History tells you how people of the past lived, what they did, and why. A society which does not know its own history has been compared to a person without a memory. How important is your memory to you? Actually, if you started to write down all the ways in which your memory helps you every day, you would find the list endless. Your memory is like a computer which stores all the information you have learned and everything you have experienced since you were born.

Your actions are based on this knowledge and experience. If you suddenly suffered total amnesia, or loss of memory, you would become almost helpless. Try to think what you would do in such a case. How would you piece together your identity? You might turn to your parents or friends—but wait! Who are your parents and friends? Of course you don't know, for you can't remember. You could turn to the police for help, but if you had no papers or documents, it would be hard. And anyway, you wouldn't even know about such things as policemen.

Do you begin to see how difficult this task would be? You would have nothing to rely on to guide your actions. Where you live, who your friends are, even your name, would all be lost to you.

In a similar way, the country that did not know its own history would be lost. It would have no "memory" or experience to rely on when the time came to make decisions.

People who write about a country's past are called historians. Like the ball-carrier in the game of football, historians often receive much of the credit for the results of their work. However, like a football play, piecing together a country's past requires a great deal of help. Historians too are part of a team—a team of social scientists. Together, they work at the difficult task of gathering the information necessary to write a country's history.

In this unit you will learn how social scientists work, and see how teamwork is needed to achieve their aims. Later in the unit, you will be asked to work like a social scientist and piece together the history of your community.

2
The Role of the Social Sciences

Read the following account of the Beothuk Indians who lived in Newfoundland about four hundred years ago:

The Beothuks were Indians who inhabited the island of Newfoundland and were probably the first Indians seen by the white men who came from Europe in the sixteenth century. In many ways they were not as advanced as some of the other Indian tribes of the Maritimes. Their weapons consisted of wooden bows, arrows and spears. They had no dogs to use as pets or for work purposes, and they made no pottery, cooking their food instead in containers made of birch bark. From birch bark they also made their canoes, which they used for transportation and fishing.

Their homes were wigwams also made of bark, and for beds the Beothuks dug pits in the ground and covered them with pine branches.

Very little is known of their language or their form of government, but they probably lived in small groups of several families with perhaps one man being the leader of each.

When they were discovered by the white man, there were probably fewer than six hundred Beothuks on the island. Over the years they were hunted both by the white fishermen and their own Indian neighbours, and they soon became extinct. The last known Beothuk, a girl named Nancy, died in captivity in 1829.

The Beothuks no longer exist. They left among their remains few tools, very little art, and no written records to help future students learn about their society. How then do we know so much about these people—what they ate, how they hunted, what they wore, when they lived?

Finding out the answers to these questions is the work of historians and other social scientists. Social scientists are concerned with learning all about human activities. They study societies of both the past and present to find out about their beliefs, their customs, their forms of government and their work. These activities make up what social scientists call human culture.

As social scientists, historians are concerned with the events and people of the past. In their efforts to discover the past, historians are often faced with problems, such as the lack of written records or other information about a certain society. In such cases they must rely on the skills of other social scientists to help them in their work. Some of those who help historians in their work are: archaeologists; ethnologists; political scientists; and economists. We shall learn more in this chapter how each of these scientists works, and how they help historians uncover the past.

Social Scientists at Work

Social scientists, as we might guess from the name, are concerned with studying society. Like scientists in any field who are trying to solve a problem, social scientists follow certain rules in their investigation. This procedure is sometimes called the scientific method. Here are the steps usually followed in the scientific method:

> *Step. 1. Find a Problem.* For example, you might set about writing the history of the Native People of Canada.

> *Step 2. Gather Information.* This may include reading such things as books and newspapers, and also conducting interviews to obtain first-hand information about the subject.

> *Step 3. Suggest a Possible Solution to your Problem,* even though at this stage it may still be just a guess. This is called a hypothesis. For example, if you were studying the living conditions of the Canadian Indians, you might form the hypothesis that Indians once lived under harsh conditions and had a difficult time surviving in their environment.

> *Step 4. Conduct Tests.* Use your solution or hypothesis and conduct tests to determine if it is right or wrong. For example, you might study many Indian groups in many parts of Canada to see if all of them lived in a harsh environment, where survival was difficult.

> *Step 5. Form a Conclusion.* If your hypothesis stands up under testing, it is time to form a conclusion or theory about the subject you are studying. You might have discovered that while in general some tribes lived under harsh conditions, many others were well off, and actually prospered in their environment. Using this information, you are ready to state your conclusion about the condition of the Canadian Indian.

While all social scientists use the above principles to a great extent for their work, their methods of study, and their areas of investigation can of course differ greatly. Let us examine each of the social scientists in detail to discover how each one works.

The Case Study

Imagine that a hundred years from now, visitors from a distant planet were to land in Canada to find out about our society. Imagine also that Canada and the rest of the earth had been long deserted and all human life had mysteriously disappeared. Under these conditions, what could the visitors learn of our society?

If they were to uncover the cities of Toronto, Ottawa, and Montreal, they might find much information about Canadians from the remains we left behind. Among other things they would discover our skyscrapers, our automobiles and subways, our libraries and government buildings, our newspapers and TV sets, our supermarkets and our museums, our billboards and our garbage dumps.

These visitors have among them a historian, an archaeologist, an economist, a political scientist and an ethnologist. What could each contribute to the task of piecing together the puzzle of this "lost civilization"?

The Historian.   Historians do much of their work using the written evidence left behind by a society. Can you think of what this might include? Some very useful sources are: newspapers; letters and diaries; government records and books. This society might also have left behind photographs and film records. Can you think of any other possible sources of information for the historian?

Historians call some sources of evidence PRIMARY SOURCES. These include eyewitness accounts, or stories written by people who were present at an event. If you had witnessed a car accident, your story about it would be a primary source. Stories written long after an event has taken place by people who were not present are called SECONDARY SOURCES. One example might be a book about the ancient Romans written by a historian in this century.

There are many legends and stories surrounding the history of most countries. Canada too has such stories and legends. Some are accepted as true, others are not. Historians sometimes have a hard time deciding which stories are true and which are false. In making a decision, they must rely on the available evidence.

One such legend concerns Viking explorations in North America. It is known that in the period after the year 1000, Vikings landed on Canada's East Coast. Did they also explore the interior of Canada? One story tells of an expedition which sailed up the St. Lawrence and the Great Lakes, and reached the central United States. At this point the members of the expedition were supposedly killed by Indians. Is the story true?

In deciding this question the historian can make use of primary and secondary evidence. It is important to be able to tell the difference between these two types of evidence. Suppose that in trying to decide the question of the Viking legend the historian had the following types of evidence available. Which would be primary sources? Which would be secondary sources?

1. The diary of a Viking leader.
2. A book called *The History of the Vikings,* by a modern author.
3. A photo of the Viking expedition on Lake Superior.
4. A letter written by a member of the expedition to his wife.
5. A newspaper article appearing in the *Winnipeg Free Press.*
6. A Viking axe found in the central U.S.
7. A television special on the expedition made in 1976.

Which type of information would the historian find most useful, primary or secondary evidence? Why?

Once all these sources have been collected, the historian now asks some important questions about the society being studied:

1. Who were these people?
2. Where did they live?
3. When did their society exist?
4. How were they governed?
5. What were their beliefs?
6. How did they live from day to day?

Read the following passage. Which of the historian's questions would you be able to answer from the information in this reading? Which questions would require further information?

The Sekani Indians lived in the Rocky Mountain area in the Valley of the Peace River.

Their main occupation was hunting, and they lived mainly on caribou, moose, bear, beaver and small game. They hunted both summer and winter, using bows and arrows, spears and clubs made mostly from wood and bone.

Their canoes, as well as their cooking implements and their dishes were made of bark. Their clothing was made of animal skins and sometimes these would be decorated with porcupine quills and grizzly bear claws.

Since they followed the game animals around, the Sekani did not build permanent camps, but instead built lodges and lean-tos covered with bark, branches and skins.

The tribe was divided into several main groups, each with its own leader, although this individual did not possess much real power. Although they had many close family ties and spoke the same language, these groups quarrelled often, and sometimes started feuds which resulted in many deaths.

This historian must not only collect facts but must also decide which ones are important. The fact that Canada has more lakes than any other country in the world is most interesting, but it may not be of historical importance. It may tell us nothing about the people or their society. On the other hand, the fact that Jacques Cartier landed in Canada in 1534 and claimed the land for France has great historical significance, since it marked the beginning of the French presence in Canada.

Here is a series of facts about Canada. Which would you consider historically important? Why?

1. Canada has two official languages—English and French.
2. Canada is the world's largest producer of nickel.
3. Champlain founded Quebec in the year 1608.
4. Canadians use the telephone more often than any other people in the world.
5. Canadian soldiers fought in two World Wars.
6. Canada consists of ten Provinces and two Territories.
7. Newfoundland was the last Province to enter Confederation.

Lastly, the historian must decide what the facts mean. This is usually a more difficult task than it sometimes appears to be. As we have seen, historians get much of their information from letters, diaries, and other personal written accounts. But these accounts do not always agree with one another, even when they are describing the same thing, for it is a natural thing for people to disagree, especially when a matter very controversial is being discussed. It often happens that two people looking at the same object can see different meanings in it. What do you see in these pictures?

In the same way it is possible for eyewitnesses of even the most important events to get different meanings from them. Historians must decide which one is more correct. Of course, they cannot always be right.

Sometimes too, historians must rely on lifeless objects such as bones, wooden tools, or pottery for their information. What can such things tell us about a society? To answer this question, historians often depend on the skills of the archaeologist.

The Archaeologist Archaeologists are members of a group of social scientists called anthropologists. Anthropologists study our cultural activities, both past and present. As members of this group, archaeologists try to find evidence of human beings and their culture, usually by digging up places where people once lived.

Archaeologists and historians are both interested in finding out about the past. Historians begin their account when people first started to write, about five thousand years ago, and continue to the present day. This is sometimes called the historic period. Human beings, however, had been on earth for almost two million years before this, a period which is called pre-history. To find out about people and their activities in prehistoric times we must rely on discovering the remains left behind—that is, human tools, weapons, food remains, clothing, shelter, and bones. Discovering these remains, or artifacts, is the work of the archaeologist.

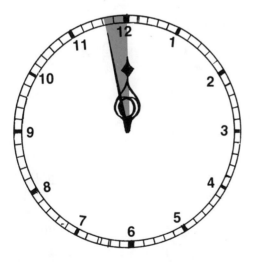

Compared to the time we have spent on earth (2 000 000 years) the length of time we have been able to write about ourselves is very short (5000 years). If we could compress our stay on earth to a 24-hour day, then our historic period shown on a 12-hour clock would be less than 120 seconds!

Often the archaeologist works on remains which are much more recent. Many groups around the world did not learn to write until the very recent past, and some have never learned to write at all. To find out about some of their activities and customs archaeologists are called upon to investigate remains which may be no more than ten or fifteen years old.

To find out about archaeologists and how they work let us go through the steps of what they do.

The first problem facing the archaeologist is—where to look? Sometimes months and even years of searching for the hidden remains of a people will lead to nothing; however, skilled archaeologists look for certain clues to guide them. They know that for people to exist in an area, two elements must be present—food and water. Water is most important, not only for drinking, but also because where there is water, there will be animals to hunt for food and clothing. The presence of water also makes possible the growth of vegetation providing berries, nuts, and other natural foods.

Sometimes the presence of unusual earth formations such as a large mound on an otherwise flat area will be a clue. Mounds often form when a town or village is destroyed or deserted for some period of time, allowing layers of earth to build up around it. Perhaps a later group of people will settle on the same spot and also abandon the site later on. This cycle may be repeated over and over again, allowing the mound to build higher and higher.

How Mounds Are Built

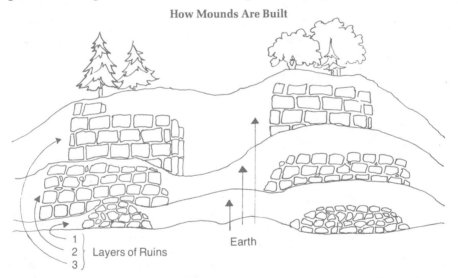

Layers of Ruins
Earth

The archaeologist may be lucky and find remains such as bits of pottery or other tools on or near the surface of the ground. Such finds are usually proof that human beings once lived nearby.

Study this map of an archaeological site. How many of the questions can you answer?

1. *What does the map show?*
2. *How old is this site?*
3. *How many people lived here?*
4. *How many people lived in each dwelling?*

5. *What kind of food did they eat?*
6. *What kind of tools did they use?*
7. *Were these people warlike?*
8. *Did they have a government?*

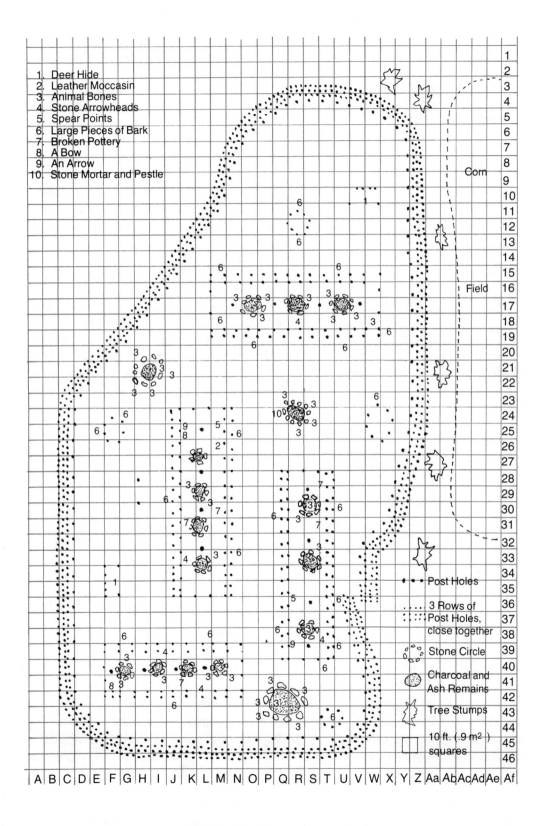

1. Deer Hide
2. Leather Moccasin
3. Animal Bones
4. Stone Arrowheads
5. Spear Points
6. Large Pieces of Bark
7. Broken Pottery
8. A Bow
9. An Arrow
10. Stone Mortar and Pestle

Corn

Field

Post Holes

3 Rows of
Post Holes,
close together

Stone Circle

Charcoal and
Ash Remains

Tree Stumps

10 ft. (.9 m²)
squares

Once the archaeologist has decided where to search, the next step is to decide how to plan the search. The actual digging takes up the most time, and because each piece of evidence may be valuable, digging must be done very carefully. A small brush and trowel are usually more useful than a shovel.

The archaeologist makes a map of the area of the dig, and then divides the whole area into squares of five feet each (about half a square metre). One square is dug at a time, working straight down by uncovering one layer of earth after another.

When a valuable object has been found in this way, the archaeologist gives it a number and marks a spot on the map where the object was found. At the end of the dig, the archaeologist will have a clear picture of where everything was found, simply by looking at the map.

Back at the laboratory, the archaeologist conducts tests on the objects found to determine their age. There are several different ways to find the age of these objects, though none of them is very exact. Two common methods are: dating by tree-rings; and Carbon[14] measurement.

Dating by tree-rings (called *DENDROCHRONOLOGY*) is a good method for things two thousand years old or less. Do you know how to find the age of a tree? A tree adds one ring of new wood for each year it grows, so a tree with thirty rings will be thirty years old. A very old tree may have two hundred rings or more.

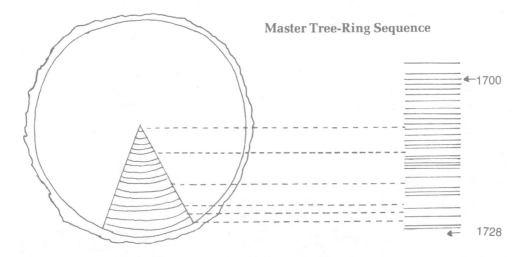

Master Tree-Ring Sequence

←1700

← 1728

Archaeologists also know that the size of a ring depends on how dry or how wet the season was in the year the ring was added. This is why tree-rings vary in size. Using this information, archaeologists have made a master chart of tree-rings for the past two thousand years. If any wood is found by an archaeologist on a dig, all there is to do is to match its rings against the chart to find out its age. Knowing what year the wood was cut, the archaeologist will also know the age of the site where it was found. Wood, however, rots with age quite easily so it is usually not found in sites which are very old.

By taking a sample of the rings of any tree and placing it on this master chart, archaeologists can find out the age of their finds. If this tree had been a log in an old log cabin, for example, the archaeologist would be able to find out the age of the cabin. Our chart starts at the year 1700.

1. How old is the tree itself?   *3. In what year was it cut down?*
2. In what year did it start to grow?

For very old objects, the archaeologist uses the Carbon[14] (or C[14]) method. Scientists know that all living things—plant and animal—take in C[14] atoms from the atmosphere as long as they live. When they die, their C[14] atoms return slowly to the atmosphere at a very steady rate. One-half the C[14] atoms disappear in about 5730 years. In the next 5730 years, one-half of what is left (or one-quarter) disappears, and so on until all the C[14] is finally given off. This whole process will take about 60 000 years.

It is easy to see that by measuring how much C[14] is left in the remains of a body, scientists will be able to tell exactly how old that body is. For example, if only one-quarter of the C[14] atoms are left, scientists know that 2 × 5730 = 11 460 years have passed since the body died. This system is fairly reliable for anything 60 000 years old or less.

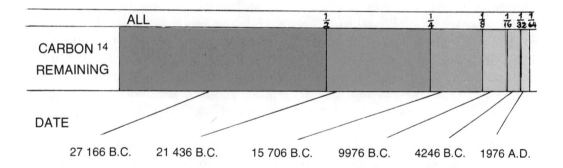

The archaeologist can now gather all the information to put together an interesting picture of the people being studied. Where and when they lived has been discovered, and by a careful study of their remains, a great deal about their customs. Much of what we know about Canada's past comes from the work of archaeologists.

In our case study of the destroyed earth society, what sources would the archaeologist examine? Some of the evidence would include the remains of buildings such as houses, offices, movie theatres, supermarkets, and schools.

What would each of these remains tell about earth's past civilization? Can you think of other sources of information which might interest the archaeologist?

Archaeologists can often tell a great deal about a society, even from things which at first do not seem important. Do you think you could be a good archaeologist? Here is an experiment each member of the class can try, which might give the answer to this question.

Select one boy and one girl volunteer from your class and ask them to empty out the contents of their wallets or purse on their desks. Make a list of the items in them, and ask any questions about them which you think might be useful. Now imagine that you as an archaeologist of the future had only these items to help you discover what this society was like. What would they be able to tell you about these two people? What would they tell you about their society? Some questions you might want to ask are these:

1. How old were the boy and girl?
2. What year did they leave this evidence?
3. What kind of government did they have?
4. Did their society have machines?
5. Did they have a religion?
6. What were their methods of transportation?

How many of these questions can you answer? Remember, you must use only the evidence provided by the items in the wallets.

The Ethnologist Ethnologists, like archaeologists, belong to the group of social scientists called anthropologists. However, unlike archaeologists who study things in the past, ethnologists study societies which are still living. They study such things as the language, customs, and physical appearance of cultural groups which are often quite different from our own, or in some way unusual to us. Some cultural groups which are often studied by ethnologists are: the Aborigines of Australia; the Bushmen of South Africa; and the Inuit of Canada.

These studies can be very helpful to historians. Much of what we know of the history of some people comes down through the years by word-of-mouth or through songs, tales, and legends. This is especially true of those groups which had not developed a written language. These stories, songs, and legends will be carefully passed on from generation to generation right up to the present day. From these stories, ethnologists have been able to learn a great deal about the past customs of these people. Also, in many cases the customs and living habits of these people have not changed greatly over the years, and so a study of their present lifestyles can tell us much about their past.

Here is an Inuit legend. What does it tell us about the customs and beliefs of early Inuit?

Long ago among the Inuit there lived a strong man with many sons but only one daughter. Because she was the only daughter, her parents and brothers gave her special treatment and soon spoilt her. She always got the best pieces of seal and caribou meat, and eyes of cod to eat. Still, she grew up to be very beautiful and a very fast runner.

The rest of the family was always careful to pay respect to the many spirits of their village and to obey all their rules and laws, but the girl, Nauya, was very headstrong and did not believe in the spirits. She went out of her way to break the rules and offend the spirits.

One day her brothers were busy cutting up frozen seal meat with small knives, because that is the way the spirits said it should be done. But Nauya came by, picked up a stone axe, and soon cut up the meat with a few chops. Her brothers were afraid the spirits would do something terrible to her, but Nauya just laughed.

She went along month after month disobeying the spirits and causing her family to fear for her. One day when everyone was out of the igloo, she put some caribou meat in a pot to cook along with some seal meat. Now this was one of the worst things possible in the eyes of the spirits. When her family discovered this, they told the rest of the village what Nauya had done. The villagers also became afraid of what the angry spirits would do to them, so they resolved to catch Nauya and punish her.

Nauya ran away, and as she was a good runner, the others had trouble catching her. But as she ran for hour after hour, she soon began to gasp for breath, and her breath froze behind her in thick clouds. The clouds of fog her breath created grew bigger and bigger until the villagers lost sight of her forever. And that is why to this day we can still see great clouds of fog on certain mornings.

In our case study, the ethnologist from space may not be of much help. However, if some earthlings had managed to survive, they would be research subjects for the ethnologist, who would be able to find out much about their present way of life. This would include their beliefs and customs, their language, their stories and legends of the past. In this way the ethnologist could perhaps uncover some clues about the history of their planet.

The Political Scientist   One of the important parts of any society is its form of government. It would be almost impossible for us to think of a society without some form of government, no matter how simple. If you were to try to make a list of all the things the government of Canada does for you, it would be a very long list indeed. Without a government, we would probably have no roads, or schools, or hospitals, or hundreds of other things that we take for granted every day.

Political scientists study the kinds of governments people around the world have created. They study how certain kinds of governments began and how they have developed into their modern form. For example, England has had a combination of a *MONARCHY* and a *PARLIAMENTARY* government for many centuries. It was the model for Canada's own form of government. But the type of government we have in Canada and Britain today is vastly different from that of earlier times. In the beginning, Parliament did not even have a Prime Minister or a Cabinet. What changes have taken place? Why were these changes made? How do governments affect the lives of people? These are some of the questions political scientists try to answer.

Political scientists also study people in politics to discover how they make decisions and what their motives are for making such decisions.

In modern times, one of the jobs of political scientists is to conduct polls during elections to find out before hand how people will vote. After an election they will analyse the results to find out why people voted the way they did. In this way they can be very helpful to politicians and to the public. They can also help historians explain political events of the past such as election results and political decisions made by our leaders.

Here is an example of a poll taken before the 1974 Canadian federal elections; and the result of the elections:

Prediction of Popular Vote before the 1974 Election

Liberal	Conservative	New Democrat	Other
43%	35%	16.5%	5.5%

Actual Result of the 1974 Election

Liberal	Conservative	New Democrat	Other
43%	35%	16%	6%

How accurate were the polls?

The Economist   Economists study how people make their living, investigate what products a country makes, and what it should do to develop or maintain a high standard of living. Most people spend the greater part of their lives in trying to make a living. Perhaps you are concerned even now with what kind of a job you will have when you finish school. Since this is so important a part of people's lives, it is sometimes said that people are motivated to do things more for their own economic benefits than for any other reason. If this is true, it helps to explain their behaviour at certain times.

For example, if we studied the behaviour of Canadians during the Great Depression of the 1930s, we would find that some unemployed people stole food to keep alive, or joined long soup lines for free food. We would also find that many people who had once been wealthy were now forced to sell apples on streetcorners or shine shoes to make a living.

Men eating in a government soup kitchen during the Depression.

The economic conditions of this time also affected the government of Canada. With unemployment at such a high rate, the government introduced unemployment insurance for the first time, in order to relieve some of the conditions of poverty and starvation.

We can see through this example that understanding the economic conditions of any period can help to explain the actions and attitudes of the people and their government during that time. In this way we can better understand the history of a society during that period of time.

Conclusion

Writing the history of a society is first and foremost the historian's task. But as we have seen, the historian makes great use of the skills of a number of other social scientists who are involved in related areas of research. The history of any society then is the product of the combination of the work of different scientists using different skills. Without this co-operation, our own history might still lie undiscovered.

Word Study

anthropology	economics	political science
archaeology	ethnology	prehistory
artifact	history	primary sources
Carbon[14]	hypothesis	scientific method
culture	monarchy	secondary sources
dendrochronology	parliamentary	site

Things to Do 1. *If you could put some of your belongings in a five-foot square box to show some future archaeologist or historian what your society was like, what things might you put in that box? Explain how each item is really typical of you or your society.*

2. *This chapter made reference to the fact that two people viewing the same event may see different meanings in that event. Conduct an experiment to see how often this happens in the newspapers. If your family receives more than one newspaper, or if you have a friend who receives a different newspaper, compare two newspaper accounts of the same stories to see how similar or how different they are.*

3. *Make a scale model of a cross-section of a five-foot (one and a half metre) square showing some of the things which might be found in the square. Clay strips or putty can be used to represent the different layers of earth. Assume that each layer represents five hundred years of history. What artifacts might you put in each layer to represent Canada's history?*

4. *Here is a simple exercise to help you practice dating by the Carbon[14] method:*
(a) *How old would an object be if it had the following amounts of C^{14} left:*
   i. *1/4*
   ii. *1/8*
   iii. *1/16*
   iv. *1/32?*
(b) *What fraction of C^{14} would be left in an object that was*
   i. *11 460 years old*
   ii. *17 190 years old*
   iii. *22 920 years old*
   iv. *45 840 years old?*

3
The Study of Local History

Do you know

—when your community was founded?
—how your community got its name?
—why this particular site was selected for settlement?
—who lived on this site before the coming of the European settlers?
—who the first pioneers of your community were?
—what the patterns of growth of your community have been?
—how your street got its name?
—how large your community is?
—how your community is governed?
—what the prospects for the future of your community are?

Perhaps these questions have already occurred to you. Perhaps you have already investigated and found the answers to some of them. But it may surprise you to learn that while many students are familiar with the history and current events of distant parts of the world, very few are aware of the history or affairs of their own community. Even though they may be born and live and work all their lives in the same place, most people have never taken the trouble to study its history and growth. Yet this can be a very interesting and important topic.

As a young Canadian, you probably live in a town or large city. Over seventy per cent of all Canadians today live in urban communities, and the number is growing constantly. By the end of this century over ninety per cent of Canadians will live in towns and cities. However, a hundred years ago only twenty per cent of Canadians lived in towns larger than five thousand people. As you might guess, this represents a very drastic change in conditions and living habits from when your great-grandparents were young, and an even greater change from the time your community was first settled.

In this chapter you will have an opportunity to study the history of your community, to answer the questions posed at the beginning, and to discover what changes have taken place in your community over the years. Naturally as there are hundreds of towns and cities in Canada we cannot study them all in this chapter. We will focus our study on only one, the Borough of Scarborough, which is part of Metropolitan Toronto. This will serve as a case study to provide you with a model by which you can launch your own study of the history of your community.

In carrying out this study you will be asked to apply the skills and techniques of the social scientists which you learned in the previous chapter. Can you remember the skills performed by the social scientists, and the steps of the scientific method?

As you search for materials to help you study the history of your community, some of the following may be very useful sources of information:

—local libraries and museums
—local newspaper offices
—family diaries, old letters and photograph albums
—old buildings which are still standing
—old churches and cemeteries.

The History of Scarborough

The Township of Scarborough, which since 1954 has formed one of the 5 boroughs of Metropolitan Toronto, is one of the largest and fastest-growing communities in Canada. Its large population of over 300 000 people, its land area of over 182 square kilometres, its many housing developments, great shopping malls, numerous businesses and industries all suggest that the Township has had a long history. Yet it was only 350 years ago that the first French explorers spotted the towering grey walls of the Scarborough Bluffs on the Lake Ontario shoreline. It has been less than 200 years since the first European settlers took up residence there. Compared to the history of the cities of many other countries this seems a very short span of time. Yet like many other Canadian communities, Scarborough has managed to accomplish a great deal in this short time.

The Natural History of Scarborough   Although the human history of Scarborough may be brief, its natural history is a long one. Geologists tell us that the Scarborough Bluffs began to develop about one million years ago. It was during this period that the great ice ages advanced and retreated in Canada, leaving behind many of the formations we see today, including the Great Lakes, the St. Lawrence River and the Scarborough Bluffs.

With each retreat of the ice, layers of deposits were left behind which gradually built up certain parts of the land. The last ice age retreated about 12 000 years ago. The top sixty metres of the Bluffs show the layers of sand and clay deposited during the Great Ice Age. Below these layers we see the Scarborough Beds—fifty metres of stratified sand and layers of clay. These Beds ex-

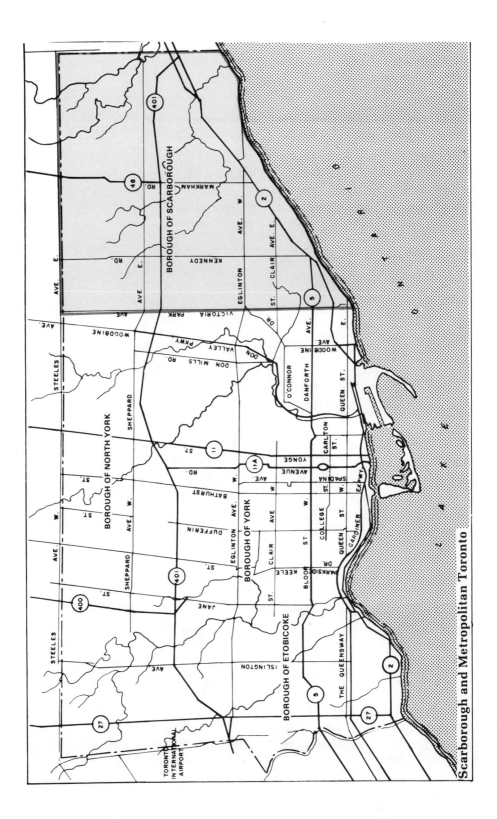

Scarborough and Metropolitan Toronto

tend below the level of Lake Ontario. Below the Beds is a layer of slate which makes up the bedrock of the Bluffs. Of course, since it is below the waterline, it cannot be seen.

At one time the Scarborough Bluffs extended out much farther than they do today. However, natural erosion due to wind and water have been cutting the cliffs back at a rate of more than seventy-five centimetres each year. The sand and clay from the Bluffs has been carried westward by the currents in Lake Ontario where it has built up Toronto Island. Each year over thirty-six thousand cubic metres of sand and clay are still deposited on Toronto Island.

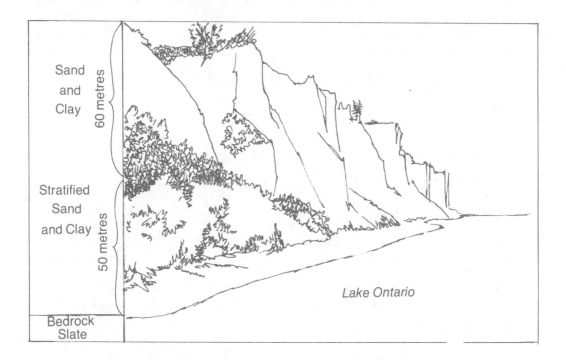

Since 1900, many people have built houses close to the edge of the Bluffs. Can you think how the process of erosion might be a concern to them? If the erosion is not stopped in some way, what will happen to these houses in the next fifty years? Does your community have any problems with land erosion or other natural forces? What is being done to solve these problems?

Local History Projects 1. *Find out how long ago natural forces formed the soil and other natural formations of your community.*
2. *What kind of soil is most common in your area?*
3. *Construct a model to represent the thicknesses and types of soil found in the various layers of the landscape in your area.*

The Indian Period

Long before the first Europeans settled in Scarborough, and shortly after the last ice age had disappeared, a few bands of Indians made the Scarborough area their home. Archaeologists using Carbon[14] dating indicate that they were present in the area by at least 7000 B.C. (Do you remember how Carbon[14] works?) They probably came in search of game, which at that time was plentiful and included such animals as deer, caribou, beaver, and even huge mastodons, large elephant-like creatures which roamed North America then.

Very little was known of the life of the Indians in Scarborough itself until 1957, when a paving company accidentally uncovered some skeletons at a site in Pickering Township just east of the Scarborough boundary. In the next few years archaeologists from the Royal Ontario Museum excavated a whole village. The village had been surrounded by a stockade, and inside the walls the archaeologists found remains of longhouses, firepits, tools and weapons. Carbon[14] tests indicated the site was inhabited about eight hundred and fifty years ago.

Here is a sketch of a typical Huron-Iroquois village. What sources of food might such a village have? Look at the construction of the walls. What indicates that the village was prepared for war?

In the previous year, 1956, an archaeological expedition had uncovered remains of Indian burials at a site called Tabor's Hill, near the corner of Lawrence Avenue and Bellamy Road in Scarborough. From these remains much was learned about Indian customs and burial practices. The two discoveries show that the Indians who lived in the area were Iroquois and that they were present in large numbers.

In time, farming became more widespread among the Indians. It appears that the heavy clay soil common in the Scarborough area was not very good for crops. Gradually the Indian population of the area began to migrate to regions with better soils. When Etienne Brûlé, the first European in Ontario, visited the Toronto region in 1615, he found it practically uninhabited.

Etienne Brûlé at the mouth of the Humber, 1615.

From about 1690 onward the Indian population of the entire region began to change. Mississauga Indians, who were more interested in hunting and the beaver trade, began to replace the Iroquois. The French set up a small trading post at the mouth of the Humber River and called it "Toronto" after an Indian name which probably means "the place of meeting". As the beaver trade grew, bigger forts were built in the area in 1751 and 1752. However, the last fort was destroyed in 1759 at the end of the Seven Years' War between the French and English.

When the English took control of Canada from the French in 1763 they decided to use the lands in southern Ontario for settlement and so began to buy the land from the Indians. Portions of eastern Ontario were bought in 1783. The Toronto region itself was purchased on Sept. 23, 1787 for about £1700 and some goods, such as four dozen handkerchiefs, a few butcher's knives, blankets, and scissors. The total purchase price paid to the Indians probably amounted to less than five thousand dollars.

The sale of Toronto did not actually include the Scarborough region, although in the following years many settlers flocked to the area to take up homes and farms. To this day there is no document to prove that the Indians ever sold the land to the British.

Local History Projects 1. *Find out what tribes of Indians settled in your community before the coming of the Europeans. How long ago did they first settle in your area?*
2. *Have any Indian remains been uncovered in your community? If so, research their findings and learn what archaeologists can tell you about the* *daily life and customs of the Indians.*
3. *Who was the first European to come to your area? In what year was the visit?*
4. *Did the government buy the land in your community from the Indians? If so, find out the purchase price. Do you think this price was fair to the Indians?*

The Pioneer Period

The Township east of Toronto was surveyed in 1791 and at first named Glasgow. However, in 1793 Elizabeth Graves Simcoe, wife of the first Lieutenant-Governor of Upper Canada, saw the high bluffs on the Lake Ontario shoreline. They reminded her of an English town with similar grey cliffs, by the name of Scarborough. In her diary she wrote: "We came within sight of what is named in the Map the high lands of Toronto . . . they appeared so well that we talked of building a Summer Residence there and calling it Scarborough." In that year the name Glasgow was dropped, and replaced with Scarborough. Nearby Toronto also had its name changed to York in honour of the English hero the Duke of York.

The year 1793 also saw the beginning of the first migration of settlers to the Scarborough area. Charles Annis and his family passed through the Township, and although they did not have land grants, they set up squatters' rights in the area. In following years, army officers, government officials, and other citizens were able to receive large grants of land from the government. Most of these did not intend to settle, but hoped to sell the land later for a profit.

Among the first true settlers to come to Scarborough were David and Mary Thomson, who became the parents of the first European child born there.

Compare the work this woman would do with that of a modern housewife. What changes have taken place over the years? What has made these changes possible?

Life was still very difficult for the first pioneers in Scarborough. The land was heavily wooded and each tree and stump had to be cleared by hand before the land could be farmed. There were almost no roads, so travel and communication were very difficult. This made the first settlers very isolated. They sometimes went for weeks or even months without seeing other people or hearing news about the outside world. For those of us who have the conveniences of telephones, radios, televisions, books, and daily newspapers to inform and entertain us, it is hard to imagine what daily life without them might be like. What do you think these first settlers might have done for amusement and entertainment in the evenings and on free days?

David and Mary Thomson

Two of the very first settlers of Scarborough were David Thomson and his wife Mary. They came from Scotland to settle in Scarborough in 1796. In the first few years while their farm was still being cleared and was producing little, David Thomson often had to find work in the Town of York to support his family. This meant that Mary would sometimes be left alone on the farm for weeks with her children. During this time she would do all the chores and look after her family. The wilderness was so close that she could hear the animals at night.

In 1800 Mary and David became parents of the first European child born in Scarborough, a girl. David Thomson died in 1834 and Mary in 1847, at the age of eighty. Today a large modern high school in Scarborough is named in their memory.

As more and more settlers made Scarborough their home, the first streets were carved out of the wilderness. One of them was built by an American contractor, Asa Danforth. Other roads built during this period include Kingston Road, Dundas Street, and Kennedy Road.

Scarborough Roads

Danforth Road. The first major road built through Scarborough, Danforth Road was built in 1799 at the cost of $36 per kilometre. At first it was known as Dundas Street, but later was named after the contractor who built it, Asa Danforth. Today, major roads can cost as much as $15 million per kilometre to build.

Kingston Road. Kingston Road was the second main road to be built in Scarborough. Started in 1801 as a narrow, winding trail, the road ran close to the Lake Ontario shoreline. In 1817 it was completed as far as Kingston, Ontario, and this is how the road got its name. In time, the road was extended as far as Montreal. Later it became part of Highway #2.

Over its first few decades the Township grew slowly but steadily. Here is a chart of the early growth of Scarborough:

Year	Population
1820	477
1830	1135
1842	2750
1850	3821

During this early period Scarborough was a community consisting of numerous farms and several small scattered villages, including Highland Creek, Malvern, Ellesmere, Wexford, and Woburn.

Life in the Pioneer Period

Education   The first schools in Scarborough were small, privately run schools, operating entirely on the fees of parents and students and some private donations. Until well into the nineteenth century this is the way education operated in most parts of Canada, since at that time there was no system of government aid to education. This meant that many poorer children could go to school for only a short time, or perhaps not at all. It was not until 1847 that schools were made free to all students.

These early schools were of the one-room cabin type and usually quite small, perhaps no more than five by six metres in dimension. These schools of course were much more uncomfortable than those of today. For desks there were long benches without desks. On the walls there were no blackboards or maps. Writing paper was very scarce and pens were made of goose quills. For students who misbehaved or failed to do their assigned work there was always the threat of punishment by the birch rod.

Teachers at this time were usually not qualified instructors, but old retired soldiers or officials from England. Their pay was very low and usually depended on how many students they had in their classes. Their duties often included sharpening the students' pens twice a day and keeping the schoolhouse clean and warm, as well as teaching reading, writing, and arithmetic.

The first school in Scarborough was built in 1817, although classes had been taught in some private homes as early as 1807. As the population increased many more schools were built since it was felt that students should not have to walk more than three kilometres to attend school. These schools taught primary grades only; it was not until 1922 that Scarborough had its first high school. Until this time students who wished to continue their education had to travel to Markham High School or Toronto Collegiate Institute.

Religious Activities   In the early years of Scarborough, while the population was still very small, it was not possible to support a church and a full time minister. For religious services the people of the township had to depend on meetings conducted by travelling preachers, or travel to St. James Church in the Town of York. Sometimes the settlers had to drive eighteen kilometres or more on bad roads and under harsh weather conditions to attend these services.

The need for a regular church in Scarborough grew with the population, and in 1818 St. Andrew's, the first church in Scarborough, was built on land donated by David Thomson. This first church was a very simple building, measuring only ten by twelve metres, and lit only by lamps and three windows.

After this churches in Scarborough grew both in number and size. The Anglican religious community built St. Margaret's Church in 1833, St. Paul's in 1841, and Christ Church in 1846.

Churches of other religious denominations were also built during this period, including Presbyterian, Methodist, and Catholic. At last people did not have to travel long distances under hard conditions to attend their religious services.

The Reverend William Jenkins

The first minister of Scarborough's first church was the Reverend William Jenkins. To conduct services at St. Andrew's the Reverend Jenkins had to drive twenty-four kilometres from his farm north of the Township, often on horseback or sleigh over country that had hardly any roads. On one occasion, he and a friend had to spend the night by the side of the road in the middle of the winter when their sleigh overturned as they were trying to get to the church. For the services he provided, Reverend Jenkins was paid only $100 a year. He died in Richmond Hill in 1843.

Sometimes, instead of the people going to the minister, the minister went to the people. Why were so few churches built during the early pioneer days?

Social Life   As in farming communities in every part of Canada, the farmers' first concern was looking after their farms. This left very little time for recreation and social events. Leisure time activities usually followed a standard form.

Barn-raising bees are very hard work. Yet most people pitched in cheerfully to help a neighbour. Some people even looked forward to such events. Why? Can you think of any communities in Canada today where people continue to live this way?

Fairs   The first fair held in Scarborough was in the year 1844. Before this time farmers would flock to fairs in York or other nearby communities. At these fairs farmers proudly displayed their best cows, bulls, horses, sheep, and pigs, and also their farm products, such as wheat, peas, and potatoes.

Bees   "Bees" were gatherings usually held to help a friend or neighbour put up a house or barn, or to do a farm job which required many people, such as clearing land of trees and stumps. Not only were these "bees" useful in helping out a needy neighbour, but they also provided farming families with an opportunity to meet other people. The work was often followed by a dance. The music for the dance was usually provided by fiddlers and tunes such as "Pop Goes the Weasel" were most popular.

Inns   The most popular meeting places in the Township were the inns and taverns. Here tired and dusty men could discuss such things as religion and politics, or simply the state of the weather.

Sometimes, however, they tended to drink too much beer or whiskey. Despite the fact that ministers would denounce drunkenness at church on Sundays it did not appear to have much effect on some of their audience. One minister wrote: "The Scarborough folk are noted drinkers."

The most popular of these early inns were *The Painted Post* near the city of York, the *Blue Bell Inn* on the corner of Kennedy Road and St. Clair Ave., and the *Halfway House* on Midland Ave.

Local History Projects   *1. Find out when the first European settlers came to your community. When did your family first settle in the area?*
2. Find out when and where the first churches and schools were built in your community.
3. If you have a camera, begin a scrapbook by taking pictures of some of the historic buildings in your area.
4. One interesting thing you might want to do as a project is to trace your family tree.

Do you know what a family tree is? You have one. Everyone does. A family tree traces the branches of your family's past. It includes your parents, grandparents, great-grandparents, as far back as your ancestors go.

Most people know something about their grandparents—where they lived, what they did, etc. Some people may even know something about their great-grandparents. Very few people can trace their family line past this point. Not many people even bother. Yet finding out your family history can be very rewarding. If you like mysteries or puzzles, you will enjoy tracing your family tree. Who knows what you might find!

Discovering your family tree is not very expensive, but it will take a few minutes of your time each day.

Step 1: Make a Master Chart, filling in as many names as you can.

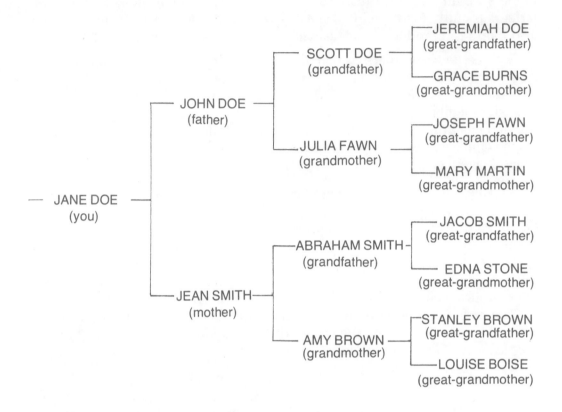

Step 2: Make a Family Sheet for each nuclear family group. A nuclear family is made of mother, father, and children. One such sheet should be made for parents, grandparents, great-grandparents and so on.

Father—   John Doe   Married: Feb. 18, 1958
          Born—Dec. 11, 1933   Where: Hamilton, Ont.
          Place—Ottawa, Ont.   Died:
                                Where:

Mother—   Jean Smith
          Born—Nov. 19, 1937   Died:
          Place—Liverpool, Eng. Where:

Children— 1. Jane Doe
             Born—June 13, 1960
             Where—Hamilton, Ont.
          2. James Doe
             Born—July 29, 1962
             Where—Hamilton, Ont.

Your parents will probably be able to help you fill out the information sheet for your grandparents. Your grandparents may provide the information you need for your great-grandparents.

Beyond this point gaps will probably start to appear in your information sheets. How will you uncover this information? Here are some useful places to look:

1. *Family Records* These may include:
   - —family Bibles
   - —old letters
   - —old photographs
   - —deeds and wills
   - —cemeteries
   - —newspaper clippings
   - —diaries
   - —old report cards
   - —wedding, birth, and death certificates

2. *Census Records* In certain years, each country makes an official list of the people in that country, and records some information about them. This information includes the name, age, place of birth, and occupation of each member of a household. This is called a census. Census records began in Canada in 1851. The last census was held in 1971. Census information may obtained from most local public libraries.

If your ancestors lived in another country, you will have to write for the census information to that country. If you know the town or city in which your ancestors lived, getting this information will be easier and faster, for you can write directly to the library systems of those places.

3. *Parish Records* Before census records were taken, this information was usually kept by the parish in which your ancestors lived. Parish records have information regarding births, marriages, and deaths. Most parishes have kept records dating back hundreds of years. If you know the name of the parish, you may write directly to the authorities for information.

The Growth of the Community to 1945

In 1850 Scarborough became officially the Township of Scarborough, with its own government. The first Reeve of the Township was Peter Secor, a miller. The growth of Scarborough from this time to the end of the nineteenth century was very slow and uncertain. In fact, after 1871, when the population had reached a high of 4615, it actually began to decrease. By 1900 there were only 3711 people in the Township. This shows that the trend being felt in other farming communities in Canada was also affecting Scarborough. At this time began the movement of large numbers of people away from the farms and into the larger towns and cities. This pattern was especially strong among young people, who hoped to find jobs in the cities working in industries. For the young of Scarborough, nearby Toronto with its numerous industries and its population of over 200 000 at this time was a great attraction. Throughout history, large cities have always held an attraction for people. Job opportunities are one reason for this. What are some other possible reasons?

The Scarborough Oil Company

Scarborough had a few thriving industries of its own, but some of the more adventurous ones were doomed to failure. In 1866 the Scarborough Oil Company was formed to drill for oil in the Township. One hundred and sixty shares were sold to the public at twenty-five dollars each. On each occasion the drilling proved to be a failure. However, a local smith would sometimes pour a few gallons of coal oil down the holes at night and this would create much excitement the next day as people believed they had struck oil. They did not seem to realize that oil wells produce crude oil, not refined oil. Would you have been fooled by this trick?

The growth of Toronto soon meant prosperity for Scarborough as well. As the city of Toronto began to burst its boundaries, some of the population began to spill into Scarborough. The first arrivals were wealthier Torontonians seeking summer cottage space. For this purpose Scarborough seemed a natural location. At the turn of the century the Township could still be described in this way:

The Heights of Scarboro are noted for their romantic beauty. The shore from Toronto along the front of the Township is fast becoming the permanent or summer residence of gentlemen who belong to the city. ... Not only Torontonians, but excursionists from a distance, have there held numerous picnics, entertainments and demonstrations.

The turn of the century however, also introduced great new inventions which would make Scarborough an attractive site as part of the growing Metropolitan Toronto. Try to imagine how these new inventions might make possible the creation of much larger cities than had existed in the past.

Before 1900, the horse, buggy, and bicycle were the only means of transportation to and from the city. However, in 1898 the Toronto Railway Co. began laying tracks along Kingston Road to expand trolley services to the Scarborough area. At about the same time automobiles were introduced to the area. These new vehicles would hit speeds of up to fifteen or twenty kilometres per hour, creating great clouds of dust on the unpaved roads and frightening people and horses alike. In 1903 there were only two hundred and twenty automobiles registered in Canada.

The common means of public transportation in Metro Toronto before 1900. How can you tell that this area was not yet ready for automobiles?

Name all the different methods of transportation this photo shows. Compare it with the preceding one. What changes have taken place to make all the improvements in transportation possible?

By 1907 the McLaughlin Motor Car Company in Oshawa began making them. By 1912 there were over twelve thousand cars in Ontario alone. It seemed that among some people, cars were popular. Yet many people viewed these vehicles with disgust. Many taxpayers objected to automobiles because new and better roads would have to be built for them. There were other complaints. These were some typical complaints.

> Automobiles keep women off the roads.
> We can't keep the windows of our house open, because of the
> dust, especially on Sunday.
> They are very noisy and scare passing horses.

In some countries, "Red Flag" laws were passed to put restrictions on automobiles. These laws put speed limits of eight kilometres per hour on automobiles. They also required someone to walk ninety metres in front of the car holding a red flag to warn passersby that a car was coming.

Ontario passed a law in 1908 stating the following restrictions:

—all automobile operators require a licence
—no person under 17 shall operate a motor car
—if a horse becomes frightened by a car, the motor will be turned off
  until the horse passes
—upon meeting a funeral, a car must turn down a lane
—if someone is injured by a motor car, the driver must give his name
  and address without being asked.

At first cars were very expensive, and only the wealthy could afford them. In 1909 the cheapest Ford cost $1150 in Canada. By this time, however, Henry Ford, founder of the Ford Company, had developed a new way of mass-producing cars, using the assembly line. The "Tin Lizzie", as the new Ford was called, cost only $455. The car was now available to most Canadians and the age of the big city was on its way.

Another great invention was introduced to Scarborough in 1903, the telephone. Within a few years the Scarborough Independent Telephone Company was providing services to subscribers, and the familiar telephone lines began to appear in the area.

In 1909 electricity came to Scarborough, in the form of street lamps along Queen St. near Victoria Park. By 1917 the population of the Township had grown enough to allow extension of hydro services to the more heavily populated parts of the area.

These new inventions not only made travel and communication easier and faster for ordinary people, but they also began to change Scarborough from a farming community to an industrial community. Industries need rapid transportation, communication, and a large population base to work efficiently. Can

One of the first cars in the area. Compare it with a modern vehicle. Can you list the changes of the past seventy years? What problems might this car have in bad weather, dusty roads, or night driving? What new jobs would the invention of the automobile create?

you think of why these ingredients are necessary to industrial growth? By the 1920s Scarborough had all these ingredients and so during this period there was great prosperity in the Township.

In the 1930s came the hard times of the Depression. Do you know what happened during these years? If you do not, ask your parents or grandparents. Ask them if they can remember the hardships they faced at that time.

Scarborough felt the hard years of the Depression much as other parts of Canada did. During this time many people were out of work and over thirty per cent of the population needed government help to survive. The costs of the relief program were almost half a million dollars each year, and these high expenses put Scarborough heavily in debt.

Local History Projects 1. *Find out when the following inventions were first introduced into your community: telephone, electricity, trains, buses.* 2. *Find out what type of automobile first travelled the roads of your community. When did it first appear?* 3. *Investigate the effects of the Depression on your community during the 1930s.*

These two aerial photographs indicate the tremendous growth of Scarborough over the past twenty years. What physical features of the original landscape are still visible? Are any of the original buildings still standing?

Modern Scarborough

By far the most important period of growth for Scarborough was that after the end of World War II in 1945. The Township grew from about 25 000 people in 1945 to over 300 000 today. Scarborough in fact became the fastest growing community in Canada. During this period over five hundred industries were set up in Scarborough, including makers of auto parts, home appliances, typewriters, glass products, and candy.

With the growing population came the need for new schools. In 1954 there were still only two high schools in the Township, Scarborough High School and Agincourt High School. By 1973 this number had increased to twenty. As well, there were over one hundred public schools, and the school budget now takes up over forty-five per cent of the total Scarborough budget.

There is no university in Scarborough, although the University of Toronto has a college campus in Scarborough. However, in 1965 the Government of Ontario started a program to set up community colleges throughout the Province. Centennial College in Scarborough was one of these.

In 1954 the Township of Scarborough officially became part of Metropolitan Toronto. The population of Metro Toronto has been growing at the rate of 50 000 a year. This has added to the number of social and economic problems of the area. New jobs have to be created, homes have to be provided, old areas have to be renovated, transportation systems must be improved, supply and waste disposal services have to be increased. It was felt that these and other problems could best be solved if all the townships ringing Toronto were joined to form one large metropolitan area.

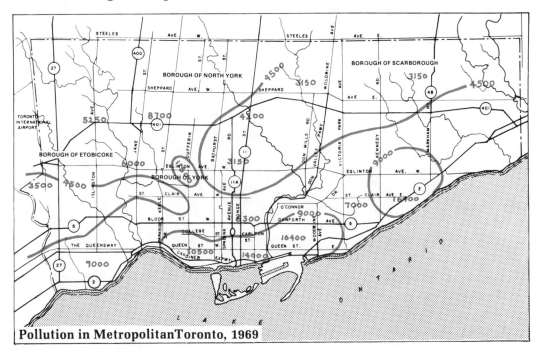

Pollution in MetropolitanToronto, 1969

A 1974 map showing dustfall in Metropolitan Toronto. The figures indicate the number of milligrams of dust per square metre, every 30 days.

How serious is the air pollution problem in your community? What is your local government doing to fight it?

AnneMorris

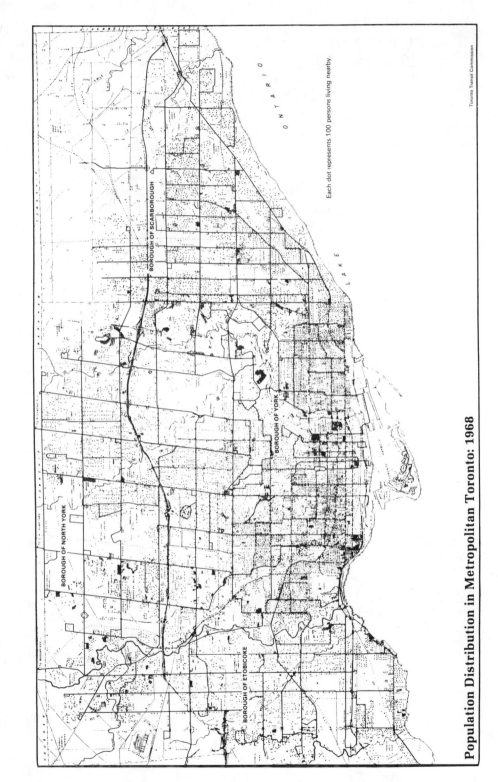

Each dot represents 100 persons living nearby.

Toronto Transit Commission

BOROUGH OF SCARBOROUGH

ONTARIO

LAKE

BOROUGH OF YORK

BOROUGH OF NORTH YORK

BOROUGH OF ETOBICOKE

Population Distribution in Metropolitan Toronto: 1968

The Scarborough Civic Centre, opened in 1973.

Scarborough continues to grow. The new Metro Zoo, which opened in the Fall of 1974, is located in the northeast sector of Scarborough. In 1959 when Queen Elizabeth II visited Scarborough, Reeve A. M. Campbell summarized the history and achievements of the Township in these words:

> To this new land, where great cliffs rising sheer from Lake Ontario spoke of the English Scarborough, in the year 1796 came settlers from the British Isles and Loyalists from the former British colonies of America. Here in the forest they bravely built their first log cabin homes and hewed out farms which became one of the richest agricultural areas of Canada for over a century. Here in the open fields of Scarborough were bred men who served their King and Country and fought for freedom with their comrades of the Commonwealth in two World Wars. Today, in a Township transformed into one of the great industrial and commercial centres of Canada, enriched by the skills of men of many countries, in modern and attractive factories we share the creative work of the nation; and in new schools and churches, parks, libraries, and homes we strive to build yet better, happier citizens, loyal to those high principles which are our British heritage.

Local History Projects *1. Find out the names of the schools in your area, and the origin of their names.*

2. Do a study on how your area is governed. What are the main jobs of your elected officials?

3. *Draw a map of the area showing major roads, rivers, and railways. What effect have these had on the development of your community?*
4. *On a map showing the outline of your community, indicate where one might find the downtown area, the in-* dustrial area, and the residential area.
5. *What factors do you think account for the rapid growth of Scarborough? What factors account for the growth of your own community? Which of these factors do you think is the most important?*

Word Study

urban community	mastodons	Community Colleges
rural community	bees	township
family tree	reeve	Upper Canada
ice age	trolleys	parish

Things to Do   1. *Interview some people who have lived in your community for a long time. Here are questions you might wish to ask.*
(a) *Why did they come to your community? When?*
(b) *What problems did they face when they first settled?*
(c) *What important changes have taken place since they first settled?*
d) *Which of these changes do you think are improvements?*
e) *What are some ways in which the community will change in the future?*
(f) *Is the quality of life better now than in the old days?*
2. *Plan a class visit to Upper Canada Village near Kingston, Black Creek Pioneer Village in Toronto, or any such location where the lifestyles of the pioneers can still be seen. Such a trip will give you an opportunity to see the houses, tools, clothing, and cooking of the early pioneers.*
3. *As a class project, organize a* "local history newspaper" *to report on the changes which have taken place in your community. The theme might be* "Yesterday and Today". *For example, one student might write a column dealing with entertainment in the days of the pioneers. Another might compare this with modern forms of entertainment. Other areas of comparison might include:*

—*size of the community*
—*dress styles*
—*average income*
—*styles of education*
—*hardships faced by immigrants*
—*changes in roads and transportation.*

4. *Some members of the class can be assigned roles as members of a typical pioneer family—father, mother, children and grandparents. Another student can be assigned the role of* "interviewing" *each member of the family. Each family member might be asked what he or she considers the hardest part of pioneer living.*

Unit 2
Canada's First People

A teenage Inuit music group in Churchill, Manitoba.

1
Introduction

"The Scots are stingy."
"The English are snobbish."
"Jews are money-hungry."
"Italians are criminals."
"Americans are greedy."
"Indians are lazy."

How often have you heard statements like these? Perhaps you have even made them yourself. It is common in many societies for certain groups to label members of other groups in such terms. This is especially true in countries such as Canada and the United States where people from many parts of the world have made their homes.

When you make a statement such as "English people are snobbish" you are *STEREOTYPING* the English. This means you are putting all English people in the same category. How does such a practice begin? It is very clear that this attitude is something you have learned rather than something you were born with. Perhaps on one occasion you were snubbed by an English person. Because of this experience, you now consider all English people as "stuck-up" and "snobbish". You have stereotyped them.

Stereotyping can lead to *PREJUDICE*. To be prejudiced means to pre-judge a person. You may have heard that the Scots are stingy. At school you meet someone from Scotland. You may believe that person is stingy, because of the stereotype. In this case you have made up your mind before getting to know the person. You have pre-judged someone.

Prejudices may be passed on from one generation to the next. If a set of parents does not like one minority group, they may pass this attitude on to their children. This is one of many ways by which prejudice is spread. Of course if you are prejudiced against an individual or a group, but keep this attitude to yourself, you are not harming anyone except yourself. However, if you voice your prejudice, or take other action against this individual or group, then you are practising *DISCRIMINATION*. One example of this would be an employer refusing to hire someone because he or she does not like that person's colour or religious beliefs. Discrimination is prejudice put into action. Of course, you can also be prejudiced *in favour* of certain people. In such cases you might discriminate in their favour by going out of your way to be friendly toward them, or to give them special treatment.

Unfortunately the practices of stereotyping, prejudice, and discrimination against certain groups are present in many societies. Often it is applied by one race of people against another or by one ethnic group against another. This sometimes leads to conflict and violence. The racial problems of the United

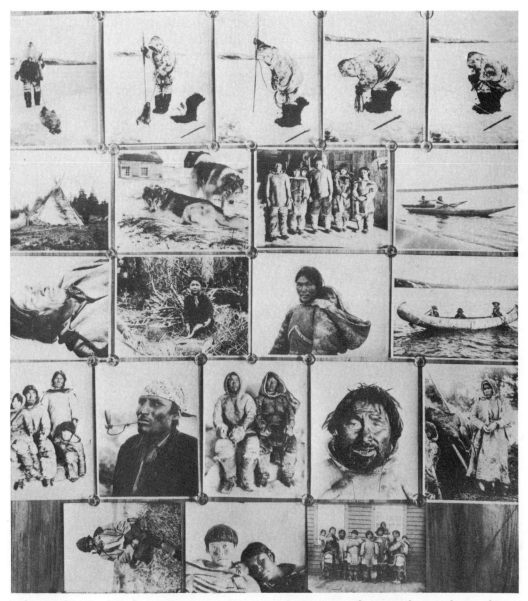

Indian and Inuit of Hudson's Bay, 1906. Can you point out some distinguishing Indian and Inuit characteristics?

States in the past have been examples of the results of prejudice and discrimination.

Canadians have long prided themselves on their sense of fairness toward all people. Is this feeling justified? In this unit you will be studying the treatment of the Indians over the centuries.

The European's misunderstanding, and mistreatment, of the Indians of North America began with Christopher Columbus' first landing. Thinking he had found the Asian country of India, Columbus called the inhabitants of North America "Indians". Today, many social scientists call the first North American People *AMERINDS*, a combination of the words "American Indians".

The second error came when the explorer John Cabot landed in Newfoundland in 1497. There he met a group of Beothuk Indians who had painted their faces red. Cabot reported his meeting with the "red Indians". The mistaken notion that Indians are "red" has existed ever since.

Actually Amerinds belong to one of the three main racial groups. These groups are Caucasoid, Mongoloid, and Negroid. Races are divided according to certain physical features. Social scientists have shown that there is no such thing as a "pure" race. Over thousands of years, there has been much mixing of people of different races. These are some of the ways in which the three major racial groups are divided today:

	Caucasoid	Mongoloid	Negroid
Physical Features Skin	white to dark brown	yellowish-white to copper brown	light brown to ebony black
Hair	blond to black, curly to straight	black straight	black tightly curled
Eyes	blue to dark brown, oval shape	dark brown, oval shape with skin fold over inner angle of eye opening	dark brown oval shape
Nose	narrow	medium	broad or flat
Mouth	thin to medium	medium	thick
Location (where most of the population lives)	Europe, North America, Near East, South America, India	China, Southeast Asia, Japan	Africa

Compare the photos of the Indians and Inuit on page 45 with the categories in the chart. To which racial group do Indians and Inuit belong?

Both the Indians and Inuit of North America belong to the Mongoloid racial group. Yet there are considerable differences in appearance between Indians and Inuit, and even between one tribe of Indians and another. In general there are the same physical differences between Indian groups that one might find between various groups of Europeans.

Despite these differences, there are basic similarities among Indians throughout North America. These include: skin colour, which is some shade of brown or copper; the hair of the head, which is black and straight; the eyes, which are medium to dark brown, and have the mongoloid skin fold; the face, which is usually wider than a European face; a full chest, and evenly proportioned body and limbs.

Inuit tend to have lighter skin than Indians, faces which are broader and flatter, and smaller noses. Anthropologists feel these differences may be due to climate conditions and diet. The Indians and Inuit probably belong to the same racial group, but differences in their environment have produced physical differences.

The Indians and Inuit were Canada's original people. But as a racial minority in Canada, they have not always received fair treatment. Much of this is due to ignorance and lack of understanding of their problems and needs by other Canadians. Perhaps you have never met an Indian or Inuit. Much of your information concerning their way of life probably comes from comic books, movies, and television. The Indian "stereotype" has been fixed in your mind from the time you were very young.

The image you might have is that all Inuit live in igloos and all Indians have painted faces, wear feathered bonnets, and do nothing but trap and hunt or collect welfare money from the government.

The practice of stereotyping the Indians and Inuit has often stood in the way of understanding between these people and other Canadians. Recently, as Indians and Inuit have become more outspoken in demanding certain rights, more and more Canadians have begun to listen to them.

In this unit you will be studying some aspects of Indian and Inuit life before the coming of the European. You will also see how the Europeans affected this way of life. Finally you will be able to study some of the issues facing the Indian and Inuit in modern Canada.

Before you begin, try to sum up in a paragraph or two your feelings and attitudes towards Canada's Indians and Inuit. Which of the following words would you use: fierce, savage, brave, fearless, noble, warlike, lazy, proud, kind, ancient? Do this exercise again at the end of the unit. Have your attitudes changed?

We and They

Father, Mother, and Me,
    Sister and Auntie say
All the people like us are *We*,
    And everyone else is *They*.
And *They* live over the sea,
    While *We* live over the way.
But—would you believe it?—*They* look upon *We*
    As only a sort of *They*!

All good people agree,
    And all good people say,
All nice people, like *Us*, are *We*
    And everyone else is *They*:
But if you cross over the sea,
    Instead of over the way,
You may end by (think of it) looking on *We*
    As only a sort of *They*!

1. *What prejudice is expressed in the poem?*
2. *Does the poet think "they" are "inferior" or only "different"?*
3. *Does knowledge of other groups and cultures help reduce prejudice? Explain.*
4. *What experiences have you had in learning about groups against whom you were prejudiced? Do you think that knowledge always makes people more understanding of other groups?*

2
The First Discovery of America

Moscow, June 14, 1974

The Soviet news agency Tass today reported that archaeologists have found new evidence that the Indians of North America emigrated to the New World from Siberia.

The leader of the expedition, Professor Dikov, working at sites in northeast Siberia and the Kamchatka Peninsula, claimed that the latest finds show that Indian ornaments had their origin in Asia.

He added that the migration of the Indians took place during the ice age when Siberia and Alaska were joined by land across the Bering Strait.

This news report is not really news at all. It simply confirms what many historians and anthropologists have believed for a long time. The proof of their theories is only now being uncovered.

Canada had no true native peoples. Traces of our origins in other parts of the world go back more than two million years. Yet in neither North nor South America do human remains date back more than fifty thousand years. Anthropologists conclude that human beings did not originate here. They migrated here from other parts of the world.

Although the Indians were not native to Canada, they were certainly the first people in this country. Because of this they can truly be called Canada's original people.

In this chapter we will look at the settlement of Canada by the Indian and Inuit people. The evidence we will examine tries to answer the questions: where did they come from? how did they get here? when did they migrate to Canada?

The Origin of the Indians and Inuit

The Europeans who first had contact with the Indian tribes of North America were amazed at the richness and variety of the cultures they saw. In Central America, where Indian culture reached its highest peak, the wealth and luxury of the Aztecs astounded the explorers. They found it hard to believe that the Indians of Central America could have built the magnificent temples and monuments that are still to be seen today.

The Aztec capital at Mexico City, first visited by Cortez in 1519, was as splendid as any European city of the time. All this was achieved without metal tools or even the wheel. The Mayans, an Indian society which lived in Mexico before the Aztecs developed a system of irrigation, grew corn, knew arithmetic, and invented a calendar which was even more precise than the one we use today.

Mayan Arithmetic Table

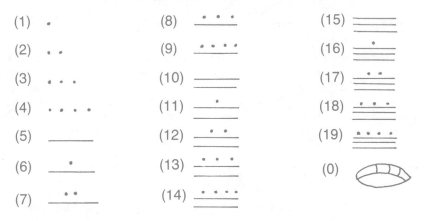

In other parts of North America Indian cultures did not reach such levels. Yet they also developed complex societies. They were able to adjust very well to their environment although they too lacked such basics as metal tools, the wheel, and horses.

Right down to the present, many people have found it hard to believe that the North American Indians could have achieved what they did on their own. They considered the Indians "primitive" and so believed they must have developed their culture somewhere else. The idea developed that the Indians must have been the descendants of a group of "advanced" people from the Old World.

One theory suggests that the Indians are the descendants of one of the "lost tribes" of Israel mentioned in the Bible. Others suggest that Indian culture came from the ancient Egyptians, or perhaps from the Pacific islands of Polynesia. The noted adventurer Thor Heyerdahl has shown how this was possible. He built boats of the kind in which the Polynesians and Egyptians of thousands of years ago might have sailed across the oceans. In these he too sailed to North America.

Most experts today do not believe in these theories. Neither do they believe that the Indians are native to North America. Where then, did the Indians come from? The answer they give is—Asia. We have already seen their reasons for believing this. The physical features of the American Indian seem to resemble very closely those of Asian people. Recent archaeological finds also suggest the close ties between prehistoric Asian people, and the first Indians. This seems to answer the question of Indian origin.

The next question is, how did they get here? Again there are several possibilities.

1. They may have sailed directly across the Pacific Ocean. This theory is unlikely, simply because the length of the voyage and the poor quality of boats would make the success of the trip doubtful.

2. They may have come across the Bering Strait. The distance between Siberia and Alaska across the strait is only sixty-seven kilometres and the land on each side is so high that on a clear day it is easy to see across. Eskimos still often travel back and forth across this route in their kayaks.

3. They may have crossed on a land bridge between Siberia and Alaska. Even today, the water is only forty-five metres deep in this area. If the water level dropped lower than this it would expose a mass of land connecting Siberia and Alaska. How could such a drop in the water level have occurred?

Scientists tell us that many thousands of years ago, during the last ice age, huge glaciers developed over large parts of North America. To make these glaciers large amounts of water would have been drawn from the oceans. This would have lowered the ocean level by more than ninety metres.

> You can do a simple experiment to illustrate this. Place a glass of water in your freezer. After one hour, remove the ice which has formed in the glass. What has happened to the level of the water? The effect of the ice age on the oceans was the same. In this case the glaciers moved onto the land and so lowered the ocean level.
>
> We still have many glaciers in the world today. Scientists calculate that if the Greenland and Antarctic ice sheets were to melt suddenly, the ocean level would rise by seventy-five metres!

In the past 100 000 years the land bridge between Asia and North America, called Beringia, was exposed several times. About 20 000 years ago, it probably looked like the map at the top of page 52.

The theory indicates that the Indians may have migrated at several different periods across Beringia. Since the land itself was probably very fertile, they may actually have lived in Beringia for many years waiting for the glaciers in Alaska to melt. How could this theory be proved? There would probably be a great number of tools and weapons to be found by archaeologists in Beringia. Of course, since it is now under water, these relics may never be uncovered.

Once the glaciers began to retreat from the coast, the Indians would have moved south to warmer climates in Central and South America. As the glaciers disappeared from most of North America, they would then have moved northward again, finally settling in Canada.

1. *Which of the three theories concerning the possible route of Indian migration do you think is most likely? Why?*

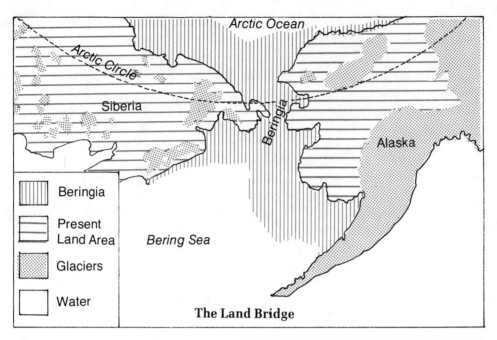

The Land Bridge

Legend:
- Beringia
- Present Land Area
- Glaciers
- Water

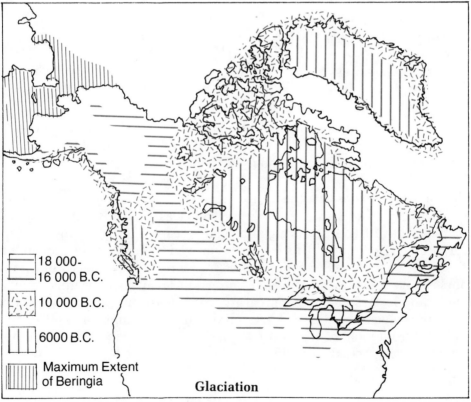

Legend:
- 18 000–16 000 B.C.
- 10 000 B.C.
- 6000 B.C.
- Maximum Extent of Beringia

Glaciation

2. *If the Indians came to North America by way of Alaska, explain why Canada was probably the last part of North America to be settled.*

3. *Consult a book on the history of the Jewish people, or talk to your priest or minister, or rabbi. Try to find out who the "lost tribes" of Israel were.*

This leaves the question of when these migrations took place. For many years archaeological findings indicated a fairly recent date for this migration. Some of the discoveries and suggested dates are:

Items	Place	Date
spear points	New Mexico	8 000 B.C.
spear points, tools	Oregon	9 000 B.C.
human bones, spear points	Patagonia in South America	6-700 B.C.
human bones	Minnesota	11 000 B.C.
human bones	Texas	13 000-17 000 B.C.

Other findings which showed an older date for Indian migration were often thought to be fakes. However, recent findings may throw new light on this subject.

San Diego, May 15, 1974 (Associated Press)

A team of scientists said yesterday that new findings show man may have existed in the New World 50,000 years ago. "A new chapter in the history of man" may have been opened up by a set of human fossils found in Southern California.

The bones were at first believed to be only 7,500 years old, but a new technique in dating shows one skull to be 48,000 years old. Another skull was dated at 44,000 years.

The scientists said man could have walked across the Bering Strait far longer than that. "We know that the sea level was low enough to allow the formation of a land bridge about 140,000 years ago and perhaps also 70,000 years before the present", they said.

Evidence concerning the migration of the Inuit is even more vague. Some scientists once believed that the Inuit were offshoots of North American Indians. They believed the physical differences were due to differences in climate and diet.

Most scientists now believe that Inuit are a group separate from, though related to, the Indians. They are believed to have crossed to North America from Siberia much later than the Indians, perhaps 4000 years ago.

1. *At what date do you think the first Indians crossed into North America? According to the scientists, at what two dates would this have been possible?*

2. *Why do you think it is difficult in present day North America to find more evidence of early Indian settlement?*

3. *What route would the Inuit have used to get to North America?*

3
Indian Society Before the Arrival of the Europeans

It is the opening scene of the movie *Red River*. The hero, John Wayne, is seen parting from a westward-bound wagon train and his sweetheart, in search of his own land. In the next scene we learn that Indians have ambushed the wagon train and massacred all the settlers. That same night, the hero and his friend are attacked without warning by a number of these Indians, but of course, are able to kill all their attackers. On one of the dead Indians the hero finds a piece of jewellery belonging to his sweetheart.She too has been killed. The hero suffers a moment of grief, and in his anguish we the viewers are made to feel resentful toward Indians and their ways. *Red River* is considered one of the greatest movies yet made.

Almost any week of the year, if you consult your television listings you will find movies of this kind on the late show. They show the "winning of the West" and the struggle between Indian and European. The next time you see such a movie, try to make notes of the number of times these lines are heard:

"The only good Indian is a dead Indian."
"Them dirty redskins are attacking again."
"The savages never attack at night."
"We've been ambushed."
"The red devils have massacred every man, woman and child in the wagon train."

Almost every generation since movies were invented has been exposed to this sort of entertainment. The North American view of the Indian has been shaped over the last fifty years by the image created in movies, television, and novels. The Indian can only ask in wonder, "Why is it always that when the Indian people win a victory over the Europeans in defense of their land it is a massacre, yet when the Europeans kill Indian women and children it is a victory?"

There are several images people have of the condition of the Indian before the coming of the Europeans. One paints the picture of a warlike, bloodthirsty, backward primitive, the other of the "noble savage" who invented the canoe and the snowshoe.

In fact Indian cultures in Canada were quite varied. There was as much difference between Indians in Newfoundland and in British Columbia as between Europeans in Italy and in Finland. This was true despite the fact that at the first coming of the Europeans there were perhaps no more than two hundred and twenty thousand Indians in all of Canada.

In this chapter we will look at several aspects of Indian culture in different parts of Canada. As you read, try to account for the differences in Indian cultures. Try to note also the attitude of the Indians toward their environment.

Language Groups

The Indians of Canada did not divide up their land into "countries" as the Europeans did. Because of this, it is difficult to find the boundaries between one Indian cultural group and another. One way to classify Canadian Indians is by language groups. Groups, or tribes, speaking a similar language, are placed in the same language group. This does not mean that they shared a similar culture. Picture a large, modern Canadian city. In this city there are many people from different parts of the world. Most of them have learned English or French, and so speak a common language. Yet they may still retain their own different cultures. So it was with the Indians.

The opposite was often true also. Several tribes in one culture area might belong to different language groups. This was usually due to the large areas of land involved. The Plains tribes, for example, all lived by buffalo hunting. Because of the large area covered by the buffalo herds, there was room for the tribes of more than one language group. The map below shows the distribution of the culture groups.

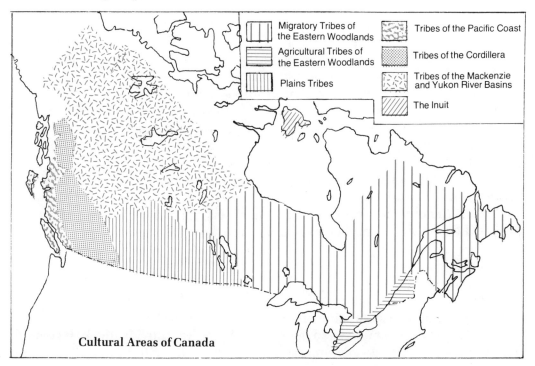

Migratory Tribes of the Eastern Woodlands

Agricultural Tribes of the Eastern Woodlands

Plains Tribes

Tribes of the Pacific Coast

Tribes of the Cordillera

Tribes of the Mackenzie and Yukon River Basins

The Inuit

Cultural Areas of Canada

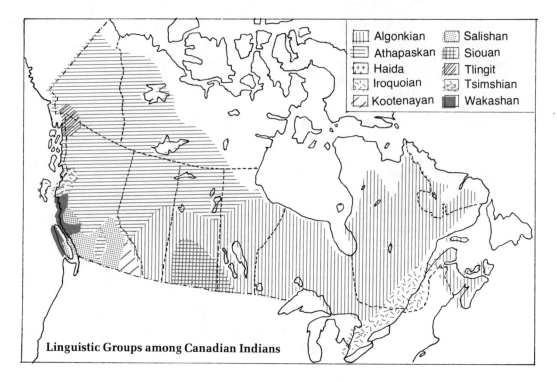

Algonkian	Salishan
Athapaskan	Siouan
Haida	Tlingit
Iroquoian	Tsimshian
Kootenayan	Wakashan

Linguistic Groups among Canadian Indians

The Canadian Indians did not develop a true system of writing. This was perhaps the major obstacle in the way of developing a higher technology. Some experts have said that writing has been the most important human invention. Try to imagine what writing has meant in human society. It enabled people to preserve their knowledge, pass it on from generation to generation in a form more lasting and accurate than memory, and to build on to this knowledge. Without such a system rapid progress would be difficult. Each generation would have to learn slowly through experience, rather than quickly through education and books.

Can you make a list of the inventions which have been made possible by the invention of writing?

In fact, the Indians did develop a form of writing, sometimes called picture writing. Look at the example on the next page.

1. *Can you tell what the message is?*
2. *What drawbacks are there in this system of writing?*
3. *What might this message have been written on? What might it have been written with?*

The message is a love letter from an Indian girl, who belongs to the tribe represented by the bear's paw, to her boyfriend, represented by the fish symbol. It says she would like to see him, and shows him the path to her village. Her teepee is beside the tents occupied by Christian missionaries, represented by the

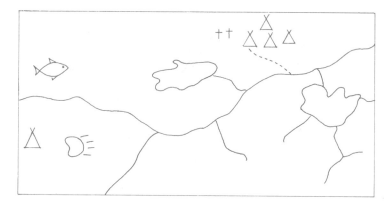

crosses. Perhaps now you can see some of the disadvantages of this form of writing.

Despite their lack of a developed system of writing, the Indians were able to develop a fine oral tradition. By word of mouth, they were able to hand down from one generation to the next most of the knowledge and skills which they considered necessary and valuable for survival in their kind of society and environment.

Political Life

The political organization of Canadian Indian tribes differed greatly from area to area. Some tribes had a very simple organization. They were led by a chief, who was chosen for his hunting ability. Others developed systems which were very complicated. The best example of this was the Iroquois Confederacy. It has been described as one of the wisest political systems ever invented.

It may surprise you to learn that the first Confederation in North America was developed by the Iroquois. The Iroquois were actually not one tribe, but five. They lived on the southern shore of Lake Ontario in the region of present-day New York State and Quebec. From east to west the Five Nations of the Iroquois were the Mohawks, Oneidas, Onondagas, Cayugas, and Senecas. Later the Tuscarora tribe joined to make the Iroquois six nations.

Unlike most Canadian Indian tribes, the Iroquois did not depend only on hunting for their food. Although the forest were rich with game, the Iroquois had also developed agriculture. They grew maize, or corn, as well as beans, pumpkins, and squash. The important task of looking after the crops was carried out by the women of the tribe.

The Iroquois way of life was actually based on agriculture. They were not nomadic as other tribes were, but rather built permanent villages near their crops. They would live in these villages until the land could no longer produce crops. Then they would move to another location and begin again.

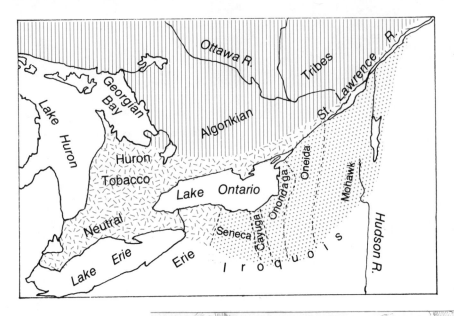

Breaking ground and sowing corn.

A small fish often went
into each hill as fertilizer.

Gathering the corn.

What tools might the Indians be using to break the
soil? What tools are used
today?

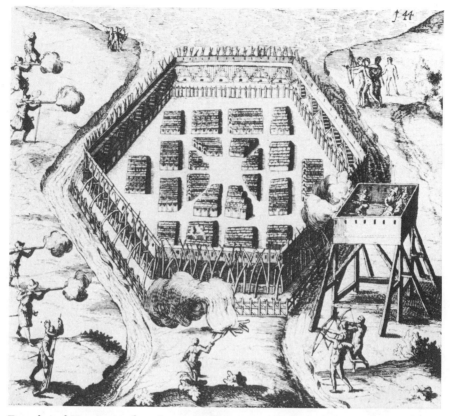

French and Huron attack an Iroquois village. How many longhouses can you count in this village? What protective features does it have?

Compare the Iroquois village with this Ojibway village of the Plains. Which is more heavily fortified? Can you think of reasons why?

The smallest unit of Iroquois society was the Fireside family, which consisted of the mother and her children. It was the mother who counted in this unit, for the Iroquois traced their lineage through the mother's side rather than the father's.

Each Fireside family was part of a larger group, the Maternal family, which consisted of a head woman and all her children, grandchildren, etc. Some Maternal families numbered more than two hundred people.

Interior of an Iroquois longhouse.

Several Maternal families combined to form a Clan. There were at least four clans in each tribe. The main point about the Clan was that no member could marry someone from the same clan. In the following diagram, a member of the Turtle Clan, for example, would have to marry someone from one of the other three clans of the tribe, or perhaps from another tribe.

The clans together formed a nation, or tribe. The five tribes together formed the Iroquois Confederacy or League.

The Iroquois Confederacy

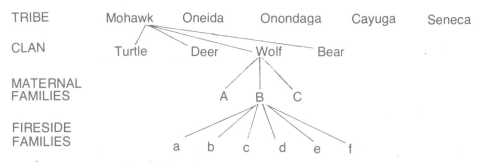

Are you surprised that the Iroquois women were regarded so highly? So were the first Europeans. They were even more surprised to discover that:

— Marriages were arranged by the mothers of the couple.
— Each longhouse was in the charge of a head woman.
— The Iroquois League was ruled by fifty chiefs. Each candidate for this position was selected by the head woman of a maternal family.
— The head woman could also depose, or impeach, a chief who did not carry out his duties properly.

Women in Iroquois society were still considered inferior to men. They could not hold office themselves, nor were they recognized at council meetings, for example. Yet, compared to European women, they held many important roles in their society. It was not until three hundred years later, in 1917, that women were first allowed to vote in Canada.

The fifty chiefs of the Iroquois League were considered equal. They dealt with matters that were important to all the Iroquois tribes, but could not interfere in internal matters of an individual tribe.

Some tribes, because of their size or important geographical position, had more representative chiefs than others:

Mohawk	9
Oneida	9
Onondaga	14
Cayuga	10
Seneca	8
Total	50

The Iroquois sometimes viewed their political organization as a symbolic longhouse. Geographically, the two tribes at the eastern and western extremes were the Mohawk and the Seneca. They were the guardians of the "doors" and were responsible for the military protection of the League.

The Onondaga in the centre were in charge of the "central fireplace". They called the meetings of the League, and in a close decision they would cast the tie-breaking vote in the meetings. Even though they were smaller in number than the Senecas, the Onondagas had more representatives at the meetings of the League. The Senecas, who formed the largest tribe, had the fewest representatives.

Why do you think the league would give more representatives to the more peaceful Onondaga, and fewer representatives to the two tribes responsible for military action, the Senecas and Mohawks?

Iroquois government was one of the earliest democratic governments in the world. Each man had an opportunity to be selected as chief, regardless of age or birth. His selection was based on personal qualities admired by Indians, such as skill in battle, courage, wisdom, and speaking ability. There were no upper classes or lower classes in Iroquois society, and even the chiefs were not considered to be above their people.

1. *Why were the Iroquois villages permanent?*

2. *Who looked after raising the crops? Why would agriculture be considered so important by the Iroquois?*

3. *How would you account for the important political role played by women in Iroquois society? Why might women not play so important a role in other Indian societies?*

4. *Compare the role of women in today's society with their role in Iroquois society. In which case do the women have more influence?*

5. *What qualities do we look for in a leader in Canada today? Compare these with the qualities considered important by the Iroquois.*

6. *How would you define "democracy"? Do you think the Iroquois government was really democratic? Explain.*

Economic Life

The economic activities of the Indian were as varied as the Canadian countryside. The economy of the West Coast Indians depended mainly on fishing. The Plains tribes relied upon the migration of the great buffalo herds for their survival. The Iroquois could count on their mixed hunting and farming activities to supply them with all the necessary food.

By far the majority of Canada's Indians depended upon hunting and fishing. It was in these activities that they used their skill and knowledge of their surroundings. Not only did the Indians hunt, they studied the background and habits of the animals they hunted. For example, the Nootka Indians of Vancouver knew every stage of a salmon's development, from egg to adult. This

Model of an Iroquois bark longhouse in the Rochester Municipal Museum. Compare the types of shelter shown here. Which is the quickest to build and take down? Why would the Iroquois have more permanent houses than the Plains Indians?

Indian teepee at Gods Lake, Man., 1925.

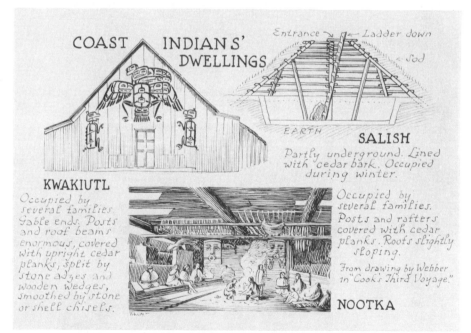

COAST INDIANS' DWELLINGS

Entrance — Ladder down — Sod

EARTH

SALISH

Partly underground. Lined with cedar bark. Occupied during winter.

KWAKIUTL

Occupied by several families. Gable ends. Posts and roof beams enormous, covered with upright cedar planks, split by stone adzes and wooden wedges, smoothed by stone or shell chisels.

Occupied by several families. Posts and rafters covered with cedar planks. Roofs slightly sloping.

From drawing by Webber in "Cook's Third Voyage."

NOOTKA

Why might these houses not be suitable for the Plains Indians?

knowledge enabled them to stock rivers by moving the eggs from one location to another.

Such knowledge was vital to the Indians. Their very survival depended on it. In times when game was scarce, knowledge of an animal's movements, places of hibernation, and food sources gave the Indian hunter an edge. Often it was the difference between life and death.

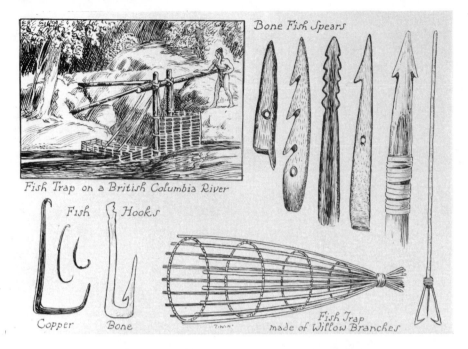

Bone Fish Spears

Fish Trap on a British Columbia River

Fish Hooks

Copper   Bone

Fish Trap made of Willow Branches

The Indians were also very observant of the plant life in their territory. They knew which plants were edible and which were poisonous, which plants could be shaped into tools and weapons, and which could cure sickness. They discovered the medicinal qualities of many plants unknown to white doctors. In 1536, the Indians of Quebec saved the lives of Jacques Cartier and his men by curing them of scurvy.

Indians show Jacques Cartier the cure for scurvy.

One day our Captain, seeing the disease so general and his men so stricken down by it . . . caught sight of a band of Indians . . . and among them was Dom Agaya whom he had seen ten or twelve days previous to this, extremely ill with the very disease his own men were suffering from; for one of his legs about the knee had swollen to the size of a two-year old baby, and the sinews had become contracted. His teeth had gone bad and decayed and the gums had rotted and become tainted . . . . The Captain inquired of him what had cured him of his sickness. Dom Agaya replied that he had been healed by the juice of the leaves of a tree and the dregs of these . . . They showed us how to grind the bark and the leaves and to boil the whole in water. Of this one should drink every two days, and place the dregs on the legs where they were swollen and affected. . . . The Captain at once ordered a drink to be prepared for the sick men . . . after drinking it two or three times, they recovered health and strength and were cured of all the diseases they had ever had . . . .

1. *What are the symptoms of scurvy?*   *find out what the modern cure for*
2. *What was the Indian cure? Try to   scurvy is.*

Of course, hunting skill varied from tribe to tribe. The Cree Indians were recognized as probably the best hunters in the Eastern Woodlands. Their neighbours the Chipeweyans were not as skilled in hunting, but were probably better fishermen.

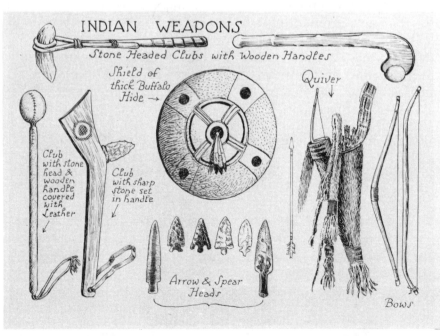

Most tribes adopted a number of different hunting techniques. The most basic was the individual hunt. This pitted the skill of an individual against an animal. For success, the hunter had to have tracking ability, speed of foot, endurance, patience, and marksmanship. The Indian was one of the most skilled hunters known to history.

Hunting animals which travelled in herds required a community effort. Women and children were often enlisted to help. While the hunters stationed themselves on one side of the herd, the women and children approached from the other, making as much noise as possible, hoping to drive the animals toward the waiting hunters.

A second method was simply to surround the herd of animals and shoot as many as possible before the rest broke through.

A third method, which could be wasteful at times, involved stampeding a herd over a cliff. This was sometimes used by the Plains Indians in the buffalo hunt. Hundreds of buffalo were often killed this way in a single hunt. Their bones can still be found from time to time. But Indians did not kill game for sport, nor did they usually kill more than they needed for food.

Some tribes used more complicated methods, such as building traps and luring in herds of deer or buffalo. The trap might consist of a circular compound made of trees, twigs, and branches. When a herd of buffalo was found, a lone Indian wearing a buffalo skin would approach the herd, and try to get the buffalo to follow him. If this succeeded, he would lead them into the compound, or "pound", leap out, and close the gate. Since a herd might sometimes be more than eighty kilometres from the compound, this was a very difficult job. When the horse came into use in the eighteenth century, it made this task much easier.

Winter hunting was often more difficult because the game was scarcer. Deep snow was also an obstacle. On the other hand, certain types of animal pelts, such as beaver, were more valuable when taken in winter. This became important when Europeans began to trade for these furs.

Samuel de Champlain describes one winter hunt in 1604:

During the winter they go hunting for moose and other animals when the snow is very deep. They make use of certain racquets which they tie to their feet, and with these they are able to travel over snow without sinking. They follow the tracks of animals until they catch sight of a beast. They shoot at him with their bows or kill him with spears. This is easily done, since these animals cannot travel in the snow without sinking in.

1. What are the "racquets" to which Champlain refers?

2. What advantage does the hunter have over the animal in winter?

3. Would hunting be easier for the In-   4. Why would certain pelts, like bea-
dian in summer or in winter?   ver, be more valuable in winter?

A Deadfall for trapping foxes, wolves, etc.

Montagnais hunting Moose in Winter

Shooting the Wild Turkey

If successful in the hunt, the Indians were faced with a problem few of us would think about today—preserving the food. Today we have refrigerators which can keep our food for long periods of time, even in summer. What could the Indians do to preserve food beyond a few days? For one thing, they stored extra food in caches, leather bags which were buried in the ground or hung from trees. Unfortunately such caches were often discovered and eaten by animals.

A second method, one which could be used in the winter, was to sink an animal carcass in a shallow stream. A layer of ice on the surface of the water would prevent animals from finding the meat. In the ice-cold water, the meat would keep for several weeks.

Finally, there was PEMMICAN, the most ingenious of the food-preserving methods invented by the Indians. Pemmican could be made from any kind of meat—buffalo, moose, deer, etc. Meat was dried slowly over a fire, or by the sun. It was then ground into a powder which could be flavoured by adding fruits and berries. Fat was added for a binder, and the pemmican was stored in a leather pouch. Food in this form was almost as nutritious as regular meat, but was easy to carry and could last for years.

An important practice in Indian society was the system of food-sharing. Hoarding food was unthinkable if another were starving. All Indians knew how difficult survival was. In bad times, men, women, and children could, and often did, starve to death. Sickness, bad luck, and accidents might prevent a hunter from bringing in game for weeks at a time. Under such conditions, co-operation and sharing of goods were necessary. Yet because of the pride Indians had in their own hunting skill, no hunter would take advantage of the system by loafing. The hunter's values enabled him to contribute to the welfare of his tribe and his family.

Blood Indian ponies and travois, Aug. 23, 1910. The travois was the chief method of transportation on the Plains. Why did the Indians not use carts or wagons?

Indian Religion

Although the Indians were called "pagans" by the first Europeans, they had a deep religious life of their own. Indian religion was not concerned so much with the afterlife as with the here and now. Practices and customs varied greatly from tribe to tribe. Yet some characteristics of Indian religion were common to all parts of Canada. The belief in a Supreme Being who ruled over the earth, the presence of souls in people, and often in other creatures, the respect for nature, are all common features of the Indian religion. Some of these will be seen in the following Indian prayers and legends.

From the Delaware Indians of Ontario:

> There is a Great Spirit, a leader of all the gods, called Manitou. Through his agents he created the world and everything in it, the water, trees, fire, and the Delaware themselves. People pray to him in ceremonies and thank him for his gifts. We also pray to his agents who are closer to man, and more easily hear our prayers.

From the Dakota Indians of the Plains:

> All things in the world have spirits. The spirits of trees and stones are not the same as the spirit of man, but they too are given by beings who are greater than mankind. These beings together are called Wakan Tanka. They were not born and they never die. The greatest of these is the Great Spirit.

Prayer to a slain beaver:

> O friend, tree-cutter, thank you for coming to me. I wanted to catch you so that you might give me your ability to work. I wish to be like you, for there is nothing you cannot do, friend.

1. *What did Indians believe about the Great Spirit?*
2. *What are the qualities of the gods to whom the Indians prayed?*
3. *Why did an Indian hunter pray to the beaver he killed?*
4. *How is the Indians' deep respect for nature shown in these writings? In what way is the Indian view of nature, and nature's creatures, different from that of the Europeans?*

The Indians believed that both good and evil came from the gods. It was important to avoid offending the gods, and also important to pray for favours. Success in the hunt or in war depended on the favour of the gods. Sometimes this could be obtained through prayer alone. When a young boy reached his teens, he would often try to get the help of a supernatural power. This sometimes meant seeking a guardian spirit as protector. The guardian spirit might take different forms, including that of an animal or bird such as the beaver or the eagle.

This practice usually meant the young boy had to undergo a period of fasting, prayer, and self-sacrifice, hoping to see a vision. A Christian missionary describes a vision which came to a young Huron boy:

> When he was fifteen he prepared for his vision by going into the desert. After he had fasted sixteen days without eating anything, drinking only water, he saw his vision. An old man came down from the sky, and approached him saying "Have courage. I will look after you. You are lucky to have me as your master, for no devil will have power to harm you. You will have four children, the first two, and the last will be male, the third female." The spirit returned into the sky, but appeared often after that and promised to help the young man. Almost everything he predicted at that time has come true.

Shamans singing to drive away evil spirits causing sickness.

Many Indians placed their dead on scaffolds or trees above ground.

Conjuring Tent inside which a Medicine Man is supposed to be wrestling & communicating with spirits.

Those who had special powers of healing and seeing into the future were called medicine men, or *SHAMANS*. A shaman was not a priest in the modern sense. It was believed that he had the power to cure illness, restore souls, or even to cause illness and death. A shaman could be either male or female.

Besides his healing powers, the shaman was expected to regulate all religious ceremonies, especially those in which young boys and girls entered adulthood. The institution of shamanism was common to all Indian and Inuit

What is the purpose of these dances? In what parts of Canada would the Green Corn Dance have been performed? Where would the Buffalo Dances have been held?

societies in Canada. The shamans usually possessed very strong personalities. Because of this, they sometimes became both religious and political leaders. The power of the shaman decreased with the coming of the Europeans. New diseases from Europe afflicted many of Canada's tribes. The shaman most often could not cure these diseases. In fact, he often fell victim himself. Today the shaman is still influential among many Indian bands, although he is more a psychologist than a religious leader or doctor.

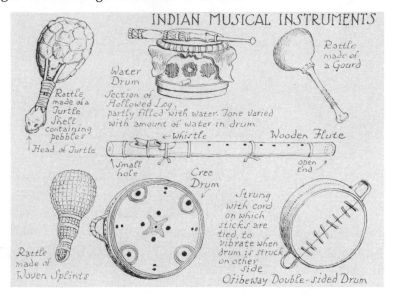

1. What do you think was the main purpose of religion to the Indians?

2. In what way did their religious beliefs cause the Indians to have a greater respect for nature?

3. How was the function of an Indian shaman different from that of a Christian priest or minister?

Indians were very fond of playing games. The most popular was lacrosse. How are the Indian sticks different from those used today?

Word Study

pagan	shaman	Sun Dance
Manitou	Conjuring Tent	Iroquois Confederacy
Wakan Tanka	pemmican	

Things To Do   1. Some people have said the Iroquois Confederacy was the model on which the United Nations and the government of the United States were based. Find out the structure of the United Nations or of the government of the United States. Do you see any similarities among these systems of government?

2. Find out more about Indian burial practices. How did they vary in different parts of Canada?

3. In what ways were the religious beliefs of the Indians similar to and different from your own?

4. What was the Indians' view of nature? What evidence is there that non-Indians are beginning to come closer to the Indians' view of their environment?

5. Plan a trip to a museum which displays Indian art and cultural objects. Look closely at the workmanship of these items. How would you compare them to modern Canadian paintings and art objects?

Haida totem poles from the Queen Charlotte Islands.

Examples of Indian art. The Pacific Coast Indians seemed to work on a larger scale, and on stationary objects like houses. The eastern Indians made movable objects, like pottery. Can you explain this difference? Which group would have more reliable food sources? More leisure time?

INDIAN POTTERY
Some Typical Designs

Algonkian
Cooking done by setting pot in embers, and dropping hot stones in water in pot.

Iroquoian
Cooking done as above and also by suspending pot over fire.

No.2 was made by a cord twined around a stick and pressed on the wet clay. Circles made by end of hollow stem or bone. No.10 made by pointed thumb nail.

Iroquoian Pot found near Roebuck, Grenville County, Ont.

Sharpened pieces of bone used for marking designs.

Notched bone used for marking rows of small dots.

4
The Inuit

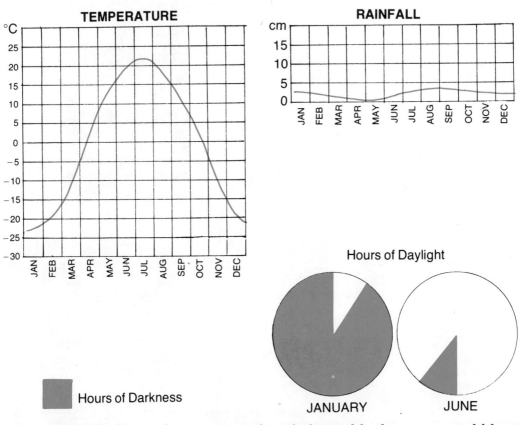

Hours of Daylight

Hours of Darkness

JANUARY   JUNE

If you were asked to pick one area in the whole world where you would *least* like to live, which would it be? If you compared all the places in the world where people live today, chances are your answer would be—the Arctic. Why would you choose this area? Here are some facts to consider:

— The ground is covered with snow for nine months of the year. The frost remains even longer.
— Temperatures of −55° C and lower have been recorded in Canada's Arctic.
— Most forms of agriculture are impossible.

— In the winter months, the sun disappears almost completely, except for a few hours of twilight at mid-day.
— In the summer, the land is almost completely bathed in sunlight for two months.
— In the summer swarms of black flies and mosquitoes can be such a problem that they have been known to cause large animals to stampede to death.

Examine the charts opposite, of Dawson City, Yukon. Compare the figures shown with those of the place where you now live.

1. *How much snow falls on Dawson City in one year? (One centimetre of rain = twelve centimetres of snow.)*
2. *The temperature range is the difference between the highest and the lowest average temperatures in* *one year. What is the temperature range in Dawson City? What is the temperature range in your home town?*
3. *What special problems might Arctic people face in mid-winter and mid-summer?*

Arctic Hazards   Newcomers to the Arctic are often given the following warnings. Why would it be dangerous to ignore them?

— Do not touch metal with your bare hands.
— Shoes, socks, and gloves should be worn loosely in cold weather. If your hands and feet hurt, this is a good sign. If they stop hurting, this is a danger signal.
— Do not handle gasoline or other liquids in very cold temperatures with your bare hands.
— Be careful of walking on ice where you see many seals. Seals must come out of the water to breathe through air-holes.
— Do not wander more than a few metres from your house during a blizzard. The visibility at this time is zero.

The Arctic world, as you see, can often be harsh. It is also very fragile. Much of the Arctic has a ground cover of very delicate plants over a thick layer of permafrost.

In the far North, the temperatures are below freezing much of the year. This means that only a very thin layer of ground, at the surface, ever thaws out. The layer of ground below remains frozen all year round. This layer is called permafrost. Usually there are few trees north of the permafrost line. Can you think why this might be? What problems might the permafrost create if people tried to erect the kinds of buildings that we have in the South?

Because of the climate and soil conditions, plants grow very slowly in the Arctic. A tree no larger than a sapling may actually be hundreds of years old.

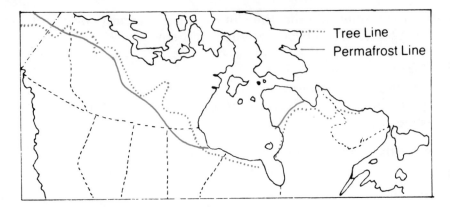

For this reason, people must take great care when dealing with the northern environment.

Our industrial society has not always taken such care. In their search for energy sources, oil companies have sent crews with huge machines to explore the Northland. In the winter this has not created problems, since the land is covered by ice and snow. In the summer these explorations have sometimes caused great destruction. As the machines pass over the ground, the thin layer of vegetation is destroyed. Once damaged, the natural ground cover is slow to grow back. When the permafrost is exposed, it sometimes melts into ugly holes and ruts of mud. These ruts may then actually continue to grow. How might this happen? Can you think why it may take years and even decades for these ruts to heal? Can you offer any solutions which may preserve the Arctic environment and still permit exploration for resources to continue?

In 1964 a group of men working for Imperial Oil set up camp at Fort Macpherson in the Northwest Territories. The group, known as Seismic Party 23, had come to the Canadian Arctic in search of oil. They would spend the next seven years in this task. Here is part of their story:

Surviving in the Arctic

The crewman was doubled up on his bunk with stabbing chest pains. A heart attack? His boss, Clarence McIntosh, chief of Imperial Oil seismic party No. 23, didn't know, but the man obviously needed a hospital. Which was a scarce commodity up there on the shores of the Beaufort Sea.

Party 23 was camped at Kay Point, N.W.T., 20 miles [32 km] north of the 69th parallel. The nearest hospital was at Inuvik, 140 miles [224 km] southeast—a short trip by air, but how could a pilot find this little cluster of trailers at 10 o'clock [22:00] on a bleak Arctic night?

McIntosh raised Inuvik headquarters on the radio. Yes, came the reply, an Otter would fly in, if Party 23 would somehow light the landing strip. Today, Arctic camps are equipped with portable landing lights but there were none in this winter of 1968-69. No matter. Party 23 was famous for its ingenuity. If a thing could be invented, concocted, or improvised, Party 23 would do it. What was so hard about lighting a runway?

First the crew emptied all the soup cans from the kitchen trailer into a big pot. Then they put a roll of toilet tissue in each can, added diesel oil and lit it. The blazing torches lined the packed-snow airstrip and brought the plane right in on target. 'As good a set of lights as I've seen anywhere,' said the pilot, as he rushed the crewman off to hospital.

'And we ate soup for quite a while after that,' McIntosh recalled recently.

No matter how excellent the technology, working in the Arctic is still essentially a matter of man against nature. Machines break down, weather becomes overwhelming and getting the job done comes second to sheer survival . . . .

"There's no other place in the world where you have to spend so much time on survival,' says Ory Gorgichuk, chief of Party 23 during part of its Arctic tour, and later field supervisor.

Northern Alberta's winters had been harsh, but the really cold periods were short, and there were trees to break the wind. Now, everything south of the Arctic Circle seemed like paradise. It was tediously cold. Once Party 23 worked 38 days at temperatures of 40 below [−40° C], or colder. Most of the camp thermometers bottomed at 50 below, [−45° C], and the last man to bed sometimes brought in the thermometer so it wouldn't burst.

Even that kind of cold is tolerable if you can see the sun. But most of the working days were black. Between latitudes 65 and 70, the hours of daylight in December and January range from about five hours to none, depending on time and place. So, generally, the crewmen set out in the dark and came home in the dark. They tried miners' lamps strapped to their heads or arms, but the lamps were more trouble than they were worth.

. . . At extreme temperatures a motor will soon freeze solid if it's not kept running. One Party 23 man slept all day and stayed up all night, solely to tend the motors: starting each one up for an hour, shutting it off for a half-hour, starting it again.

One night, according to a thermometer at Fort McPherson (Party 23's thermometer had gone to bed inside a trailer), the temperature hit

74 below [−58° C]. At this point the tracked vehicles broke down. The rubber pads to which the steel treads were attached turned brittle and cracked.

The real terror of Arctic operations is the sudden storm. 'They're like the sand storms of west Texas,' Gamble says. 'When you saw a white wall of snow coming you headed home fast. But first you grabbed up all the cables and geophones, because the snow packs hard during a storm. It's great for building igloos but not for digging out buried equipment.'

In such storms, visibility is nil. The camp's office trailer had a constantly flashing beacon on a high pole to help both aircraft and ground vehicles locate it. (In later years, crews painted an orange fluorescent band around the silver trailers; today, entire trailers are painted bright colors.) Even so, vehicles could be stranded a mere half-mile [.8 km] from camp.

Drivers soon learned to stay put, and to ask for help over their two-way radios only in dire emergency. A search party was equally likely to get lost, and every vehicle carried a survival kit of extra clothing, blankets, food and propane fuel bottles. With those supplies you could be as comfortable in the vehicle as you could in camp.

One winter morning after a three-day blow, party chief McIntosh couldn't open his trailer door. The entire camp was snowed under. The men climbed out the rooftop hatches in each trailer, cleared their doors and then dug tunnels from trailer to trailer.

'It was like living in a culvert,' says Gorgichuk, field supervisor at the time. 'You had to duck-walk from place to place.'

There *were* some awkward moments. Once, during a move, the lavatory trailer was left behind. For a while the crew had to make do in the outdoors, which at 40 below [−40° C] tests a man's speed and fortitude. And there was always the danger of fire during a storm. The wind—so strong that sometimes a man couldn't face it—swooped down the trailer chimneys and blew out the oil stoves. If this happened while the camp was asleep, and unburned oil continued to build up in the heater, it could be dangerous when the men lit up again in the morning. Consequently crewmen sometimes shut off the stoves overnight during a storm, and crawled into their sleeping bags.

After one such night Bill Gamble rose, lit the morning fire, and belatedly realized the chimney was snowed in solid. Before he could shut off the heater the trailer was on fire. Gamble and his three roommates dove for the door.

'I was pulling on my snowmobile suite with both feet in the air at the same time,' claims Gamble. 'With that wind fanning it, the trailer burned in 20 minutes. We lost all our clothing and equipment.'

Some of the best employees were the dozen-or-so Indians and Eskimos who worked for Party 23 over the years. They were trained in most of the skilled jobs of seismic operations and, says McIntosh, 'in a few more years they could have taken over.' One of them also became something of a legend, by strolling casually between trailers in his T-shirt on the coldest days.

When Party 23 disbanded in 1971, the crewmen scattered. Many of them still look back on the Arctic years as a great adventure. 'You either like the North or you don't,' says McIntosh, from Imperial's gas plant at Devon, Alta. 'Actually I think the cold is worse down here.'

1. What do you think were the most difficult problems faced by Seismic Party 23 in the Arctic?
2. Give some examples of how the crewmen had to use their ingenuity to survive in this environment.
3. What problems could a sudden snowstorm cause?
4. What problems were caused by the wind?

The Inuit

We have seen why the Arctic has sometimes been described as one of the hardest environments on earth. Many newcomers to the North last only weeks or months before returning to the more comfortable southern climates. Only a very few make their homes in the North for a lifetime. Yet one group of people, the Inuit, have surved here for over two thousand years. How have they managed to adapt and come to terms with the Arctic?

The Inuit came to Canada long after the Indians. Only the harsh northland was still unoccupied. Travelling eastward from Siberia, the Inuit spread across the Arctic all the way to Greenland.

At its maximum, the Inuit population numbered about 100 000. Today there are only about 80 000, although their numbers are rapidly increasing. Of this total about 17 000 live in Canada.

Canadian Inuit Population

Group	Number	Group	Number
Mackenzie	2200	Iglulik	2700
Copper	1600	South Baffin Island	3300
Netsilik	800	Quebec	4000
Caribou	2200	Labrador	1100

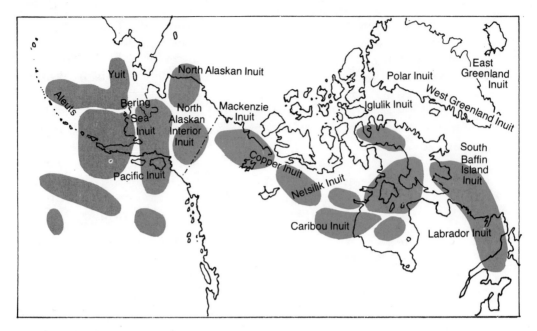

The word "Eskimo" is a Cree Indian word which means "eaters of raw meat". It was used by the Indians as a term of disrespect. The Arctic people call themselves *INUIT*, which means "the men." The singular is *INUK*.

Inuit Hunting. Most Inuit lived along the Arctic shores, especially during the winters. Agriculture in any form was of course impossible in the region of permafrost. The only real source of food for the Inuit was the game they hunted.

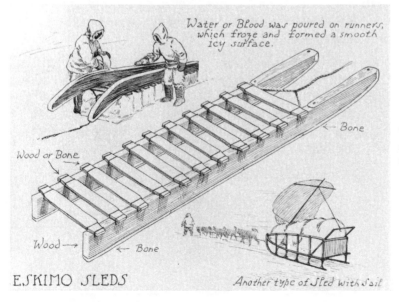

Was this drawing done recently? How can you tell?

In the winter, seal and walrus were the main targets. In the summer the migrating caribou herds provided the Inuit with their food. The caribou was more than just food. Its fur provided the Inuit with the finest winter clothes, its antlers and bones furnished the materials for tools and weapons, and its sinews were made into thread for clothing.

During the summer months, seal, walrus, bear, geese, ducks and fish were also hunted. Some ground vegetation was also gathered, but the Inuit diet consisted almost entirely of meat. Although they were called "eaters of raw meat", the Inuit in fact preferred their meat cooked unless conditions made this impossible. In the winter meat was boiled in pots of water heated by seal-oil. The same seal-oil also heated their houses. In the summer, the fuel for fire was provided by twigs, dried moss, and driftwood.

Berry pickers.

An Inuk hunter in a kayak. What is the kayak made of? What is the hunter using to throw the harpoon? What animals might he be hunting? How is he disguising himself from his game?

Building an igloo. Starting at the top left picture: (1) The blocks are cut. (2) First block set on edge. (3) First tier complete. (4) Beginning of second tier.

"Ae," said everyone. And the dogs sank into the snow, too tired to fight, and they buried their noses between their paws and let the snow-smoke drift over them, and while our women sat in the shelter of our sleds and nursed the small children, Annunglung and I went off with our snow knives and harpoons, and by good luck we found along a crack in the ice a deep drift of snow. We cut out a block of snow. The edges cut sharp and did not crumble and then we cut out block after block and built our igloo.

The dogs between sleep kept watching us and when we had built our igloo and from the inside cut out the door and crawled out, they were all around us howling for their seal. I had to use my long whip to keep them away, and then our wives crept inside and they were all smiling for they were away from the burn of the cold, and they lit our seal-oil lamps and put our willow mats and deerskins down while the children chewed their pieces of raw seal. Outside we gave our dogs their meat, and then they bedded themselves in the snow in the shelter of the sleds and the igloo, and let the snow cover them again. Annunglung and I went inside, and our wives cut seal meat and filled our mouths, and we said the night was full of good signs, though there were growls now and then running through the ice, growing louder and louder as they came toward us, and sounding in our ears like Nanook the bear rushing toward the spear, but I said, "Never

(5) Third tier. (6) Roof. (7) Last block. (8) The camp ready for the night. Actually, very few Inuit lived in igloos. Most built houses of stone and earth of used skins for tents. They used wood where it was available. Yet igloo construction shows the ingenuity of the Inuit in using all the resources of nature when they had to.

mind, there is always growling from the sea.'' So we fell asleep, cold though our igloo was, as a new igloo always is when there is no wind.

The Inuit were social people, and dancing and singing were pastimes in which both men and women participated.

During the period of darkness, the Inuit hardly left their igloos. When the days shortened and the sun was but a little dot on the horizon, the Inuit from the surrounding area would assemble at Kitigariuit for the winter festivities.

Brown bear skins were stuffed to appear alive, and the heads were ingeniously made to produce grunting sounds. White bears were also stuffed, and the paws and claws made to move. As soon as the sun had left the sky the merry-making began. In those days these holidays took the place of Christmas and New Year festivities. The day was spent watching wrestling matches and eating. As deeper darkness set in, we children would not dare leave the igloo: we were afraid of the bears!

The village had a Chief to organize things and launch the games. This Chief was quite old. When night fell the children squatted on the sleeping platform of the igloo, afraid of the brown and white bears.

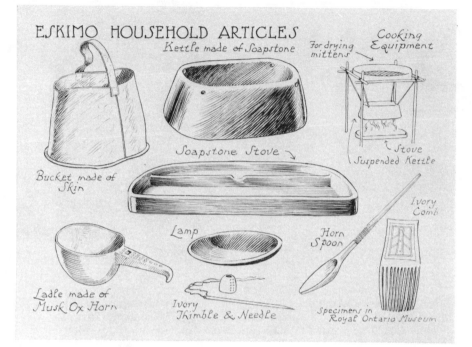

ESKIMO HOUSEHOLD ARTICLES
Kettle made of Soapstone
For drying mittens
Cooking Equipment
Soapstone Stove
Bucket made of Skin
Stove
Suspended Kettle
Ivory Comb
Lamp
Horn Spoon
Ladle made of Musk Ox Horn
Ivory Thimble & Needle
Specimens in Royal Ontario Museum

Suddenly someone would shout "Aaa!" "Bears" would enter through the katak in the floor, while the Inuit sang amusing songs. Since I was very little, I did not memorize them.

Once the bears were gone, the Inuit would challenge each other in tug-of-war contests; tugging at someone's arm was another way to prove one's strength. Another game was called *Orsiktartut*, they-make-a-loop. Two ropes were fastened to the vault of the igloo. Some-one sitting on the floor would grasp the ends of the ropes and raise himself from the floor. Once raised, he must bring his hands under himself and sit on them. Then he was to return to his first position without touching the floor, and begin all over again. Some would do this five times in a row, while others could not raise themselves from the floor at all. It was not easy. At the end there was a champion! . . .

During the times of merrymaking that were the night festivals a host of interesting and amazing things was shown. There was such an abundance of meals, games and things to admire that these sunless weeks sped by as if they had been only a few days.

As the sun reappeared and the gatherings were close to an end, we ended our festivals with dart shooting. The dart, there was only one, was balanced by little wings made from a duck's tailfeathers. It flew straight and true. It was carried to each contestant by the one who had made it. The target was a little piece of caribou fat (tunu) thinned out and formed into the shape of a candle, about four inches [10 cm] long and an inch and a half [3.75 cm] in diameter. It was set in the middle of the floor. The igloo was large and the onlookers many. Men, women and children were all admitted. Someone would set up a prize and another would aim for the target. The greater the stake, the higher the interest rose. Peals of laughter echoed all around. The winner, the one who hit the target, was in turn expected to put up a prize for the next contestant.

Thus ended the last game of the kaivitjuik, the time of dancing and rejoicing which began with the departure of the sun and ended with its return.

The Inuit also enjoyed telling stories. Some of the tales which have survived tell us much about Inuit values.

The Story of the Magic Wife

A certain young wife was so badly mistreated by her husband that one day she decided to run away from him. For several months she lived on her own, eating roots and berries. As the cold weather approached, however, she knew she would soon have to find shelter.

One day by luck she stumbled into a house when there was no one home. Here she found everything an Inuk requires—meat to eat, seal-oil for the lamp and warm skins to lie on. When the hunter who owned the house returned, she told him who she was and why she had run away from home.

"Very well," the hunter said, "You may stay here as long as you like. I have no wife, and I promise I will treat you well."

They lived happily for several years and had two sons. The woman was very happy, for her new husband took care of her very well. One day, however, an old woman appeared. The old woman said, "Let me comb your hair for you so that you will appear beautiful to your husband."

Unaware of any danger, the young wife agreed. The old woman combed the wife's hair but at the same time scratched her head. She then turned into a red fox and disappeared, for she had been secretly sent by the young wife's former husband.

When the young wife awoke, she began to turn into a caribou, and ran away. When her husband returned, he realized what had happened for he saw his wife's footsteps in the snow, and noticed that they changed to those of a caribou. He decided to search for her.

For years he searched with no luck. One day he heard a mother telling her children a story which sounded very much like his own experience. He asked the woman to help him find his wife.

The woman told him "Your wife is on the other side of the mountain, with a herd of caribou. You will recognize her because she runs about more than the other caribou. You must capture her, turn her on her back and skin her, but be careful to do no harm to her flesh. Then, make a small cut in her stomach, and your wife will come out."

The man did as he was told, and regained his wife. They lived in happiness until the end of their days.

1. *Were Inuit marriage customs the same as ours? Explain.*
2. *What household goods did an Inuk consider most valuable?*
3. *What evidence is there that the Inuit had a high regard for nature?*
4. *Is there any evidence that the Inuit believed in magic?*

Art   The Inuit are perhaps the most artistic of Canada's original people. With care and grace they shaped tools and weapons such as bows, arrows, spears, knives and saws out of bone, flint, and glassy stones. They have become famous for beautiful soapstone carvings. Inuit art is considered among the most beautiful in the world.

Typical Inuit carvings. The Inuit have become famous throughout the world for their art. What kind of stone is used for these carvings?

Religion   Even more than their Indian cousins, the Inuit had a deep respect for magic. They often carried lucky charms for protection against the evil spirits. Due to this fact, the shaman, or medicine man, had a great influence in Inuit society.

Ceremonial mask.

The Inuit believed all people had two souls: a breath-soul and a name-soul. The breath-soul gave a person life, and stayed with that person until death, although it might leave for a short time during sleep or illness.

A person's name was accompanied by a soul which gave to the carrier the strength, skill, and courage of the person who had had the name before. It was therefore in the best interest of an Inuk to get as many names as possible.

It was believed illness was caused by the loss of these two souls. Like the Indians, Inuit believed souls could also be stolen by witches. When this occurred, the shaman was called in to find the lost or stolen souls.

Inuit believed that spirits lived both under the water and in the sky, but they were far more concerned with the present life than with the uncertainty of the afterlife.

Language   Inuit language is very different from English, or even from the Indian languages. The meanings of their words can often be changed by adding different endings. Sometimes one word can replace a whole sentence in English. Here is one example:

Inuit Word	English Meaning
tuktoo	caribou
tuktoojuak	a big caribou
tuktoojuakseok	hunt a big caribou
tuktoojuakseokniak	will hunt a big caribou
tuktoojuakseokniakpunga	I will hunt a big caribou

With only small changes, this language is common to all Inuit. An Inuk from Siberia could be understood all the way to Greenland, almost six thousand four hundred kilometres away.

The Inuit Today

For a long time, the hard northern environment isolated its inhabitants from other societies. The Inuit did not feel the impact of European culture until the twentieth century. However, when the Europeans finally did appear in the North, Inuit culture went through drastic changes.

Most Inuit depended on hunting for survival. As we have seen, caribou, seal, walrus, and whale were the chief game. The European hunters were mainly interested in furs, however, especially the fur of the white fox. Soon, more and more Inuit took up this way of making a living. They used the new weapons, guns and metal traps provided by the European traders. In exchange for food and supplies, they provided the traders with the valuable furs. In time, many Inuit came to depend not on themselves but on the European's trading post for their survival.

This change proved very harmful to the Inuit. Sometimes the value of the furs dropped. At other times the fur-bearing animals became scarce. When this happened, the income of the Inuit shrank greatly. Many European traders went back south, for they did not care what happened to the Inuit. The Inuit now found it difficult to make a living in the new way. Nor could they easily return to the old ways, for the caribou were now scarce, and most Inuit had forgotten how to hunt in the old ways. Many starved, and others sadly came to depend on government welfare.

The Canadian writer Farley Mowat wrote two books describing the effects of these changes on the Inuit. In *People of the Deer*, and *The Desperate People*, Mowat shows the plight of one such group of Inuit, the Ihalmiut.

By 1957 the Ihalmiut had forgotten how to provide for themselves. Men, women, and children had to depend on the government for food and clothing. The government then decided to move them inland, away from the influence of European society. It was hoped that now the Ihalmiut would learn to provide for themselves again. One of the Ihalmiut, Owliktuk, tells of their experiences:

We were surprised when the white men told us this was a good place for caribou, for we knew it was a hungry country. All the same it was the right time for the deer to come north and we needed meat. The food that had been left for us only lasted a few days. Our people were hungry and they ate a lot.

The white men had made us pitch the tents under a big hill. We knew this to be an evil place but we let the tents stay there for a while and took our rifles and went looking for deer trails and crossing places. We found no trails. We knew there had not been any deer in this place for a long time because there were no old trails. After a while we came back to the tents and we decided to move because we were afraid of the hill spirits.

We knew we could not go back to our own country, but we thought if we went a little way to the west we might find level ground where the deer might pass. Some of the people would not move, because they said it was no use. So they stayed at the camp the white men had chosen for us. They were Pommela, Alekahaw and Onekwaw. All the rest of us walked for a day to the southwest until we had

Inuit at a summer camp. What evidence is there of contact and trade with Europeans?

crossed the big hills and reached some little lakes where we could see flat country to the west. Here we set up our camps. There was lots of wood here, and we had fires, but we had no food. There were some ptarmigan but not enough to be much use. We tried to fish in the lakes, but the ice was very thick [it would then have been from six to eight feet (1.8 to 2.4 m) in thickness], and when we had cut through it we did not catch any fish by jigging. I do not think there were any fish in those lakes.

It was on the second day after we had come to Henik that we moved to the new place. While we were making the new camp we heard some airplanes flying to the southwest and Anoteelik thought they were landing. So he and Mounik and another walked that way. They found some white men with a big camp, and with a tractor, and one of the white men gave them some food.

The next day all of the men walked to that camp and they gave us food again, but they did not have very much to give us.

One day Alekahaw arrived at our camp and said that Pommela had died and that he had starved to death. He said there was nothing to eat at the first camp and so he had come to see if there was food where we were. We did not have any food, for no deer had come at all and we could not get any fish.

Some thought we ought to walk back to our own country but it was too far when the children were hungry, and anyway the white men had told us we had to stay where we were.

One day a white man from the camp came to visit us with Anoteelik. He slept with us and went back the next day. He said he would send a message that we were hungry and that some food would be brought in. Nothing happened for a long time. We were all hungry, but the white men at the camp could not give us much food. Mostly we stayed in the tents and some people wished they had run away and hidden when the plane came to Ennadai to take us away.

One of the white men at the camp tells of what followed:

One day shortly after a Canso had landed and taken off I was sitting in my tent when the flap was thrust open and a figure stepped in. He was a grotesque looking fellow and I was momentarily startled. He introduced himself as Anoteelik. I offered him tea and food which he readily accepted. He asked if I had seen any caribou and I said I had not. I asked where his village was and he said it was some hours off to the northeast and that there were many of his people there. I kept offering him food and he ate in such a famished way that I thought he had not eaten in some time. Later I discovered that this was the case, not only for him, but for his whole tribe. Later more Eskimos came and I offered them food, but they were eating so much that I became apprehensive about our fresh meat supply which was limited.

The following day the Eskimos returned and brought some of their fellow hunters. They seemed to be in desperate need of food and accepted every opportunity to take it. Unfortunately we were not fully aware of their dire circumstances and had to save our meat for ourselves, so we did not offer them too much.

In the afternoon Anoteelik brought another Eskimo named Uhoto. I learned from Uhoto, who could speak a few words of English, that the little group was in need of food for they were starving and already one of their elder tribesmen had died of starvation.

A few days later an old Eskimo woman with two children came to the tent. [This appears, from the photographs, to have been Nanuk, Ohoto's wife, who was then forty-one years old.] I gave them a sack of flour, thirty pounds, [13.5 kg] which they eagerly accepted. I noticed that the old woman's eyes were in poor shape; red-rimmed and almost completely swollen shut. I gave her a pair of sun-glasses for I thought she was going snow-blind.

After the Eskimos had been dropping in for about a week I made up my mind to visit their village. . . . As we approached, the whole village turned out to greet us. I noticed that bark had been stripped away from some of the trees. I questioned Anoteelik about this. He said some of the people had taken this bark and boiled it for a long time and then drank the liquid and ate the bark. . . .

Many changes have taken place in the Arctic in the last thirty years. Radar stations and airfields from the D.E.W. line, Canada's northern defense system, now dot the North. Exploration teams searching for new energy sources have also become common. Schools, health-care centres, and new homes have been built for the Inuit. This has encouraged more and more Inuit to move away from the traditional small hunting camps to large settlements.

So many changes from their old lifestyle have made it hard for the Inuit to fit smoothly into the new ways. The Canadian government is trying to help them. It has started programs to help the Inuit in the following areas:

— low rental housing assistance
— full support of primary, secondary, and higher education
— social organization to help Inuit retain their culture
— a medical care plan
— legal aid to help Inuit retain right to their land.

The future for the Inuit of the Arctic is uncertain. Here are some comments from observers of Inuit life:

> A lot of people will say the native way of life should be preserved, but they don't know what they're talking about. Their way of life was changed forever from the moment the first trading posts were established.

> What's going to happen when they bring TV in here next?

> If these people think they've been subject to culture shock in the past, they haven't seen anything yet.

> It's hard to educate them fully in the North. Yet on the other hand sending them south isn't the answer either. Many won't want to come back north where they're really needed.

What does it mean to be one of the Inuit? One man said:

The bow drill can be used to drill holes in wood and bone, and to make fire. Can you tell how this tool works? Do you think it is still used?

We should learn as much as we can from this new culture but we must not forget our own culture . . . Keep our language alive. Tell the old stories, sing the songs, dance the old dances, make jokes, enjoy this great power for thought developed from long ago by our ancestors . . . There are only very few Eskimos but there are millions of whites, just like mosquitoes. It is something very special and wonderful to be an Eskimo—they are like the snow geese. If an Eskimo forgets his language and Eskimo ways, he will be nothing but just another mosquito.

Word Study

bow-drill	permafrost	kayak
Inuit	shaman	igloo
Inuk	tree line	breath-soul
name-soul	soapstone	

Things to Do 1. *Divide the class into small groups of six to eight people each. Now imagine it is October and you will be stranded in the Arctic all winter. You have food to last two weeks, and the following supplies:*

knives	*sunglasses*
sleeping bags	*rope*
warm clothes	*axes*

How will you solve the problems of surviving in the Arctic for the next few months? Remember, you will have to find ways of providing shelter, food, clothing, warmth, and a system of choosing leaders.

2. *A university graduate of Inuit origin returns to the North after many years of schooling in the South. What problems might she or he have readjusting to the northern environment? What changes in climate, housing, entertainment, and job possibilities will such a person have to face?*

3. *Many people speak of a "generation gap" between the old and the new generation of Inuit. How would you account for these changes?*

4. *The search for raw materials in the North is continuing at an ever faster rate. This is having a great effect on both the Native People and the environment. If you had the power to do so, what laws would you pass to regulate exploration in the Arctic?*

5. *Of the following four choices open to the Inuit, which do you think is the best?*

(a) *Return to the traditional hunting society.*

(b) *Migrate to the South and become part of industrial society.*

(c) *Remain in the North and learn the new skills of technological society.*

(d) *Place themselves under the care of the Canadian government.*

5
The Impact of the Europeans

The entire Indian way of life was changed by the coming of the Europeans. Of course, this change did not take place all at once. The Indians in the East, who had contact with the French as early as 1534, felt this change first. The Indians in the West were not as greatly affected until the nineteenth century.

In the end every aspect of Indian life was affected. The Europeans' technology changed the Indians' hunting and farming methods. Their demand for furs changed the Indians' economic pursuits. Their greed for land eventually pushed the Indians into small corners of a land that once belonged only to them.

Were these changes good or harmful to the Indians? Did the Europeans want to improve the condition of the Indians or to eliminate them as rivals?

The European Views the Indian

The first Europeans to settle in Canada were the French. After their first contact with the Indians, they were faced with the question: "What should be done with the natives?" The French attitude naturally had much to do with their treatment of the Indians. As you read the following accounts, make a list under two columns of the "good" and "bad" qualities of the Indians as described by the French. Do you think the Indians would agree that some of these qualities were "bad"? What suggestions are made for "civilizing" the Indians?

Pierre D'Avity, 1637:

> Except for some tribes, which are clever thieves, they do not steal from each other. They do not fight each other, for they are fearful and cowardly, although they boast that they are brave, and want to be held in high regard.
>
> Most of them are good natured, have a good, clear mind, and good memories. In spite of the fact they have no police, army, literature or money, they despise other nations and think highly of themselves. They are witty and are extremely good speakers.
>
> Some tribes such as the Iroquois are very cunning and treacherous.

Early painting showing Jesuit missionaries martyred by the Iroquois. What effect would this picture have on people in Europe? What effect does it have on you? How might the image of the Indian be affected by such a picture?

Sieur de Corbes, 1608:

They are handsome men, who let their hair grow to their waists, both men and women. They have well-formed bodies, high foreheads and eyes which burn like candles.

In their manner of living they are very coarse, but they are beginning to take on our ways. They are easily converted to Christianity, and I believe that if preachers were sent to them in a short time the whole country would give in to the Christian faith.

Father Jean Brébeuf, 1635, on the Hurons:

They are gluttons, but they endure hunger much better than we do. They are very lazy, are liars, thieves, and beggars.

They also have many shining qualities. They care for each other, often exchanging presents. Their hospitality, even to strangers, is remarkable. Of their amazing patience in poverty, famine and illness, what shall I say? They are never heard to make a complaint.

Unfortunately, because the Indians left no written documents we do not have any accounts of the first contacts with Europeans from the Indian point of view. There are some hints that the Indians were not very impressed with Europeans as a group, although they were awed by their technology.

Brother Sagard, 1623, on the Hurons:

> They think we have little intelligence in comparison to themselves. They hold us missionaries in a little higher regard, but compared to other Frenchmen, they think their own children wiser and more intelligent.

The French answer to the Indian question was Christianity. The priests led the way, setting up missions in the wilderness and living among the Indians. These early attempts to convert the Indians to European religion and ways of life were mostly failures. The constant wars with the Indians spurred French and English to acts of hatred and revenge. These made it difficult for the Indians and the Europeans to accept each other as equals.

1. *According to the first Europeans, what were the good and bad qualities of Canada's Indians?*
2. *Do you remember the Indian attitude toward private property? Why might they object to being called "thieves"?*

Technology

The most obvious changes to the Indian way of life were made by the Europeans' superior technology. When they came to North America, the Europeans brought steel tools, domestic animals, the wheel, firearms, matches, paper, a system of writing and arithmetic, and knowledge of agriculture and housebuilding, among other things. The Indians lacked almost every one of these.

Think of the advantages these gave to the European. Domestic animals such as cows, sheep, and pigs provided food even in hard times. The horse made transportation and farm work much easier. The only domestic animal known to Indians was the dog.

Steel axes, saws, hammers, and nails allowed one person to build a log cabin in less than a week. To build a similar house with stone tools twenty Indians might have to work several months.

The Europeans' technology gave them similar advantages when it came to clearing land, hunting, travelling, and communicating with faraway places.

Where did the Europeans get this technology? Examine its sources:

domestic animals	The Near East
paper	China
writing	The Near East
numbers	Arabia
gunpowder	China

Many of these things were first invented in other parts of the world and learned by the Europeans. The Indians, cut off from other civilizations, did not have this advantage.

It was European social organization which made individual skills possible. In Indian society, everyone did much the same job as everyone else. In European society, jobs were specialized. One person knew how to make paper, another made cloth, or bricks, or weapons. Taken together, these skills produced an advanced technology. Individually, however, one person would have a difficult time surviving. A brickmaker may have known nothing about making paper or steel axes. It was co-operation among these different workers which made progress possible.

The same is true today. What would you do if the water tap in your home broke? If your car did not start? You would probably call a plumber or an auto mechanic. If these people were not available, you would not be able to get a glass of water or drive to the supermarket.

You depend a great deal on people around you who are experts in their fields. If they did not exist, your whole way of life would be changed. You would have to give up all the wonderful technology you make use of every day, or learn how to run it yourself. You can see how difficult this would be. Without specialized skill, our technological society could not operate.

In your daily routine, how many people do you depend on? Make a list, making sure you include people on whom you depend for food, clothing, transportation, entertainment, etc.

Individually our ability to handle technology is probably less than that of an Indian of five hundred years ago. This is something to keep in mind when we ask why the Indian technology was so primitive.

The Fur Trade

The Europeans' first price for this technology was furs. The Indians agreed to become the supplier. In exchange for certain goods the Indians sought out beaver pelts and the skins of other fur-bearing animals. The fashion houses of Europe demanded these pelts in great quantities. Here is a typical list of the items exchanged by Europeans for furs. Explain why these items would be desirable to Indians. Which would be considered most valuable?

gunpowder	fish-hooks	iron arrowheads
ball and lead	linen shirts	soap
axes	needles	swords
knives	thread	brandy
kettles	beads	

The fur trade had far-reaching effects on the life of the Indians. It completely changed the way of life of many tribes. Some tribes became completely occupied in hunting furs. Other tribes, such as the Iroquois, Huron, and Cree became "middlemen". When the fur supply ran short in their territory, these tribes could do little trapping of their own. They obtained furs from the western tribes, then sold them for a profit to the English or French. The competition for furs led to wars, not only between Indian and European, but between Indian and Indian. The Hurons were allied to the French, the Iroquois to the Dutch and the English. Soon whole tribes perished. The Hurons, once one of the proudest tribes in North America, were among the first victims.

In 1649, the Iroquois made one of their many attacks against the Hurons. A French missionary describes the results:

> The band of Iroquois appeared at the gates of the village, striking terror in all the poor people. Some fled, others were killed on the spot. Many were taken prisoner, but they put to death all the old men and children, and others whom they thought could not keep up with them in their flight.

1. What advantages did the Iroquois appear to have over their enemy?
2. Why might the Iroquois make frequent attacks on the Hurons? What happened to the Hurons in 1649?
3. The Iroquois were described by the French fur traders and settlers as cruel, savage warriors. Compare this image with your earlier study of the Iroquois. Are these two views similar? Why might the French describe them in such a way?

In time, the Indians became almost completely dependent upon European technology. A fur trader gives an example:

> The Indians in this quarter have been so long accustomed to use European goods, that it would be with difficulty that they could now obtain a livelihood, without them. Especially do they need fire arms, with which to kill their game, and axes, kettles, knives, etc. They have almost lost the use of bows and arrows; and they would find it nearly impossible to cut their wood with implements made of stone or bone.

Warfare lasted for almost two centuries, and in the end almost destroyed the Indians of eastern Canada.

One of the saddest and cruellest events in Canada's history was the murder of the Beothuk Indians of Newfoundland. These were harmless people, numbering about five hundred men, women, and children when they were first seen by Europeans.

In time the Europeans who settled along the coast of Newfoundland resented the presence of the Beothuk. They hunted them like animals for sport, and shot them at every opportunity. They even placed bounties of fifty dollars on their heads. Soon even the Micmac Indians crossed over from Nova Scotia and shot them.

The entire Beothuk tribe was wiped out. The last survivor died in 1829.

1. *Europeans often gloated that they had "cheated" the Indians by giving them cheap knives and axes in return for expensive furs. Present an argument from an Indian point of view indicating why you think you are getting the best of the bargain.*

2. *List the positive and negative effects of the fur trade on Indian tribes. In the balance, do you think the introduction of European technology was good or harmful for the Indians?*

Disease

In July, 1969, Americans Neil Armstrong and Buzz Aldrin became the first men to walk on the moon. After their return, they were kept in isolation for several weeks as doctors gave them a complete check-up. Do you know why this was done? One of the main reasons was the widespread fear that the astronauts might have picked up a disease-carrying germ on the moon for which earth doctors had no cure. The results might have been disastrous for mankind. A plague without cure would have spread throughout the earth. A recent book and movie, *The Andromeda Strain*, showed how this was possible.

If you can imagine that possibility, it will be easier for you to understand the position of the Indians in North America when the Europeans first came. Before this time, North America was very isolated from Europe, and many European diseases were unknown. The Indians had suffered diseases of course, but in most cases they had skilfully found cures from the plants in the forests around them.

The new European diseases left them helpless. These diseases, tuberculosis, measles, fever, typhus, and smallpox, between them killed more Indians than all the wars fought over the centuries. By 1900, there were only about one hundred thousand Indians in all of Canada. European war and disease had killed more than half of Canada's Indians.

The worst disease was smallpox. It left a trail of death across Canada. Whole tribes were wiped out. Some others moved about to different parts of the country to escape its horrors.

Here is an account of the effects of smallpox on the Indians of the Bow River. It was told by an old Indian to a European explorer in 1788:

> We caught it from the Snake Indians. Our scouts informed us of a large camp, too large to attack, but they saw none of the men hunting or moving about. We thought it was a war trick.
>
> Next morning we attacked the tents, but our war cries soon stopped. There was nobody to fight, only the dead and dying, everyone with disease.
>
> We touched no one, but took the best tents, other goods and some horses.
>
> Two days later, a terrible disease broke out in our camp and spread from one tent to another as if carried by the evil spirit. About a third of us died, but in some other camps there were tents in which everyone died. We believed the Good Spirit had forsaken us. Our hearts were sad. We shall never be the same people again.

1. *How did the Indians contract the disease if they did not touch anyone in the camp?*
2. *On what did the Indians blame the disease?*
3. *What would have been the effect of the ravages of smallpox on the position of the medicine man?*
4. *Find out what kind of diseases each of the following are, and how they affect the human body: smallpox; typhus; tuberculosis; consumption.*

Alcohol   Another corrupting factor the Europeans introduced to Indian society was alcohol. Some Indian tribes in Central America had made their own alcohol before the Europeans came. In most cases, it was used only by a certain few people, and usually for religious reasons.

The Europeans introduced alcohol to the Canadian Indian. It brought great harm to many Indian individuals, to families, and to whole tribes. Of course alcohol, when misused, can be harmful to anyone, European or Indian. How did the use of alcohol, or "firewater", affect the Indian? Why did the Indians seem to react worse to alcohol than Europeans did? Look closely at the following comments:

Montreal, seventeenth century:

> Some tavern keepers used to keep "Indian barrels", which they sold only to Indians. In these barrels they would dump the dregs from the glasses of wine, beer and whiskey which were served in their tavern.

Newspaper editorial, nineteenth century:

> The Indian could not resist the effects of drunkenness. The poison crept into his blood, and was passed on to his children. They died by the thousands.

Europeans had been using alcohol for a long time. They had learned its dangers, and so used it with care. The Indians had no such advantage. They were usually given inferior whiskey, which they drank on an empty stomach, and drank without restraint.

Chief Pontiac, 1763:

> You have bought guns, knives, kettles and blankets from the white men, until you can no longer do without them; and what is worse, you have drunk the poison firewater, which turns you into fools.

N. Denys, seventeenth century:

> They do not call it drinking unless they become drunk, and they do not think they have been drinking unless they fight and are hurt. However, when they set about drinking, their wives remove from their wigwams the guns, axes, the mounted swords (spears), the bows, the arrows, and (every weapon) even their knives, which the Indians carry hung from the neck. . . . Immediately after taking every- thing with which they can injure themselves, the women carry it into the woods, afar off, where they go to hide with all their children. After that they have a fine time, beating, injuring, and killing one another. Their wives do not return until the next day, when they are sober.

Daniel Harmon, North West Company, 1802:

> This day being Christmas our people have spent it as usual, in drink- ing and fighting. . . . Of all people in the world, I think the Canadians, when drunk, are the most disagreeable; for excessive drinking gener- ally causes them to quarrel and fight, among themselves. Indeed, I had rather have fifty drunken Indians in the fort, than five drunken Canadians.

1. *What kind of "firewater" was sometimes sold to Indians?*
2. *How would you account for the ef- fects firewater had on the Indians?*

Did Europeans seem to behave dif- ferently from Indians when drunk? Why might more Indians than Eu- ropeans be affected by alcohol?

3. In what ways would the children also be affected by the use of alcohol by their fathers?

4. What further effects might drunkenness have on the Indians' energy, and their spirit of independence and self-reliance?

The Reserve System

Do you live in your own house, on your own piece of land? If not, a house is probably a dream you and your family are working for. The great majority of Canadians probably share the same dream. It may surprise you to learn that before the Europeans came, no Indian thought this way.

The idea of private ownership of land was strange to the Indians. Each tribe had a certain area of the country in which it lived and hunted, and other tribes recognized this. Within this area, however, each member of the tribe had the same rights as any other member. No Indian would have thought of setting off a piece of land as "private property".

When the Europeans came they brought a different outlook. In their society, most people believed that "life, liberty, and property" were three sacred rights.

Why did these different views exist? Consider the differences in the two societies. The Indian lived on hunting. The European lived on farming.

As hunters, the Indians were always on the move, following the game within their territory. The farmers, on the other hand, lived in one place. They had to know where the boundaries of their land were in order to plant the crops.

As these opposing ways of life clashed, the Indians found themselves driven from their hunting grounds. They could not match the great number of Europeans now entering the country. As a result they had to make certain agreements with the Europeans. These were called treaties. Under such agreements, the Indians gave up their claim to huge portions of Canada. The area around the city of Toronto, for example, was obtained by treaties between the years 1805 and 1820.

Date	Location	Area
1805	—Townships of Etobicoke, York, Vaughan, parts of King, Whitchurch, and Markham, part of York County	128 666 hectares
1806	—parts of Peel and Halton	34 000 hectares
1818	—parts of Dufferin, Halton, Peel and Wellington	259 200 hectares
1820	—parts of Toronto and Peel	2320 hectares

The last Indian claims were given up by treaty in 1921.

In return the Indians were given areas of land called "reserves". Today there are 2241 reserves in Canada, some only a few hectares large, some almost 1300 km² in size.

Some terms used in Indian affairs today are:

BAND—usually refers to a group of Indians who had historical ties with a tribal unit, for example, the Six Nations of the Iroquois near Brantford, Ontario, were a band.

RESERVE—a unit of land set aside for the benefit and use of the Indians. However, the Indians cannot sell or lease their lands without permission of the Canadian government.

BAND FUNDS—money which is made from the sale or lease of Indian lands. This includes money made from hunting, fishing, and the sale or lease of natural resources found on the reserves.

BAND COUNCIL—a group of Indians chosen by members of the band to look after their affairs. In some bands the chiefs are chosen for life, in others only for several years.

Along with the reserves, the Indians received other payment. Here are some of the terms of the treaty signed with the Plains Indians in 1877. The government of Canada agreed to give:

—permission to hunt and fish on the lands given up to the government
—to each family of five, 256 hectares
—to each man, woman and child, a $12.00 cash present
—annual cash payments—to each chief, $25.00
           —to each minor chief, $15.00
           —to every other Indian, $5.00
—$2000.00 in ammunition for the whole band
—to each chief and minor chief, one suit of clothes every three years a Winchester rifle, and a medal
—hoes, spades, axes, ploughs, a team of oxen for the band
—provisions for schools and teachers.

1. *Do you think the treaties gave the Indians fair payment for their land?*
2. *Why do you think the chiefs were given larger payments than other members of the tribe? Who might do the negotiating for the tribe?*
3. *What do you think was the intention of the Canadian government in making these agreements?*

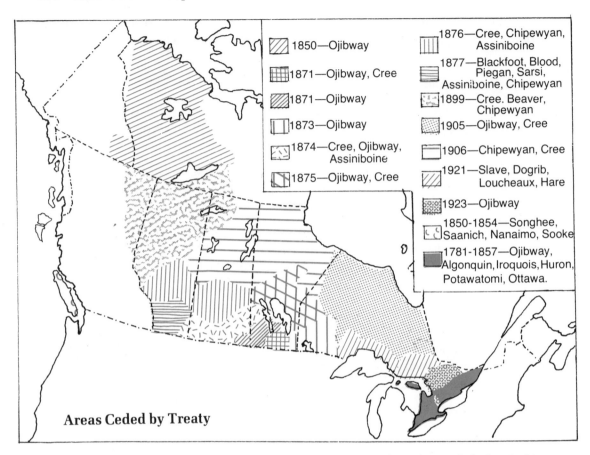

Areas Ceded by Treaty

Legend:
- 1850—Ojibway
- 1871—Ojibway, Cree
- 1871—Ojibway
- 1873—Ojibway
- 1874—Cree, Ojibway, Assiniboine
- 1875—Ojibway, Cree
- 1876—Cree, Chipewyan, Assiniboine
- 1877—Blackfoot, Blood, Piegan, Sarsi, Assiniboine, Chipewyan
- 1899—Cree. Beaver, Chipewyan
- 1905—Ojibway, Cree
- 1906—Chipewyan, Cree
- 1921—Slave, Dogrib, Loucheaux, Hare
- 1923—Ojibway
- 1850-1854—Songhee, Saanich, Nanaimo, Sooke
- 1781-1857—Ojibway, Algonquin, Iroquois, Huron, Potawatomi, Ottawa.

Many people have called the treaties unjust. Why, then, did the Indians agree to the terms? Here are some views from both Indians and Europeans:

Alexander Morris, Lieutenant-Governor of the Northwest Territories, 1885:

> The Indians are fully aware that their old mode of life is passing away. They are not "unconscious of their destiny"; on the contrary, they are harassed with fears as to the future of their children and the hard present of their own lives. . . . They recognize the fact that they must seek part of their living from "the mother earth". . . .

A. G. Archibald, Lieutenant-Governor of Manitoba, 1871:

> We told them that whether they wished it or not, immigrants would come in and fill up the country; that every year from this one twice as many in number as their whole people there assembled would pour into the province and in a little while would spread all over it, and that now was the time for them to come to an arrangement. . . .

Sweetgrass, Cree Chief, 1871; on the land transfer from the Hudson's Bay Company to the Canadian government:

> Great Father,—I shake hands with you, and bid you welcome.—We heard our lands were sold and we did not like it; we don't want to sell our lands; it is our property, and no one has the right to sell them.
>
> Our country is getting ruined of fur-bearing animals, hitherto our sole support, and now we are poor and want help—we want you to pity us. We want cattle, tools, agricultural implements, and assistance in everything when we come to settle—our country is no longer able to support us.
>
> Make provision for us against years of starvation. We have had great starvation the past winter, and the small-pox took away many of our people, the old, the young, and children. . . .

Big Bear, Cree Chief, 1884:

> We have all been deceived in the same way. . . . They have given me to choose between several small reserves but I feel sad to abandon the liberty of my own land when they come to me and offer me small plots to stay there and in return not to get half of what they have promised me. . . . The government sent us those who think themselves men. They are not men. They have no honesty.

1. *Did the Indians sign the treaties willingly? What would have happened if they had not signed?*
2. *What effect did the new economic conditions in the West have in persuading the Indians to enter the reservations?*
3. *Is there any evidence that the Indians trusted the government negotiators? Did these men appear to keep their promises?*

What was the effect of reservation life on the Indian? An observer in the 1880s noted:

> You would not know the Canadian Indian. He is all changed. Pride, vigour and sturdy independence all gone. The loss of the buffalo made the change. His living is gone. His very life is gone. He does not like the rotten pork the government gives him. He is sick. Smallpox and other white men's diseases kill them in hundreds. He talks of uprisings but he does not have it in him any more. He is just full of grievances.

Before the Europeans, the Indians were proud masters of Canada. Now they were not even full masters of their own small reserves. By 1900, the Indian population of Canada stood at less than one hundred thousand. It seemed that a unique culture would disappear.

This century, however, has seen a new start for the Indian. Today, Indians are the fastest growing segment of Canada's population. Their numbers now stand at over two hundred and fifty thousand. What is more, they are seeking recognition as full citizens of Canada, and they are beginning to demand their rights. The future holds promise for the Indian, but it also contains problems. What will be the future role of the Indian in Canada?

Word Study

reserve	band council	middlemen
band	firewater	Indian barrels
band funds	smallpox	

Things to Do 1. *Find some information on the effects of alcohol on people. Can alcoholism be passed on from parents to their children?*
2. *Find out if the land on which your home is located was obtained from the Indians by treaty. If so, what payment was made to the Indians in return for the land? This information can be obtained by contacting your Public Library.*

3. *What is the reserve nearest to you? Find out its size and population. What Indian band occupies the reserve? Do a study on how many houses in the reserve have telephones, electricity, running water, indoor plumbing, indoor washrooms, refrigerators, and stoves. Would you say the homes in this reserve are better or worse off than the average Canadian home?*

6
The Indian Today

100 Indians Armed with Rifles Seize Kenora Park

Indians Halt Massive James Bay Project

Almost every day it seems, newspaper headlines shout out some new demands made by Indian groups. Canadians find themselves asking, "What do the Indians want?"

It is a difficult question for both Indian and other Canadians to answer. Indians, like everyone else, do not all want the same things. One of the main questions has to do with the Indians' identity. Do they wish to remain a separate group in Canadian society, or become "Canadians of full status"? Prime Minister Trudeau stated his government's view:

> We can go on treating the Indians as having a special status. We can go adding bricks of discrimination around the ghetto in which they live and at the same time perhaps helping them preserve certain cultural traits and ancestral rights. Or we can say, "You're at a crossroads—the time is now to decide whether the Indians will be a race apart in Canada or whether they will be Canadians of full status."
> ... But aboriginal rights? This really means saying "we were here before you. You came and took the land from us. Perhaps you cheated us by giving us some worthless things in return for a vast expanse of land. We want to re-open this question. We want you to preserve our aboriginal rights and to restore them to us". And our answer . . .—our answer is "NO".
> If we think of restoring aboriginal rights to the Indians, what about the French who were defeated at the Plains of Abraham? Shouldn't we restore rights to them?—And what about the other Canadians, the immigrants? . . . What can we do to redeem the past? . . . We will be just in our time. This is all we can do. We must be just today.

The Indians' views do not always agree.

Harold Cardinal:

> Indians gladly accept the challenge—to become participating Canadians, to take a meaningful place in the mainstream of the Canadian society. But we remain acutely aware of the threat—the loss of our Indian identity, our place as distinct, identifiable Canadians.
>
> To all too many being Canadian means "white is right" or "be like me and all your problems will vanish".

William Wuttunee, Indian lawyer:

> I follow the experience of my father. He lived for sixty years on a reservation, and he left it when he was sixty, and he took us with him. I'm very pleased he did because if I had not left the reserve I now would have been hunting rabbits perhaps, freezing to death in the one- or two-room shacks, and having one miserable time!
>
> Whereas right now I live in a split-level home, I have running water and I have all the things that I need, and I am pleased that I live there.

1. *Do you agree with Prime Minister Trudeau that the Indian should be treated in the same way as French Canadians or immigrants? How might an Indian reply to Trudeau's arguments?*
2. *Do Cardinal and Wuttunee agree on their aims? Explain.*

To many Canadians it appears that the Indian is getting more than a fair deal from the government. Of the registered Indians in Canada, eighty per cent live on reserves. To them, the Department of Indian Affairs extends the following benefits:

—no property tax
—no income tax
—$140 million education budget
—$25 million in free medical care
—$30 million in welfare
—government-assisted housing.

These seem to be generous benefits. Yet, consider these statistics from the Indian point of view:

—47% of families earn less than $1000 per year
—75% earn less than $2000
—40% of Canada's Indians must live on welfare
—only 39% of Indians finish Grade 8; only 3% finish high school

—the national average life expectancy is over 65 years; that of the Indian is about 40 years

—over half of all Indian families live in houses with three rooms or less; less than half have electricity; only 9% have indoor toilets and baths.

1. *What services does the government provide for the Indians?*
2. *According to these two sets of statistics, would you consider the Indian better or worse off than other Canadians?*
3. *What areas do you think need improvement most?*

The Indians would certainly be considered poor by most Canadian standards. Does the problem lie with the government? Is money the problem or does the problem lie with the Indians themselves? Read the following statements, then give your opinion.

The Indian has been given a chance. But it seems that he can't or won't pull himself into an improved status in today's Canada. The fault is no one's but his own.

Leonard Crane, an Indian:

I'm pretty well agreed that if an Indian needs help, give him help, you know. But we have to get out and do these things. . . . I figure if we get out and give the Indian department a hand in buying our medical care and trying to pay for some of our way and pay for our kids' education, it will give us more footing. Like you have to do, you have to pay for your way.

We do not want welfare assistance from the government. . . . Instead of sending welfare, why does the government not send us men who would come and see our land, to see what forms of work it could provide? Why does the government not send us men who would come to teach us the skills we need to survive in the ways of the white man?

Why do Indians suffer such poverty? Why do they not go out to earn a living by getting a job? Of course, many Indians do hold jobs both inside and outside their reserves. For others, this is sometimes hard.

For those living on the reserves, there are many problems in trying to make a living:

There's 2200 reserves across Canada, and very few of them are near towns. So if you've got a house and some land on the reserve, how do you get a job?

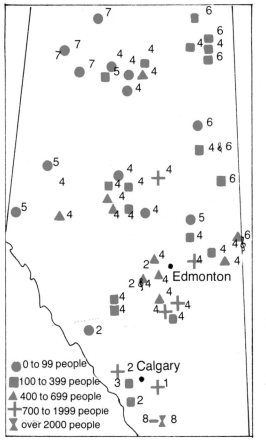

Reserves in Alberta

1	Blackfoot	5	Beaver
2	Assiniboine	6	Chipewyan
3	Sarceé	7	Slave
4	Cree	8	Blood

1. How many reserves can you count in Alberta? How many have a population of over 2000?

2. How many of these reserves are close to large towns or cities? Why might this create problems for Indians seeking jobs?

The reserves today, even in the far North, are becoming depleted of game and fish. And this will grow progressively worse as the industrialization of the marshland takes place.

Today every Indian child on a reserve or in an Indian community can receive the education he desires. . . . Not all Indian parents, however, appreciate the new opportunities. Where schools are aloof from communities, where school committees do not exist and where parents themselves lack education, the importance of learning in the lives of children sometimes is little appreciated.

1. What are the problems facing Indians seeking jobs outside the reserves?

2. What problems are there in making a living inside the reserves?

3. Are there any possible solutions to these problems?

Mrs. Doreen Jensen of the Ksan Indian village, working on silkscreen. Can you tell what she is doing?

Huron Indians were already making snowshoes when the first Europeans saw them over three centuries ago. Today in Loretteville, Quebec, Huron still make "racquettes" in small "snowshoe factories". Here an expert craftsman works on a snowshoe, using a caribou bone to make sure the spacing is even.

Loggers of the Ksan Indian village. What will the large cedar trunks be used for?

The Indian Act

The special status of Indians in Canada was confirmed in the Indian Act. This Act was first passed in 1876, and has been changed several times since then. It lists the special rights held by Indians. Some of these we have already seen. The Act also shows the control the Canadian government has over the affairs of Indians. It gives the government power to regulate these things:

Reserves and possession of lands in reserves
Sale or barter of produce
Roads and bridges
Estates and wills of Indians
Management of Indian monies
Loans to Indians
Treaty money
Election of Chiefs and Band Councils
Taxation and legal rights
Schools

These and other controls give the Canadian government wide powers over Indian life.

Who is subject to the terms of the Indian Act? The following definitions may help you see how the government classifies Indians:

STATUS INDIANS Status Indians are all those who are registered as Indians or have the right to be registered as Indians. If your name is on the Register List of the Department of Indian Affairs in Ottawa, by law you are an Indian. A status Indian is entitled to live on a reserve and have certain rights on a reserve. Many status Indians, however, live and work outside the reserves.

All children born of status Indians are considered status. Also, if a non-Indian woman marries a status Indian, she too is considered status.

NON-STATUS INDIANS Those who have their names removed from the Register are considered non-status. This may happen for several reasons. For example, if an Indian woman marries a non-Indian, she loses her status and so do her children. Indians also lose their status if they become enfranchised.

ENFRANCHISEMENT An individual Indian or a whole band may apply for enfranchisement. This means they wish to join the main part of white Canadian society. They must give up their claims as Indians and cut themselves off from the reserves, although they are given their share of treaty money when they leave. Except for a number of women who have married non-Indians, few Indians over the years have become enfranchised. Since all Indians received the right to vote in 1962, few see anything to gain in becoming enfranchised.

All status Indians have the right to live inside the reserves. However, there are almost 500 000 Indians and Métis (part Indian, part European) who live outside the reserves. These are the non-status Indians. Because they may not live on reserves, they receive none of the benefits of status Indians. Many earn less than $1000 per year. Out of this they must pay for their food, shelter, clothing. Others, like those in the James Bay area, must spend the cold winters in tents.

Joe Hill lives near North Bay. He is a non-status Indian. He used to be a carpenter, and built his own seven by seven metre cabin. He is not married, so the cabin is big enough for him. Mr. Hill is 56, and for the past twelve years he has had a back condition which has prevented him from working. Sometimes when he clears the snow from his roof he wrenches his back so that he cannot move for days.

The government gives Mr. Hill $137 a month. This is enough to buy food, but not enough for simple things like a telephone, electricity, indoor plumbing, or even a toilet. So he drinks his water from a spring close to his cabin, and even on the coldest winter nights, he must use an outdoor toilet.

1. Do you think that "status" Indians are better off than "non-status" Indians? Explain.

2. Should non-status Indians like Joe Hill be given more assistance?

3. Do you agree with this statement:

"The Indian Act discriminates against Indian women"?
4. Why do you think an Indian might want to give up his rights as a status Indian and become enfranchised? Why do you think few Indians over the years have become enfranchised?

The Future

What of the future of Canada's Indians? Many agree that the reserve system cannot last forever. It seems there are three paths which they can choose.

One choice is to become part of Canadian society. This means they would take the path that most immigrants to Canada have followed. They would speak English or French, work in Canadian society, and have the same rights as other Canadians. However, they would not be a separate culture, but only Canadians of Indian ancestry. This path is called *ASSIMILATION*. Only a few argue that it is the best path. Yet many are afraid that in the long run, they will lose their identity as Indians, lose their values, and in this way be assimilated into Canadian society.

A second choice is to retain their own culture, and set up a society separate from Canada. This society would have Indian values and be governed by Indians. This path is called *SEPARATION*. Those who wish separation argue this way:

> Canada is a white man's country, run by white man's laws. To the white man the Indian is good as long as he is quiet and it does not cost much to improve his condition. The only way to improve the Indian's condition is separation.

The third choice is to join Canadian society, but still keep the Indian identity. This means that the Indians would have to learn the kind of job skills that would enable them to compete. Their educational system must be improved, and poverty eliminated. As much as possible, the Indians would be responsible for making the decisions which affect their future. This path is called *INTEGRATION*. Those who argue for integration say:

> We have to keep the Indian values alive, but we also have to learn to use the new tools, if we are to survive. We have to learn the skills of white society, but we don't have to be assimilated into their way of life.

Among many Canadians there is a feeling of guilt about the way the Indian has been treated in the past. There is growing interest and concern about the condition of Canada's original people. Many ask, "What can we do to help?" Chief Dan George, the famous Indian actor, answers in this way:

You can stop discriminating against my people.

You can stop patronizing them in your usual manner.

You can stop feeling awful good within yourself when you make a paltry offering in the form of some money.

You can stop feeling guiltless when you buy us textbooks and blankets and houses.

You can try to understand what cultural adjustments are demanded of our younger people, who are forced to think and to work and to accept the standards of your culture.

You can stop making us look ridiculous in your plays and on your television. Go and see how we have been degraded in your social study books.

Finally, there is the question, "What do the Indians want?" A young Indian answers:

What does the Indian want? What does any man want? To be left alone with his life and have some hope of making that life what he wants it to be.

Canada can do much to help its Native People. It can also learn much from them. Indian values can provide useful lessons for modern technological society. The Indians' respect for nature is one example of the lessons to be learned. Many of the problems below might have been avoided if we had been ready to accept these lessons earlier.

—Over the past several years pollution of the environment has been recognized as one of the greatest problems we face. Only recently have anti-pollution programs been started to save our surroundings.

—Many species of animal life have become extinct over the years. Wildlife preservation is now receiving far greater attention.

—For many years Canadians have been wasting their natural resources. Most people are now beginning to see the importance of conserving resources.

Can you think of any way Canada might have benefited if it had learned these lessons in the past?

As we come to the end of this unit, can you think of any other lesson we can learn from the Indian heritage of independence and freedom? Their respect for and obligations towards others in their community? Their ideal of existence in harmony with nature?

Word Study

Status Indian	Métis	separation
non-status Indian	assimilation	enfranchisement
Indian Act	integration	

Things to Do 1. Look through your daily newspaper and clip out articles dealing with Canada's Indians and Inuit. What are these people trying to achieve? What methods are they using to gain their ends?

2. Two of the latest incidents dealing with Indian and Inuit rights have occurred at James Bay and Kenora. Find out why trouble has broken out in these two areas. What is the government side of the question? What is the Indian-Inuit side of the dispute? How have the problems been solved?

3. In some recent cases, Indians have used the threat of violence to demand certain rights. Do you think this tactic should be used by minority groups who are seeking rights from the majority? What other methods are available to the Indians?

4. Many Indians are receiving higher education away from the reserves at high schools and universities. What problems do you think they will face in retaining their values in European society?

   What problems of re-adjustment will they face when they return to the reserves after their education is completed?

5. If you want to find out more about Indian and Inuit rights, and what is being done by the Canadian government, write to the Canadian Association in support of the Native Peoples, or to the Minister connected with Indian Affairs. Their addresses will be found in the telephone directory.

Unit 3
Patterns of Settlement

A German immigrant family waits for the train west, about 1905.

1
Introduction

A Land of Immigrants

Canada is a nation of immigrants. Even our first people, the Indians and the Inuit, are not native to this land. In the distant past, they too were immigrants. Only four hundred years ago they were the only inhabitants of a vast territory. Canada was a land almost empty of people.

At the beginning of the seventeenth century, the French became the first Europeans to take permanent root in Canada. Study the map below. Where were the main French settlements? What seems to be the pattern of French settlement?

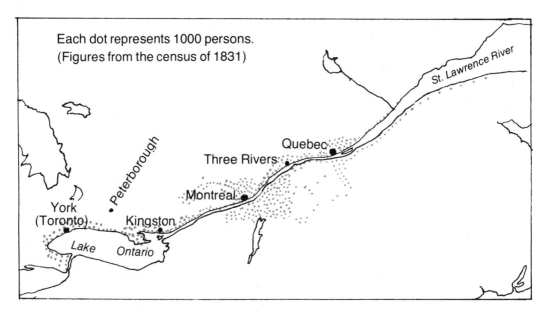

Each dot represents 1000 persons.
(Figures from the census of 1831)

The population of New Franch was small. Even at its peak it probably did not exceed 60 000. Yet these few people were scattered for hundreds of kilometres along the St. Lawrence River. Their farmlands ran in long narrow strips back from the river.

All settlers wanted farms on the river. Can you think of reasons for this? Of course water is valuable to farmers, who must irrigate their land. In a pioneer society such as New France it had an even greater importance. Rivers were the chief method of transportation and communication. In pioneer times road-building through the Canadian forests was expensive, time-consuming, and difficult. It was much easier, faster, and cheaper to ship products and to travel by boat.

In 1763 the foundation of modern Canada was set when New France fell into the hands of the English. Canada as a nation was to have two European founding peoples, English and French.

The first large wave of English immigrants to settle Canada were the Loyalists. They settled in the Maritimes and Ontario in the period following the American Revolution of 1776. These settlers too sought choice lots along the lakes and rivers. Unlike the long strip farms of the French, (see page 147) English farms were divided in the following way:

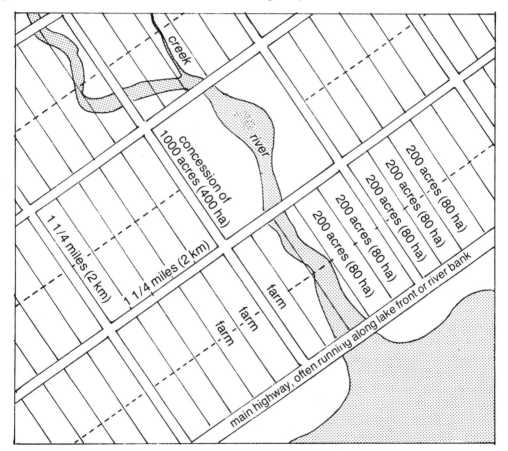

What pattern does this kind of land division seem to follow?

Between 1815 and 1850 immigrants from England, Scotland, and Ireland swelled the population of Canada to over three million. By this time most of the good farming land in Ontario was gone. Land-hungry settlers had to move farther into the interior, where the land was poor and farms were cut off from the larger communities to the south.

By 1867 Confederation had united the provinces of Canada. The new government satisfied the demand for land by purchasing the huge territory of the Northwest from the Hudson's Bay Company. In time the provinces of Manitoba, Saskatchewan, and Alberta would be carved from this territory.

The new wave of immigrants who settled the West came mainly from eastern Europe. Between 1871 and 1891 over one million immigrants came to Canada. Many settled in the West, where sixty-four hectare lots of free land were the prize.

The flat, treeless prairies were ideal farmlands. Communication between communities was not hindered by dense forests as it had been in eastern Canada. At the same time lakes and rivers were less plentiful in the West. Fortunately, the great Canadian railway, the CPR, already spanned the West. In eastern Canada settlers followed the St. Lawrence and the Great Lakes. In the West, they followed the railway.

The pattern of settlement for Canada in the nineteenth century had been set. Canada was a farming nation. By 1900 only three of every ten Canadians lived and worked in the cities. The twentieth century would bring great changes.

Toronto. Why does a city like Toronto become a magnet for immigrants?

After the outbreak the World War I in 1914, immigration slowed to a trickle. It was not until the end of World War II in 1945 that the last wave began. Since 1945 over four million immigrants have made Canada their home. Most of these have come from England, the U.S., Italy, and Germany. Unlike the settlers of earlier centuries, the modern-day immigrants did not settle on the land. They chose the city as their home.

Today the map of Canada looks like this. How does it compare with the map of the earlier settlement of Canada?

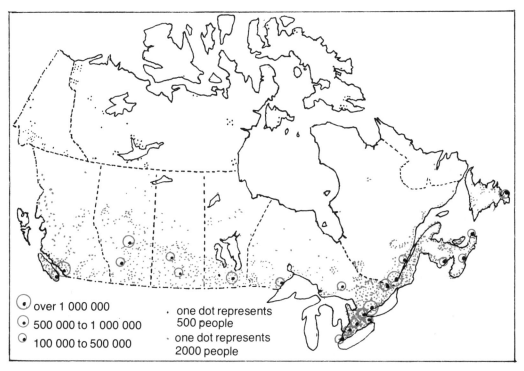

over 1 000 000

500 000 to 1 000 000

100 000 to 500 000

· one dot represents 500 people

· one dot represents 2000 people

The immigrants have been joined in the cities by large numbers of Canadians who are leaving the farm. Today 4 of every 5 Canadians live in the city. By the year 2000, 94 per cent of all Canadians will live and work in our cities. One result of this trend is the decreasing number of farms. In 1941 there were 732 000 farms in Canada. In 1961 there were only 480 000 farms.

One reason for the movement of farm workers away from the land is the increasing size of Canada's farms. In 1871 the average farm in Canada was about thirty-five hectares. By 1961 this had increased to about a hundred and forty-four hectares. Today with the new heavy machinery used in farms, fewer people are needed to work larger areas of land. More and more, people must look to the cities for jobs. Can you think what other attractions the city holds for immigrants and farm workers alike?

From the beginning, immigrants have brought their talents, skills, and cultures to Canada. They have helped to build a unique Canadian identity. Canada's immigrants will continue to play an important role in building the Canadian nation of the future.

In this unit you will be asked to study a number of questions and problems related to the settlement of Canada over the centuries:

1. What attracted people to Canada?
2. What parts of Canada did they settle? Why?
3. What hardships did they face in adjusting to a new land and a new culture?

In many cases you will be using letters and other documents written by our early settlers, to see for yourself their hopes, fears, and reactions in their new homeland.

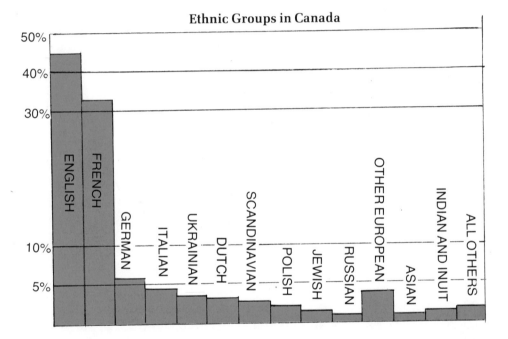

Ethnic Groups in Canada

Why They Came   Immigrants have been coming to Canada since 1605, and as you can see from the chart, they have come from many countries. In fact people from more than one hundred countries from all parts of the world have made Canada their home. Some have come because of the hope of a new life held out by Canada. Others have come because of poor conditions in their own countries. Some of the reasons for immigration most often stated are these:

—the excitement of starting a new life in a new land
—to escape poverty
—to escape wars
—to obtain cheap land
—to escape harsh systems of government
—to obtain a higher standard of living.

Do immigrants come to Canada because of the attraction of this country or because of problems at home? People usually immigrate for a combination of reasons. Divide the list above into two columns. One might be called "The Pull of Canada", the other, "The Push of the Home Country". Add any other reasons for immigration which you can think of. In your opinion, which of the two columns provides the strongest reasons for immigration?

Where They Settled   Another group of questions we will explore include the following: (1) What parts of Canada did the pioneers settle? (2) Why did these areas attract the early settlers? (3) What were the patterns of these settlements? As we look at the communities which have developed in Canada, several patterns seem to take shape. The French settled in Quebec, the English in Ontario and the Maritimes, the Germans in southwestern Ontario, the Ukrainians in the Prairies, the Italians in the cities. How can we explain such patterns of settlement?

Some reasons may appear obvious right from the start:

—friends and fellow-countrymen settled there
—the jobs were the same as those back home
—the area was close to water and roads
—the surroundings provided natural defense from enemies.

Can you suggest for yourself other reasons why people might settle in certain parts of Canada, such as in the Prairies, or along the St. Lawrence River, while other parts, such as northern Ontario or the Northwest Territories, remain empty?

How They Adjusted   Uprooting is always difficult. Have you ever had to move to a different part of the country, or to a new city, or even to a different part of town? Can you remember how you felt about it? Most of those who came to Canada hoped to find a life better than the one they left behind, but many found hardships in trying to adjust to a new way of life.

For the early French and English settlers, these hardships were both physical and social. They were often faced with harsh weather, poor soils, lack of equipment, discomforts, and disease. For many, the problems of loneliness, isolation, and boredom were even worse.

Imagine yourself in the place of an early settler on the frontier for one day. You awake at about 06:00 and begin to work your farm. Much of your day is spent cutting down trees, rooting out stumps, and clearing rocks. If time permits, you will plow a small section of your clearing, and plant seeds. At twilight you finally stop your work, and have supper. If you are lucky enough to have a book, you might spend the next few hours reading in the dim light of an oil lamp. This would provide your only entertainment.

At about 21:00 you retire for the night, ready for work the next day. Every day is much like every other day. Your nearest neighbours are many kilometres away. Roads, if they exist at all, are very poor, and travel is difficult. This means you may not see other people for weeks or even months. During this time you get no news of the outside world. For all practical purposes, you are isolated.

If you had to give up your current way of life and live like the early settlers, what would you miss most? What do you think was the hardest part of pioneer life?

Of course, today's immigrants do not have to face the physical hardships of the early settlers. Their problems are mostly social. They must adjust to a new language, new customs, and new people. Sometimes, because they are foreigners, they will not be welcomed in their new homeland. In some cases they will meet prejudice and discrimination in trying to find jobs and homes. Why does this attitude toward immigrants sometimes exist? Newcomers usually bring with them new customs, new ideas, and a whole new lifestyle. It is common for many people to be afraid of new things or things they do not understand. As a result, immigrants are not always treated fairly by Canadian society at large.

You might understand these problems more clearly if you were to put yourself in the place of an immigrant. Imagine that your family is moving to a country very different from Canada, for example, Japan. This would certainly create changes in your way of life.

You might prepare yourself in advance for your new country by finding out about the geography, culture, and types of people you are likely to meet. You could do this by reading some books about Japan. You might contact the Japanese embassy and ask its help. What other sources of information might you try?

Once there, however, you would be faced with a number of problems which you will have to deal with yourself.

Some of the obvious ones are:

—having to learn a new language
—having to make new friends
—having to adjust to new foods
—having to adjust to different fashions.

What other social changes do you feel you would have to make? Which would be the most difficult?

In this unit, you will be learning about the people who settled in Canada—their reasons for coming, the places they settled, the hardships they faced. It may be difficult for you to identify with these pioneers since conditions have changed so much over the years. Yet if you can imagine yourself in a similar situation today, the problems of settling a new country will seem much more real to you.

2
The Settlement of New France

In any list of famous Canadians, the following would surely find a place:
- —Samuel de Champlain
- —Madeleine de Verchères
- —George Etienne Cartier
- —Louis St. Laurent
- —Louis Cyr
- —Etienne Brûlé
- —Wilfrid Laurier
- —Maurice Richard
- —George Vanier

What do these people have in common? They are all French Canadians who have achieved outstanding work in their field. How many other outstanding French Canadians can you add to this list?

The French were already making their contributions to Canada more than a century before the land was ruled by the English. With courage, hard work, and patience a small group of French pioneers were able to battle loneliness, disease, and a hostile environment to create a new land. Their legacy today is the Province of Quebec. With an area of 154 440 km², it is Canada's largest province. It is the home of six million French Canadians, almost 30 per cent of Canada's population. Here the French heritage has been blended into a unique and vibrant Canadian culture.

In this chapter you will have an opportunity to study the early settlement and growth of New France. We hope that you will discover what life was like for those pioneers who were the first founders of Canada.

Reasons for Settlement

Most of us are familiar with the old rhyme: "In 1492 Columbus sailed the ocean blue." We also know that Christopher Columbus, an Italian working for Spain, was trying to find a new, shorter route to the Orient. What he found instead was North America. Other men, such as the Vikings, had landed in America before Columbus, but few knew about their findings. The existence of the New World was still very much a secret. The effect of Columbus' discovery was to spur other countries into voyages of discovery and exploration of their own. In the next fifty years such voyages were sponsored by Spain, Portugal, England, Holland, and France. Each country hoped to find a route to the fabled wealth of India and China. The Europeans quickly realized the New World was not the Orient. Nevertheless they hoped that the new lands themselves might be the source of silver, gold, and spices.

Of course, we know they were not successful in their first aim. The shape of North and South America made a short voyage to India and China impossible, until the Panama Canal was built in 1906. A few countries were most successful in their second aim. The Spanish found gold in Mexico, and the Portuguese found silver in Peru. The others had less luck. In the early years of explorations they settled for new fishing grounds in the Grand Banks off the coast of Newfoundland and in the waters off Nova Scotia. Fishermen from the west coast of France, and from England, Portugal, and Spain spent several months a year catching cod. Fish was a basic part of the diet of most Europeans. These fishermen made contact with the Indians and traded with them. Although they often spent long weeks ashore, salting and drying their cod, the fishermen did not try to establish a settlement in the New World.

While most of the exploration of this period was focused on Central America, the northern areas also captured some attention. Before the year 1534, the coastline of Newfoundland and the Gulf of St. Lawrence were known to the fishermen from England and France. However, the vast land mass of Canada still lay unexplored. Was it possible that this unexplored land might contain kingdoms with gold and silver mines such as the Spanish had found in Central America? The French certainly hoped so? In search of these treasures they sent Jacques Cartier to explore the lands along the St. Lawrence. On April 20, 1534, Cartier set out on his voyage with two ships as well as a royal charter and a grant of money from Francis I, King of France.

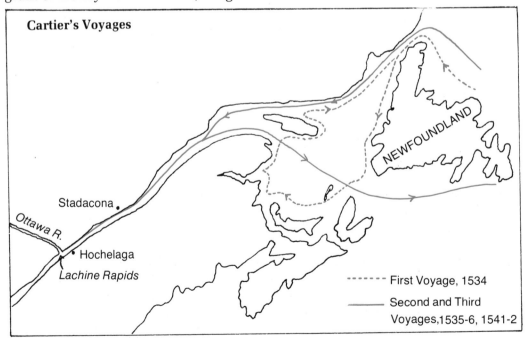

Cartier's Voyages

Stadacona

Ottawa R.

Hochelaga

Lachine Rapids

NEWFOUNDLAND

- - - - - First Voyage, 1534

——— Second and Third Voyages, 1535-6, 1541-2

Read carefully the following portion of the charter granted to Cartier:

> . . . the sum of 6000 livres tournois [over 120 000 dollars today] . . . to pay the necessary costs of the feeding, arming, and equipping . . . of ships presently in Britanny, as well as for the pay and training of those who, led by Jacques Cartier will make the voyage . . . to the New Lands to discover . . . islands and territories where, it is said, are great quantities of gold and other riches . . . .

1. What were the French hoping to find on this expedition?   *2. What do you think is meant by the term "other riches"?*

During his short stay in Canada in 1534 Cartier found no treasure, although he did manage to explore the mouth of the St. Lawrence and make contact with the Indians.

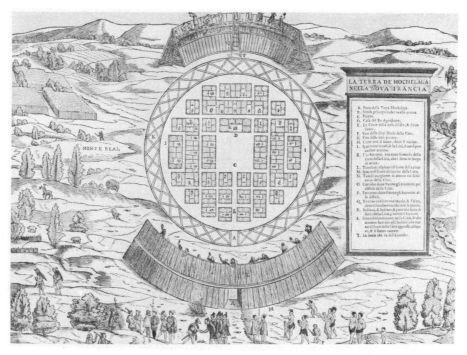

What evidence is there that the Indians of Hochelaga fortified their village against attack? What food sources did these Indians have?

Cartier returned to Canada the following year, 1535, with three ships and one hundred and ten men to continue his search. This time he went much farther inland, passing by the Indian villages of Stadacona (present-day Quebec City) and Hochelaga (present-day Montreal). He could not travel any further because rapids blocked his way and he lacked information about what lay beyond.

Cartier and his men spent that winter at Stadacona. It was a harsh winter, and many of his men became ill, yet Cartier was able to accomplish a great deal. Before his return in 1536, he explored much of the St. Lawrence, established relations with the Indians, and gained valuable information about the soil and vegetation of the new land. The Indians also told him about supplies of gold and diamonds to be found in the north. In fact, he took back to France samples of what he thought were gold and diamonds. Along with these samples, Cartier kidnapped and brought back to France an Indian chief, Donnacona, and his two sons.

In France the chief's stories seemed to encourage further exploration in the new land. Following are two accounts of the tales told by Chief Donnacona about the wealth of the New World:

> . . . And we learned from Chief Donnacona . . . that in that country the natives go dressed and clothed in woollens like ourselves; that there are many towns and tribes composed of honest folk who possess great store of gold and copper.

> . . . the King of France says the Indian King told him there is a large city called Sagana, where there are many mines of gold and silver in great abundance, and men who dress and wear shoes like we do; and that there is abundance of cloves, nutmeg, and pepper.

Partly on the basis of these accounts. Francis I decided to outfit Cartier for a third expedition:

> . . . in the past we have sent Jacques Cartier, who discovered the great lands of Canada and Hochelaga which are an extremity of Eastern Asia, in which he has reported there is much wealth . . . We have decided to again send Cartier to Canada and Hochelaga, and as far as the lands of the Saguenay . . . with a goodly number of ships and men of all rank, skills, and trades . . . .

1. *In what ways are the two accounts of Chief Donnacona's story alike?*
2. *Which parts of the story seem hardest to believe? Why? Did the King of France believe them?*
3. *If the Chief's story was not true,* *why do you think he might have told such a tale to his captors?*
4. *What evidence is there in the King's letter that Europeans were still unaware that they had found a new continent?*

Cartier's third voyage in 1541 proved to be a failure. He and his men spent another harsh winter at Stadacona. When some of his men died of scurvy and supplies ran short, Cartier decided to return to France. He had accomplished very little of his stated mission. Back in France there were further disappointments. After creating great excitement, the samples of gold and diamonds Cartier had found in his second voyage proved to be so worthless that the phrase "as false as a diamond of Canada" became popular in Europe.

The French had been disappointed in their search for precious metals. For over sixty years they gave up their ambitions and did not attempt to settle Canada. Cartier himself never returned, but he is regarded as the discoverer of Canada.

The Search for Furs

After Cartier's voyage it became clear to the French that there were no precious metals to be found in Canada. Fortunately for the future growth of Canada a new source of wealth was found—furs. At first furs were not an important business. Furs were used mainly as trim on clothing worn by wealthier Europeans, and enough furs for this purpose were usually obtained by fishermen from the Indians in return for cheap goods. By the year 1600, however, the fur trade had become a serious business. There were two good reasons for this. First, the fashions in Paris at this time dictated that every well dressed man should wear a fine hat made of beaver pelt; second, the forests of Canada contained large, easily obtained supplies of beaver.

Trapping Beaver   Trapping was quite simple. This hard-working animal was known to build houses and to dam streams, so it was easily found and killed. The supply was plentiful, since the beaver gives birth to between two and five young every year.

There were two kinds of pelts gathered by the fur traders. The normal beaver pelt had an outer coat of long guard hair, and an undercoat of soft fur. This kind of pelt was called a *CASTOR SEC*. The more expensive and valuable pelt was the one with the long hair removed. This was called the *CASTOR GRAS*.

The *castor gras* could only be obtained from the Indians. It took a long time before the guard hair would fall out. The Indians would scrape and grease the underside of the beaver skins, sew a few of them together, and wear them with the fur on the inside next to their bodies. After about eighteen months of wear, the long hair fell out, leaving the fur ready to be made into hats for the European market. Beaver hats were not what we call "fur hats". The soft fur was known as "felt".

The fur trade depended on the Paris fashion trade for its success. In some years the demand was low, in other years very high. Despite this there were big profits to be made in the fur trade, mainly because the Indians were often given cheap goods in exchange for the pelts. Here is a typical table of exchange values:

1 beaver skin	= 0.25 kg of coloured beads
	or
	0.5 kg of tobacco
	or
	2.25 kg of sugar
4 beaver skins	= 4.5 l of brandy, or
	12 large buttons, or
	20 fish-hooks
12 beaver skins	= 1 gun

Many adventurers were attracted by the chance of earning high profits in the fur trade. The fur trade was responsible for the earliest settlement of Canada, and many see it as the most important economic event in Canadian history.

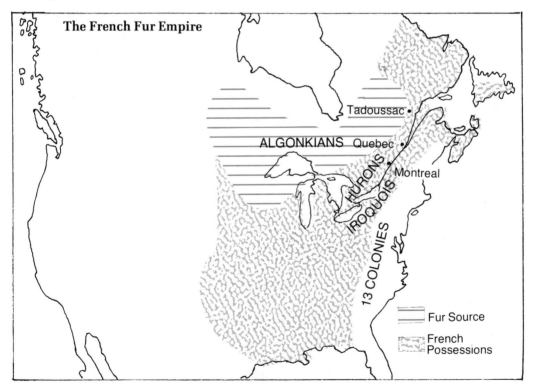

The French Fur Empire

Tadoussac

ALGONKIANS Quebec

HURONS

IROQUOIS

Montreal

13 COLONIES

Fur Source

French Possessions

However, from the very beginning there was much debate about the good and the bad effects of the fur trade. One of the concerns was about the kind of people who were attracted to the fur trade—the *COUREURS DE BOIS* ("runners of the woods"). These were the young men who endured hardship and often risked their lives to push back the frontiers of Canada in search of new supplies of fur. What sort of men were attracted to this business? What effect did the fur trade have on them and on the other colonists?

Read carefully the following accounts of the *Coureurs de bois:*

> *Coureurs de bois* are Frenchmen who were either born in Canada or who came to settle there. They are always young men in the prime of life, for older men cannot endure the hardships of this way of life. Some are of good social standing, others are merely farmers or sons of farmers; others still have no occupation . . . The profit motive is common to all men . . . .

> Since all of Canada is a vast and trackless forest, it is impossible for them to travel by land; they travel by lake and river in canoes usually occupied by three men . . . . It is in such a canoe that these three men embark at Quebec or Montreal . . . to search for beaver among the Indians . . . .
>
> They carry as little as possible in order to make room for a few bundles of merchandise . . . .
>
> If fish and game are scarce, as often happens, they resort to eating a sort of moss, which they call tripe, that grows on rocks, . . . to their moccasins, or to a glue they make from the skins they have traded. . . .

Since little time is required to carry out this trade, the life of the *coureur de bois* is spent in idleness and dissolute living. They sleep, smoke, drink brandy no matter what the cost, gamble . . . Gambling, drinking, and women often consume all their money and the profits of their voyages. They live in complete independence and account to no one for their actions, . . . no judge, no law, no police. . . .

. . . Not being accustomed to hold the plough, pickaxe or hatchet, their only tool being the gun, they must spend their lives in the woods where they have no priests to restrain them nor fathers or Governors to order them.

. . . A fashion of dressing nude like the savages is treated as a fine trick and joke . . . .

. . . I cannot tell you the attraction that all young people have for this life of the savage, which is to do nothing, to be restrained in nothing, follow every whim and be removed from all control.

. . . everyone agrees that there is almost general disobedience in the country. The number in the woods has increased to almost five or six hundred not including those who go out every day. They are the ones most capable of doing good and defending the colony.

. . . the great number of people who went to trade skins were ruining the colony because those who were most useful, being young and having the strength to work, were abandoning their wives and children, the tilling of soil and the raising of cattle.

1. *What kind of men generally chose to become* coureurs de bois?
2. *Do you think that their involvement in the fur trade had any harmful effects on their character and personality? Were there any positive results?*
3. *What objections did the government officials have to the* coureurs de bois?
4. *Have a class debate on the resolution: that the* coureurs de bois *were a bad influence on life in New France. One student may choose the role of* coureur de bois *while others take the parts of (1) a government official (2) a priest (3) a habitant, etc.*

The Canoe   The chief method of transportation for the Indians, *coureurs de bois,* and the later teams of *VOYAGEURS* who sought out the valuable beaver skins for the fur trading companies was the canoe. Canoes were among the most valuable of Indian inventions. There were very few roads in early New France, and in the small, swift rivers of the interior where the beaver were found, the larger, heavier boats of the French were of little use. Can it be argued that without the canoe, the beaver trade might not have flourished as it did in New France?

Today, canoeing has again become a popular sport among Canadians.

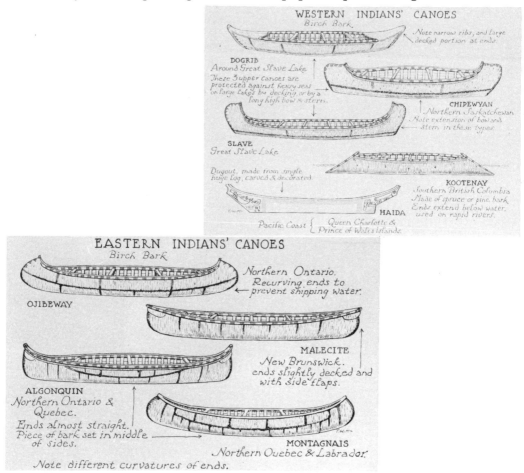

Throughout North America, canoes pop up in folklore with all the regularity of butlers in classic whodunits. The Ottawas told of a canoe made from smooth white stone, said to provide transportation to the promised land after death. French-Canadian settlers passed on to their youngsters a tale of the . . . flying canoe. The Devil used it to win over homesick lumbermen anxious to get home to their families at New Year's.

The *Relation* of 1647 records an incredible feat by a girl named Marie, widow of an Algonquin convert, Jean Baptiste. Marie was captured by Mohawk Indians but managed to escape. She came upon a large canoe that had been left unguarded by an Iroquois hunting party. When the boat proved too cumbersome for her to handle Marie, who was a skilled canoe-maker, used a hatchet to cut it down to more manoeuverable proportions, and paddled to Montreal.

The voyageurs who powered the huge birchbark freight canoes for the fur trading companies are often presented as hard-drinking, fun-loving free spirits. But this picture may bear only a slight resemblance to the truth.

. . . The larger canoes measured about 36 feet [10.3 m] in length and carried between four and five tons [3.6 and 4.5 t] of cargo, all of which had to be unloaded and lugged over each portage. Average haul per man per trip was between two and three hundred pounds, [90 and 135 kg] carried at a brisk trot of about five miles an hour [8 km/h]. Evening chores included the patching up of whatever leaks the delicate bark covering of the canoe had suffered during the day. In many respects, the voyageur's life was a decidely unglamorous one. Even the high-spirited singing seems to have been encouraged largely to boost the speed of travel, since it helped the paddlers keep a rhythmic (and more productive) stroke.

. . . After faithful service for untold centuries, the canoe fell victim to a nation-wide outbreak of public apathy. Indian craftsmen stopped handing down their intricate skills of shaping bark. In the early 1900s, the last of the fur trade freighters vanished and one bark relic after another disappeared. Fishermen started turning to rowboats and outboard motors.

Now canoeing is enjoying a brand new boom, as more and more Canadians take to outdoor recreation. It may be part of the same trend that's brought on the recent rebirth of cycling and cross-country skiing. . . .

In terms of structural design, in North America there have been few departures from the straightforward. The Iroquois in the late 1600s were known to produce a disposable canoe, made from elm bark and designed to be discarded after use. And it now appears certain that the Beothuk Indians of Newfoundland once came up with a folding canoe. Historians used to refute this suggestion, claiming bark would break if it were folded. But it's now believed that a strip of flexible hide was used along the bottom of the boat as a hinge. The centre thwarts, or cross-pieces, simply unfastened and the entire vessel folded up to allow for easy toting over trails. Generally, however, North American canoes stayed with more basic designs. Even today, though canoes are made from up-to-date materials, manufacturers still favor styles that follow the basic Algonquin or Ojibway lines of years ago. . . .

In Ontario, where canoeing mishaps account for about a quarter of all boating fatalities, the Ontario Safety League now conducts a series of demonstrations at public parks and campgrounds to teach proper techniques of handling and paddling.

Some Canoeing Tips 1. *Kneel on the floor, don't sit on the seat.*
2. *If you are going to fall over, tip the canoe with you. That way, it won't drift away.*
3. *When you paddle alone, sit toward the centre of the canoe.*
4. *Don't watch your paddle when canoeing. It can be a distraction.*
5. *Never leave your canoe if it should overturn.*

Patterns of Settlement

The fur trade was the life-blood of New France, as the French possessions in Canada were called. However, the French realized from the very beginning that in order to maintain their hold on the new lands and the fur trade itself, they would have to establish firm settlements. To support life in New France, a solid base of food production would have to be set up. But who would endure the hardships of the New World to set up farms? Where would these settlements be established? Was the land even suitable for agriculture?

Here is Cartier's description of the land on the Gaspé near the Gulf of St. Lawrence:

> . . . If the soil were as good as the harbours, it would be a blessing; but the land should not be called the New Land, being composed of stones and horrible rugged rocks; for along the whole north shore I did not see one cart-load of earth and yet I landed in many places. . . . there is nothing but moss and short, stunted shrub. In fine I am rather inclined to believe that this is the land that God gave to Cain. . . .

And his impression of the soil around Stadacona:

> . . . This region is as fine land as it is possible to see, being very fertile and covered with magnificent trees of the same varieties as in France, such as oaks, elms, ash, walnut, plum-trees, yew-trees, cedars, vines, hawthorns, bearing a fruit as large as a damson, and other varieties of trees. Beneath these grows hemp as good as that of France, which comes up without sowing or tilling it. . . .

1. *Locate Stadacona and the Gaspé coast on a map of New France. Which area is more fertile? What other factors are important in choosing a settlement? Which area would you choose for settlement? Why?*
2. *Which of these factors are present in the Gaspé Coast and at Stadacona?*

The first attempt to set up a French colony in Canada took place near the Bay of Fundy in Acadia in the year 1604. It failed, though, and was abandoned in the following year. One of the men involved in this venture was a remarkable soldier, explorer, geographer, and seaman, Samuel de Champlain, the Father of

New France. In 1608, Champlain decided to try again. This time he chose as the site for his colony the area which had impressed Cartier many years before— Quebec. Here, Canada's first permanent settlement was founded. Why was this site chosen?

Here is Champlain's own description of Quebec:

> I arrived there on July the third. On arrival I looked for a place suitable for settlement, but I could not find any more suitable or better situated than the point of Quebec, so called by the natives, which was covered with nut trees. . . .
>
> I continued the construction of our quarters, which contained three main buildings of two stories. Each one was three fathoms long and two and a half-wide. [One fathom equals about two metres.] The storehouse was six fathoms long and three wide with a fine cellar six feet [one metre, eighty centimetres] high. All the way around our buildings I had a gallery made, outside the second story . . . There were also ditches fifteen feet [four metres, fifty centimetres] wide and six deep, and outside these I made several platforms which enclosed a part of the buildings, and there we put our cannon. . . .
>
> While other workmen were busy at our quarters, I set all the rest to work clearing the land . . . since the soil seemed to be very good.

1. *What features of Quebec seemed to appeal to Champlain?*
2. *Review the aims of the French government in encouraging settlements. Why might Quebec be a good location from the govern-ment's point of view?*
3. *Make a sketch of Quebec's buildings based on Champlain's description. Compare your diagram with the following photo.*

Despite Champlain's glowing reports of fertile soil, few families took the risk of permanent settlement in New France. Moreover, the merchants involved in the fur trade did not wish to have a wave of settlers emigrate to Canada. They feared that the settlers might interfere in their trade with the Indians, or even join in the fur trade themselves, and so provide competition. The merchants also felt that once the settlers began to clear the land the sources of beaver would disappear quickly and their agents would have to go much deeper into the interior for their supplies.

In the beginning, control of the colony was given to a merchant, or company, who held a monopoly, or exclusive rights, to the fur trade. The merchant or company received the profits of the fur trade, and had the power to distribute land in New France. In return for these rights the merchants agreed to bring settlers to New France. However, for reasons we have already seen, the merchants brought very few settlers over.

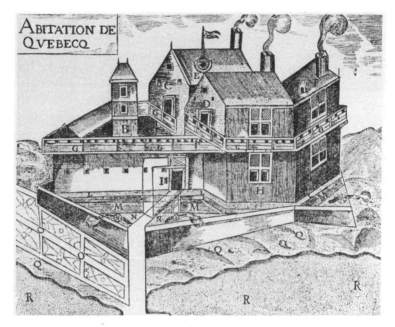

It was only through the constant efforts of Champlain that settlers were per-suaded to come to New France. The first of these families, that of Louis Hébert, came in 1617. Several others followed his example, but by 1627 the whole pop-ulation of New France was only sixty-five people.

From Champlain's Map of New France, published 1632

Many others in France who may have wished to settle in Canada were probably afraid to do so because they knew nothing about the new land, or the sort of work they might be expected to do. What kind of people would be best suited for the colony? What supplies should they bring with them? These were the common questions. To answer such questions travellers returning from New France sometimes spoke to crowds in the mother country.

Before reading the next document, try to answer the questions yourself. Describe the ideal immigrant. List the supplies you might take with you if you were sailing for Canada at that time. Remember, the first settlers knew less about conditions in Canada than you do.

You ask me in the first place whether you are fit for this country. The answer I make you is that this country is not yet fit for people of rank who are extremely rich, because such people would not find in it all the luxuries they enjoy in France; such persons must wait until this country has more inhabitants, unless they are persons who wish to retire from the world in order to lead a pleasant and quiet life free from fuss. . . .

The people best fitted for this country are those who can work with their own hands in making clearings, putting up buildings and otherwise; for as men's wages are very high here, a man who does not take care and practice economy will be ruined; but the best way is always to begin by clearing land and making a good farm. . . .

It would be well for a man coming to settle, to bring provisions with him for at least a year or two years if possible, especially flour which he could get for much less in France and could not even be sure of being always able to get for any money here; for if many people should come from France in any year without bringing any flour with them and the grain crops should be bad here that year, which God forbid, they would find themselves much straitened.

It would be well also to bring a supply of clothes, for they cost twice as much here as they do in France.

Money is also much dearer; its value increases one third, so that a coin of fifteen *sous* is worth twenty, and so on in proportion.

I would advise a man having money enough to bring two labouring men with him, or even more if he has the means, to clear his land; this is in answer to the question whether a person having three thousand or four thousand francs to employ here could do so with advantage; such a person could get himself into very easy circumstances in three or four years if he choose to practice economy, as I have already said.

Most of our settlers are persons who came over in the capacity of servants, and who, after serving their masters for three years, set up for themselves. They had not worked for more than a year before they had cleared land on which they got in more than enough grain for their food. . . .

Poor people would be much better off here than they are in France, provided they are not lazy; they could not fail to get employment and could not say, as they do in France, that they are obliged to beg for their living because they cannot find any one to give them work; in one word, no people are wanted, either men or women, who cannot turn their hands to some work, unless they are very rich.

Women's work consists of household work and of feeding and caring for the cattle; for there are few female servants; so that wives are obliged to do their own house work; nevertheless those who have the means employ valets who do the work of maidservants.

1. *How does your list compare with the suggestions of the author?*
2. *What sort of work could both men and women expect to do in New France?*
3. *What sort of people would be better off in the colony? What sort should not emigrate?*

The efforts to encourage emigration were quite unsuccessful at first. In fact, by the time of Champlain's death in 1635 there were barely one hundred settlers in New France. The government of France, however, soon adopted a policy for increasing the population of the colony. The man most responsible for this policy was Jean Talon, the *Intendant* of New France from 1666 to 1672. As *Intendant*, Talon's job was to encourage the growth of trade, industry, farming, and many other matters related to social affairs in the colony.

Talon began by determining the size of the population. His census was as follows:

Census of the Families in New France, 1666

Quebec	555
Beaupré	678
Beauport	172
Ile d'Orléans	471
St. Jean, St. François, and St. Michel	156
Sillery	217
Notre Dame des Anges and the St. Charles River	118
Côte de Lauzon	6
Montréal	584
Trois Rivières	461
Total	3418

1. *On a map of modern Quebec, try to find each of the towns mentioned in the census. How many still exist?*

2. *What kind of problems would a population separated by large distances create for (a) a merchant, (b) a general?*

Talon's census showed that only one-third of the settlers were female. He saw immediately the need to provide more wives and so increase the population. These wives were to be found in the ranks of the unmarried women in France. They included the *Filles du Roi* (the king's daughters), who were orphans and who were supported by the French crown.

Here is part of Talon's request:

> . . . it will be well to recommend strongly that those destined for this country be in no ways naturally deformed; that they have nothing exteriorly repulsive; that they be hale and strong for country work, or at least that they have some aptness for hand-labour. . . . Three or four young women of good family and distinguished for their accomplishments, would tend, perhaps, usefully to attach by marriage some officers. . . .
>
> The girls sent last year are married, and almost all pregnant or mothers; a proof of the fertility of this country.

The request seemed successful:

> The king has heard with pleasure . . . that of the 165 women who came last year there remained but 15 to be married. . . . To this effect His Majesty has taken the measures necessary to send 150 women this year. I am sure that as soon as they arrive you will see that they are established and married. . . .
>
> You did well to order that volunteers would be deprived of the right to engage in the fur trade and hunt unless they married within fifteen days of the arrival of the vessels bringing the women.
>
> With regard to those who will make the trip this year I have given the necessary orders so that those chosen will be healthy and strong. . . .

Talon next sought to encourage large families:

> . . . In order to multiply the number of children and encourage marriage His said Majesty . . . orders that in the future all inhabitants of the . . . country who have up to ten legitimate children living who are neither priests nor belong to any religious order . . . will be paid . . . a yearly gratuity of three hundred livres, and those who have twelve, four hundred livres. . . . In addition . . . it is the King's will . . . that all

males who marry before the age of twenty, and females before the age of sixteen, will receive on their wedding day twenty livres to be known as the King's gift . . . and that those inhabitants who have the greater number of children be always preferred to the others . . . and that there be established a small tax, the proceeds to go to the local hospitals, upon fathers who have not their boys married at the age of twenty and girls at the age of sixteen. . . .

1. *What measures did French officials take to encourage quick marriage and large families?*

2. *How might the encouragement to*

have a large family affect the position and role of women in New France?

The Church in Settlement

Examine closely this photograph of a small French Canadian village. It is similar to dozens of other postcard towns and villages you will see nestled along the banks of rivers in the Province of Quebec. What is the most impressive building in this village? Are you surprised that a village of this size would have such a splendid church?

Look closely at a road map of Quebec and you will notice something else. What do many of the towns seem to have in common? St. Paul, Ste. Anne, St. Ignace, St. Simeon, St. Jean—the names of saints are seen everywhere. How many such towns and villages can you locate?

The steeples, the churches, the names of saints are all symbols of what religion has meant to French Canadians in the past.

Religion has always played an important part in the exploration and settlement of new lands by European countries. In Africa, Asia, and North and South America, missionaries were usually the first to make contact with the native people. Close behind followed the settlers and traders. It has often been said that in the pattern of settlement, the flag followed the cross. What do you think is meant by this statement?

Was religion also an important factor in the early French settlement of Canada? Read carefully the following statements. The first is from the King of France; the second is from Champlain:

Francis I, 1540:

> We have brought back (from Canada) several men, and taught them to love and fear God so that when they return, they may persuade their brothers to accept our Holy Faith. We have also decided to send Cartier to Canada so that we may do actions agreeable to God our creator and redeemer.

Champlain:

> I have always had a desire of making discoveries in New France for the welfare and glory of France and also to bring these poor people the knowledge of God.

1. *What is the "Holy Faith" to which the king refers?*
2. *Who are the "poor people" to whom Champlain refers?*
3. *According to Francis I and Champlain, what was their purpose in exploring Canada?*

The merchants and fur traders of New France were not very concerned with the religious life of the new colony. They were interested in finding furs, not in settlement. It seems that only the Catholic Church took an active interest in the welfare of the colony. The Church sent priests, missionaries, and nuns to the colony. This was fortunate for the future settlement of New France. It is unlikely that settlers would have brought their wives and children to the colony without the presence of the Church. We will see shortly why the Church was so important to the young colony.

In 1615, the Récollet friars became the first missionaries in New France. They were followed by members of the Society of Jesus, the Jesuits. Soon the Jesuits came to play a very important role in the settlement of New France. From their center at Fort Ste. Marie, near Midland, Ontario, they worked very hard to bring Christianity to the Hurons. The Jesuits were also great explorers and did much to open up the interior of North America. The most famous of these was Father Marquette, who was one of the first Europeans to explore the Mississippi River.

Ursuline nuns land at Quebec.

The Jesuits worked very hard also to bring more settlers to the new colony. Their reasons for wanting more settlers can be seen in the following letter. It was written by Father Paul le Jeune, a missionary among the Hurons:

> A way of persuading the natives to receive our holy faith would be to send a number of capable men to clear and cultivate the land. They should know the language, work with the natives and settle down. When the natives see such work in their behalf they could more easily be taught and converted.
>
> With the help of a few hard working men it would be easy to settle a few families of natives and help them make a living from the soil.

1. Why would the Jesuits want more settlers to come to New France?
2. What knowledge and skills would be useful for these men?
3. What advantages would there be for New France in greater immigration?
4. Most Indian tribes were hunters. They travelled from place to place for most of the year. A missionary might see the same Indian only once every year or two. Why was it important to the missionaries to try to settle the Indians in one place?
5. The Jesuit missionaries wrote of their experiences in a collection of letters called the Jesuit Relations. If your library has a copy of this book it will make very interesting reading. From it you will get first-hand information as to the daily life, triumphs, and hardships of both the Indians and the missionaries.

The influence of the Church did not end with bringing settlers to New France. It had a great influence on the life of everyone in the colony. In the seventeenth century the Church looked after schools, hospitals, and charitable institutions, as well as missionary work and parish work. What institution looks after schools and hospitals in Canada today?

The Church was also very watchful of the moral life of the settlers. Instructions to teachers of the Ursuline Order of Nuns:

> A teacher must give her pupils lofty ideas of God's majesty. She will make them fear and avoid occasions to sin—bad friends, dances, staying up late at night, vain clothes, etc. She will inspire them to speak well of others, to avoid idleness, and love work.

On dress at Church:

> Wishing to please the men, they appear in indecent dress, showing bare arms, shoulders and throats, covering them only with a transparent material. Their head is bared or covered only with a net and the hair is curled in a way not worthy of a Christian.

On dances:

> At the proper age, parents may permit their daughters a few honest dances, but with people of her own sex and only in the presence of her mother so that indecent words and songs are not used, and never in the presence of men and boys.

1. *The Church did not allow non-Catholics to settle in New France. Can you think of reasons for this policy? What advantages and disadvantages might this policy have?*
2. *Compare the attitudes towards dress and entertainment in New France with those of modern society. How have they changed?*
3. *The missionaries had a very difficult time converting the Indians. Explain how each of the following was a factor in making the conversion of the Indians more difficult: (a) Coureurs de bois; (b) The Indians' nomadic life; (c) Problems of communication; (d) Indian medicine-men, (e) Indian beliefs and traditions.*

The Seigneurial System

The Chartered Companies had proved failures in luring settlers to New France. As we have seen, they did not even try. In 1663, the government of France took back its land from these companies. The government now hoped to encourage an increase in settlement through a system of land grants called the SEIGNEURIAL SYSTEM. The system worked quite simply. The King of France granted large sections of land called *SEIGNEURIES* to landlords called *SEIG-NEURS*. The *seigneur* in turn parcelled out smaller sections to tenant farmers called *CENSITAIRES* (later called *"habitants"*). In return for these free grants of land each party agreed to certain duties.

Tenants pay their yearly dues, in money or produce, to their *Seigneur*.

On receiving his grant of land the *Seigneur* had to kneel bareheaded, without sword or spurs, at the Governor's door and swear to be faithful to the King.

Following is a list of some of the duties of the *seigneurs* and *censitaires*:

Duties of Seigneurs	Duties of Censitaires
1. Oath of allegiance to the king.	1. Pay annual rents to the king and *seigneur*.
2. Provide census of population	2. Cultivate the land.
3. Provide tally of livestock, produce and land under cultivation.	3. Maintain permanent settlement on the land.
4. Settle tenants on land.	4. Work several days on construction of roads and bridges for the king.
5. Defend the seigneury in case of attack.	5. Aid in defence of the settlement.
6. Allow the king the right to build forts and roads on the seigneury.	6. Make payments of produce to the *seigneur*.
7. Provide a flour mill.	7. Work several days on the *seigneur's* land during seeding and harvest time.
8. Provide courts for minor disputes between tenants	

1. *Do you feel these duties asked too much of the censitaires? If so, which ones?*
2. *What social background in France might have given people the chance to be seigneurs, or to be censitaires, under the seigneurial system?*

As the large tracts of land were parcelled out by the King, the seigneuries took on a certain shape. Study the following maps:

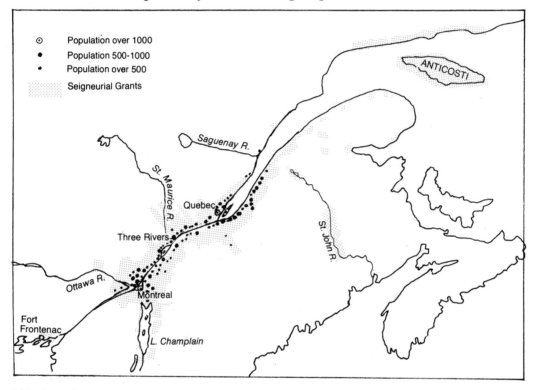

This map shows the size and location of the seigneurial land grants in New France.
What is the pattern of settlement in the colony?
Where are the largest clusters of population?
Can you account for these patterns?

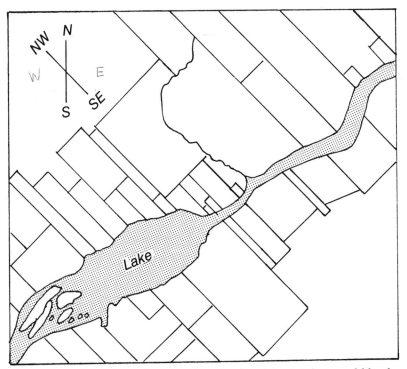

In early New France, roads were almost non-existent. What would be the easiest and fastest method of travel for a *habitant*?

In this map, the river and lake run in a northeast—southwest direction. The seigneuries are drawn up in a northwest—southeast direction. Can you account for the reason the farms run at such an angle? What valuable resource is available to most farms placed in this way?

The Government of New France

In 1663, the Company of One Hundred Associates lost its monopoly in New France. At the same time a new government was set up for the colony. It was a very simple one. Only one governing body would be in authority in New France, the Sovereign Council. The Council was made up of three main officials—the Governor, the *Intendant*, and the Bishop—and a few minor officials. The Council made laws, enforced them, and also set up courts to judge lawbreakers. Of course, New France was still under the control of the mother country, and the king had final say over any laws passed in the colony.

Sometimes the Governor and the *Intendant* would consult the ordinary people before deciding on policies which affected their welfare. On many occasions the advice of the people was followed.

The Government of New France in the Eighteenth Century

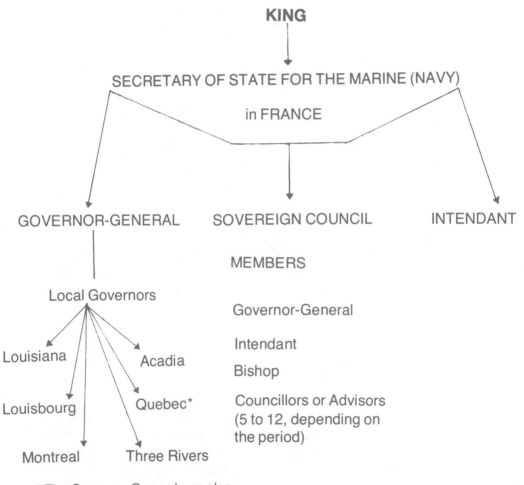

KING

SECRETARY OF STATE FOR THE MARINE (NAVY)

in FRANCE

GOVERNOR-GENERAL   SOVEREIGN COUNCIL   INTENDANT

MEMBERS

Local Governors

Governor-General

Louisiana   Acadia

Intendant

Bishop

Louisbourg   Quebec*

Councillors or Advisors
(5 to 12, depending on
the period)

Montreal   Three Rivers

* The Governor-General was also
the governor of the area of Quebec.

Jean Talon, New France's most famous *Inten-dant*. The *Intendant* was in charge of law and order, the fur trade, immigration, the seig-neurial system, public works, and trade in the colony. As you can see, he was probably the most important official in New France. *Inven-taire des biens culturels du Québec.*

Pierre de Rigaud de Vaudreuil-Cavagnal, the first Canadian to become Governor of New France. Like the *Intendant*, the Governor was appointed by the King of France, and was responsible to him. The Governor's main duties were to watch over the defense of the colony, and to handle relations with the Indians and the English colonies. The Governor could also reject the actions of other officials. What kind of background would you expect a man in this position to have?

François de Laval, first Bishop of New France. His duty was to look after the spiritual needs of the colony as well as the conversion of the Indians. *Inventaire des biens culturels du Québec.*

The Population of New France

Thanks largely to these measures, the colony of New France became stable and prosperous. That Talon's policies were successful can be seen by the growth of the population of the colony. In seven short years Talon had more than doubled the number of settlers in New France. By the time he returned to France in 1672, the population of the colony stood at over seven thousand, and would continue to grow.

This table shows some of the main sources of immigration to New France in the seventeenth century. Using an atlas, locate the regions of France indicated in this chart. Find out something about the climate and soil of these regions. How do they compare with those of New France? Would these settlers face great problems of adjusting to new conditions?

Source	Number of Immigrants
Normandy	547
Ile-de-France and Paris	508
Poitou	352
Aunis, Ile de Ré, Ile d'Oléron	332

PROVINCES OF OLD FRANCE

From whence came most of the ancestors of the French Canadians.

Note that they extend diagonally across the country from North East to South West.

The numerals indicate in their order those Provinces which supplied the greater number of colonists.

Although the population of New France continued to grow, it was far surpassed by the American Colonies to the south. Compare the growth of the two areas.

Population Growth in New France

Year	Population
1608	28
1628	76
1641	240
1653	2 000
1663	2 500
1665	3 215
1668	6 282
1679	9 400
1706	16 417
1734	37 716
1754	55 009

Population Growth in the American Colonies

Year	Population
1608	500
1641	40 000
1689	250 000
1760	1 200 000

1. Make a graph or chart using the above figures to show the rise of the populations of New France and of the American colonies. During what periods did the population of New France grow most quickly? Investigate the history of the period to discover the reasons for these spurts of growth.

Here is a list of occupations in New France in 1681. List the five occupations that include the greatest number of people. Try to find out what kind of work the other groups did. What does this list indicate about the economy of New France?

Archers	1	Gunsmiths	11
Land Surveyors	2	Bakers	7
Joiners	24	Calkers	1
Notaries	24	Carders	1
Fitters	1	Hatters	6
Wooden Shoemakers	8	Carpenters	56
Saddlers	1	Surgeons	13
Tailors	34	Rope Makers	4
Carpet Weavers	1	Roofers	5
Weavers	4	Cooks	2
Turners	4	Bailiffs	3
Armourers	2	Merchants	7

Butchers	8	Sailors	8
Hotel Keepers	1	Millers	2
Artillerymen	1	Confectioners	2
Braziers	3	Powder Makers	1
Wheelwrights	14	Locksmiths	6
Ships Carpenters	4	Edge Tool Makers	17
Shoemakers	26	Tanners	5
Cutlers	1	Riband Weavers	1
Blacksmiths	4	Coopers	9
Masons	30	Vinegar Makers	1
Farriers	2		

The Perils of Life in New France

As you read about the adventures of the *coureurs de bois* and the experiences of the early pioneers, do you sometimes wish you could live in such times? Certainly many things seem appealing—exploring unknown lands, hunting game, travelling on long canoe voyages, living among the Indians, sleeping under the open sky.

While life for some settlers was exciting, it was also full of dangers, hardships, diseases, inconveniences, and plain hard work. We can appreciate much more the debt our own society owes to these courageous pioneers when we examine some of the harsh conditions they faced.

The French were hit hard on Jacques Cartier's very first stay at Stadacona. During the winter of 1535-36, many of his men picked up scurvy, a deadly disease caused by lack of fresh fruit and vegetables in the diet. The Europeans had found no quick cure for scurvy, but as we saw in an earlier chapter, they were helped out by the Indians.

There was also the problem of the Canadian winter, particularly hard on the early settlers who were not used to it. Here is the account of the first winter spent in Canada by French settlers at Port Royal in 1606:

> . . . father Winter being come they needs must keep indoors and live every man under his own roof-tree. During this time our friends had three special discomforts in this island . . . want of wood . . . want of fresh water, and the night watch for fear of a surprise from the Indians. . . .
>
> . . . On top of this came cold and snow and frost so hard that the cider froze in the casks, and each man was given his portion by weight. . . . Some lazy fellows drank melted snow. . . . In short, unknown diseases broke out. . . . No remedy could be found. . . .

1. *How might some of these problems have been avoided with a prior knowledge of Canadian winter conditions?*

Cornelius Kreighoff, *The Blacksmith's Shop*, 1871. *Art Gallery of Ontario. Gift of Mrs. J. H. Mitchell in memory of her mother Margaret Lewis Gooderham, 1951.*

And of course there was a problem which still plagues Canadians today:

The greatest torture of all . . . is one which is beyond belief, . . . the special Canadian mosquitoes, with their cruel torment . . . there are horse flies too, and gnats. . . . There are wasps, there are hornets. . . . A cloud of mosquitoes accompanies the traveller every morning. . . . You have to wave a handkerchief continuously, but this does not in the least deter them. . . . When you relax to eat . . . you have to do battle against a whole army of them. You have to "make smoke", that is to say you kindle a big fire which you then smother with green leaves. You have to put yourself in the thickest part of the smoke. . . . I do not know which is worse, the cure or the disease. . . . You are eaten, devoured, they get into your mouth, into your nostrils, your ears. Your face, hands and body are covered with them. Their sting penetrates your clothes and leaves a red mark on the skin which swells. . . .

1. *Does this description of the tortures caused by insects seem realistic to you?*
2. *In your opinion, are insects a greater or lesser problem today than they were in the seventeenth century? Can you account for this?*

Perhaps the worst danger in the early period was the threat of attack by the Iroquois. From the beginning the French had allied themselves with the Hurons who had become their main source for obtaining furs. The Hurons and the Iroquois were deadly enemies and were constantly at war. In 1609 Champlain helped the Hurons in a battle against the Iroquois. From that point on, the Iroquois became sworn enemies of the French, attacking settlements whenever they could, and disrupting the fur trade by attacking their main supply routes.

Champlain's fight with the Iroquois, 1609. In this battle Champlain sided with the Algonkins against their rivals, the Iroquois. From this time on the Iroquois and the French would be bitter enemies. The Iroquois often managed to cut off the sources of the fur trade and to threaten small, isolated French settlements.

Did Champlain make a mistake in siding against the Iroquois? Find the location of the Algonkin and Huron tribes. Why do you think Champlain, whose main objective was control of the fur trade, sided with these tribes?

A typical seigneurial fort, Fort Remy, Lachine, 1671. (1) Mill (2) Priest's House (3) Chapel (4) La Salle's House (5) Barn (6) Palisades (7) Bastions.

PLANTING THE "MAI"

On the first of May it was a custom of the Habitants to erect a tree, decked with ribbons before the house of the Seigneur or Captain of Militia.

Do you still want to trade your comfortable ways for those of the hardy pioneers?

In 1759, the English captured the fortress of Quebec. The loss of Quebec ended a century and a half of French rule in Canada. However, the values and traditions of the pioneers of New France were to endure, and contributed to the development of a new country.

Word Study

Castor gras	Coureur de bois	Scurvy
Castor sec	Intendant	Seigneur
Censitaire	Monopoly	Seigneury
Census		

Things to Do 1. The canoe was the most important method of transportation in New France. Find out how canoes were built and why they were superior to the boats of the Europeans.

2. As a group project, construct a map of New France. Include:
  (a) the largest settlements;
  (b) the St. Lawrence River and the Lachine rapids;
  (c) the location of the important Indian tribes.

This map can be constructed with a plywood base. Plaster or flour paste can be used to make the elevations of land. The plaster can be painted various colours to show the forests, mountains, lakes, and rivers.

3. Make a replica of Champlain's original settlement at Quebec using matchsticks, plywood, or cardboard. Champlain's description of the buildings and the picture on page   can be studied for this purpose.

4. The fur trade was the most important business in New France. Present a debate on the fur trade showing its good and bad aspects. Some of the speakers in this debate might represent the point of view of:
  (a) the Church
  (b) a coureur de bois
  (c) a merchant
  (d) a farmer
  (e) an Indian

5. Write a short diary covering one summer in the life of:
  (a) a settler
  (b) a coureur de bois
  (c) a missionary

3
The English Settlement of Canada

Do you know what the words "bilingualism" and "biculturalism" mean? In the past few years these two words have been the topic of much discussion and debate in Canada. The two words mean that Canada is a very unusual country. It has two official languages and two cultures—English and French. Most of us see reminders of this fact every day. It happens whenever we read the message on a box of cereal, or a candy bar, or the traffic signs in many cities.

Most countries have only one language and culture. Why is Canada different? The answer is that modern Canada has two distinct European roots, one French, the other English. We have already studied the French root. In this chapter you will see how the English also laid their claim to Canada. You will learn why the English came to Canada, what areas they settled, what hardships they faced and what contributions they made to the development of our country.

The English in North America

For almost one hundred and fifty years after the founding of Quebec, the French were the only Europeans to settle in Canada in large numbers. During this time even more English settlers had gone to the American colonies to the south. There, the climate and soil were more suitable for farming than they were in New France. The British government had always encouraged immigration. The French government was slow to do so. We have already seen how the fur trade was partly responsible for this. As a result, by 1750 the American colonies had over one million people. At the same time, New France had fewer than sixty thousand.

Over the years, the French and English colonists had become enemies fighting for control of North America. Despite its smaller population, New France gave a good account of itself in battle in defense of the colony. The French had the advantage of two fine forts, Quebec, and Louisbourg on Cape Breton Island.

To counter the threat of Louisbourg, England built a naval base at Halifax in 1749. Halifax was the first English settlement in Canada. Former soldiers and sailors took up the offer of free land near Halifax and along the east coast of Nova Scotia. They were joined by three thousand other settlers, mostly of British and German origin.

C. W. Jefferys, *The Founding of Halifax*, Art Gallery of Ontario, Purchase, 1930.

The year 1759 was a turning point in the history of Canadian settlement. In that year a British army under General James Wolfe defeated the French in the famous Battle of the Plains of Abraham and captured the city of Quebec. You will study this battle in detail in a later unit. The fall of Quebec meant that New France was now in the hands of the British.

The American Revolution

In 1776 the American colonies to the south began their war for independence from Great Britain. With the success of the revolution, Britain lost her southern colonies, but in Canada she still had a foothold in North America. The American Revolution was a turning point for all of North America. In the south, a new country, the United States, was formed. For Canada, a new period of immigration began.

When the War for Independence began in the American colonies, a large group of colonists remained loyal to England and supported the English cause. When the Americans won their independence, members of this group, who called themselves United Empire Loyalists, were forced to leave their homes. Some returned to England, or settled in other British colonies, but a large number, perhaps fifty thousand, chose to make a new life in Canada. Who were these people who would help create a new country? Why had they remained loyal to Britain? Their decision was often a difficult one, and was inspired by many different motives.

In times of crisis, people are forced to choose sides. This choice is sometimes based on principles and sometimes on personal gain, and often on a combination of both. This was true of people in the Thirteen Colonies too. As you read the case studies of the colonists below, try to determine whether each person would have become a rebel, or have remained a Loyalist. Discuss the factors which might have led each one to make a decision.

James Miller is a merchant in Boston. He owns three ships and has carried on a brisk trade in tea with other colonists. His profits lately have been greatly reduced by British taxes, and the rival British East India Tea Company has been selling tea at a lower price than Miller can afford. This competition has been very harmful to Miller and his fellow merchants. When the revolutionary group known as the Sons of Liberty dressed up as Indians and destroyed British tea in the famous Boston Tea Party, Miller felt a great deal of satisfaction.

George Clearwater has just recently come to the colonies from England, where he still has relatives and friends. He has received a job as a tax collector for Britain. His job is a fine one and he is guaranteed a comfortable living under British government. His future wife, the daughter of a powerful English family, will soon join him in America. George is looking forward to a stable, secure future.

Sean O'Flaherty came to the colonies from Ireland fourteen years ago. During this time he has held several jobs, working as a carpenter, ditchdigger, and bartender. At this moment, however, he is unemployed. Sean had dreamed of starting his own farm on his own land, but in 1763 the British closed the frontier to further settlement. Sean's dream may never come true. Those fighting for America's independence have promised to open the frontier to settlement.

Charles Endicott, fifty-six, is a gentleman farmer who has prospered on his plantation in the more than thirty years he has been working it. Once during a trip to England he met the King. This occasion, he claimed, was the proudest moment of his life and he still treasures a small medallion the King presented to him. The crop he produces, tobacco, is sold not only in America and England, but throughout the British Empire.

Elizabeth Schnarr is twelve, and the daughter of a small but prosperous farmer living in Pennsylvania in 1776. Her parents have worked very hard and avoided becoming involved in politics since they came to America from Germany. Several months ago Elizabeth saw a person being badly beaten by a gang of men. After the men had left, Elizabeth called her father who carried the unfortunate victim back to their house and took care of him until he was well enough to leave. Elizabeth later learned that the man had made several statements showing his sympathy with the English cause and was considered a Loyalist. After this incident the girl found that because she had helped the wounded man, former friends no longer spoke to her. Once her mother found a note nailed to the door: "No friends of Britain wanted here".

Both during and after the War, those considered Loyalists were harshly treated by other Americans, who considered them traitors. Here are newspaper accounts of the kind of punishment often dealt to Loyalists:

August 8: The riflemen on their way from the southern colonies through the country administer the new-fashioned discipline of tar and feathers to . . . Tories that they meet on their road, which has a very good effect. They took a man in New Molford, Connecticut, a most incorrigible Loyalist (Tory) who called them damned rebels, etc., and made him walk before them to Litchfield, which is 20 miles, [32 km] and carry one of his own geese all the way in his hand. When they arrived there, they tarred him, and made him pluck his goose, and then bestowed the feathers on him, and drummed him out of the company, and obliged him to kneel down and thank them for their lenity.

December 6: At Quibletown, New Jersey, Thomas Randolph Cooper, who had publicly proved himself an enemy to this country, . . . was ordered to be stripped naked, well coated with tar and feathers, and carried in a wagon publicly around the town. . . .

Some of the colonies actually banished Loyalists during the war, threatening them with death if they returned; others burned their houses and destroyed their property. Several were murdered by angry colonists who felt the Loyalists might betray them.

When the war was over, in 1781, those Loyalists who remained in the United States were persecuted. Many decided to return to England or other parts of the Empire. Realizing the problems faced by her loyal subjects, England threw open the doors of Canada.

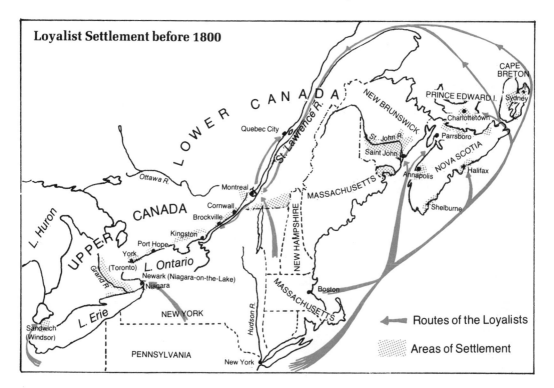

Loyalist Settlement before 1800

Loyalists in the Maritimes

The largest number of Loyalists settled in the Maritimes. Can you think of the reasons for this? Keep in mind some of the factors which concerned settlers in those days. These included:

—ease of transportation

—climate

—nearness of settled communities as sources of food and supplies.

As the ranks of Loyalist refugees swelled, the British government had to make some quick decisions. Where would these Loyalists be settled? What help would be offered to them? As you read the following letters of British officials try to discover:

1. What type of help in the form of food, clothing, land, transportation, tools, and other supplies was given the Loyalists?

2. According to the tools provided, what sorts of occupations were they expected to take up?

3. What crops would they grow? Find out if these are still important crops in the Maritimes.

4. What areas of the Maritimes were settled by the Loyalists? Why were these areas chosen?

5. How many settlers came between 1783 and 1784?

To His Excellency Lieutenant General Haldimand Governor &
Commander in Chief, & c., & c.

The request of the Companies of Associated Loyalists going to
form a Settlement at Cataraque.

That Boards, Nails and Shingls be found each Family for Com-
pleating such Buildings as they shall see Cause to Erect for their Con-
venience at any time for the space of Two years from & after their first
Arrival at Cataraque with Eighty Squares of Window Glass to be delivered shortly after their arrival there.

That Arms & Ammunition with one Felling Ax be allowed for
each Male Inhabitant of the age of fourteen years
One Plough shear & Coulter
Leather for Horse Collers
Two Spades
Three Iron Wedges
Fifteen Iron Harrow Teeth
Three Hoes
One Inch & half Inch Auger
Three Chisels (sorted)   Be allowed
One Gouge   Each Family
Three Gimblets
One Hand Saw & Files
One Nail Hammer
One Drawing Knife
One Frow for splitting Shingles
Two Scythes & one Sickle
One Broad Ax

One Grind stone allowed for every Three Families.

One years Clothing to be issued to each Family in proportion to
their Numbers in the different species of Articles Issued to those gone
to Nova Scotia. Two years Provisions to be found to Each Family in
Proportion to their [Number] and Age. Two Horses, Two Cows, and
six Sheep to be delivered at Cataraque to Each Family at Government's Expence. The Cost of which to be made known at delivery To
the End that the same may be a Moderate Tax, be again repaid to
Government at the End of Ten years if required—Our present Poverty
& Inability to Purchase these Articles as well as our remote situation
when there from Wealthy Inhabitants, will we hope pleed our Excuse
in this respect.

That Seeds of different kinds such as Wheat, Indian Corn, Pease, Oats, Potatoes & Flax seed be given to Each Family in quantity as His Excellency may think Proper.

Nova Scotia Halifax
9th July 1783.

I did myself the honor to write to Your Lordship by the last conveyance, in which I particularly mentioned the number of People that had arriv'd from New York, their numbers since that time are considerably encreas'd, to no less than 12000 Souls, the greatest part of them at Port Rosway and the River St. Johns in the Bay of Fundy, I have information of as many more, who intend coming here before New York is evacuated, as well as several who purpose coming from New England, in order to avoid Taxation, and the oppression of some of their new Masters. . . .

Shelburne, 25th July, 1783.

. . . I flatter myself that the Town will in a very few years, be worthy of so fine a Harbour, its Inhabitants at present are about 7000 Souls, which are every day encreasing from New York, as well as from other parts some of them people of considerable property, the Harbour is about five Miles long, and three and a half broad, [eight kilometres by five and a half] the depth of water from five to twelve Fathom; [nine to twenty-two metres] a safe Bay without it for Ships to Anchor in, a deep bold Shore without Rocks or Shoals, and good holding Ground.

The Town stands upon a gentle rising Ground, the situation most beautifull, the Land good with a prospect of its being very fertile, some good Timber, the Streets of Shelburne are laid out very regular at Right Angles, the Houses in great forwardness, Industry is seen in every Quarter. . . .

Nova Scotia, Halifax,
25th Octr., 1783.

I have done myself the honor of informing Your Lordship, of the several occurrences that have happened in this Province since my arrival, particularly of the great number of Refugees who have arriv'd from New York &c, they still continue to come to different parts, by two and three Ships at a time, which makes it impossible for me to as-

certain their exact numbers, but believe they already amount to about 24,000 Souls, all the Provincial Corps are arriv'd, and chiefly settled upon the River St. Johns'. . . .

Nova Scotia, Halifax,
24th Jany., 1784.

The final Evacuation of New York having taken place, closes the Emigrations from thence, as well as from other parts, with about 30,000 Souls added to this Province, all of which, except a few lately arriv'd, have got under tolerable Shelter for the Winter, and are accommodated as well as the nature of their situation would admit.

Where did the Loyalists settle? Let us follow the paths of two Loyalists from very different backgrounds as they started new lives in British North America.

The Story of Hannah Ingraham

(Hannah Ingraham was born in 1772 and died in 1868 at the age of ninety-seven. She tells of the trials her family faced as a result of the Revolution. Hannah was only eleven at the time.)

1776 to 1783

My father lived at New Concord, twenty miles from Albany. We had a comfortable farm, plenty of cows and sheep. But when the war began and he joined the regulars they (the Rebels) took it all away, sold the things, ploughs and all, and my mother was forced to pay rent for her own farm. What father had sown they took away, but what mother raised after she paid rent they let her keep. They took away all our cows and sheep, only let her have one heifer and four sheep. . . .

Little John, my brother, had a pet lamb and he went to the Committee men and spoke up and said, "Won't you let me have my lamb?" He was a little fellow, four years old, so they let him have it.

My father was in the army seven years. They took grandfather prisoner and sent him on board a prison ship.

Mother rode fifty miles [eighty kilometres] on horseback on one day when she heard it to go to see him and take him some money to buy some comforts. He had a paralytic stroke when he was there, and he never recovered, poor grandfather.

My father was taken prisoner once but he escaped. The girl who was sent to take him his supper one night told him she would leave the door unbuttoned, and he got off to the woods, but was wandering most two months before he found the army again. Mother was four years without hearing of or from father, whether he was alive or dead: any one would be hanged right up if they were caught bringing letters.

Oh, they were terrible times!

At last there was talk of peace and a neighbour got a letter from her husband, and one inside for mother to tell her father was coming home.

1783. He came home on Sept. 13th, it was Friday, and said we were to go to Nova Scotia . . . that a ship was ready to take us there, so we made all haste to get ready.

Killed the cow, sold the beef, and a neighbour took home the tallow and made us a good parcel of candles and put plenty of beeswax to make them hard and good.

Uncle came down and thrashed our wheat, 20 bushels, [7.2 m³] and grandmother came and made bags for the wheat, and we packed up a tub of butter, a tub of pickles, and a good store of potatoes.

And then one Tuesday, suddenly, the house was surrounded by the rebels and father took prisoner and carried away. Uncle went forward and promised them who took him that if he might come home then he would answer for his being forthcoming next morning. But *No*, and I *cried*, and I *cried*, and I *cried* enough to kill myself that night. When morning came they sent to say that he was free to go.

We had five wagon loads carried down the Hudson in a sloop, and then we went abroad the transport that was to bring us to St. John.

I was just eleven years old when we left our farm to come here. It was the last transport for the season, and had in it all those who could not leave sooner.

The first transport had come in May, and so had all the summer before them, to get settled.

This was the last part of September, we had a bad storm in the Bay, but some Frenchmen came off in a canoe and helped us (piloted I suppose).

There were no deaths on board, but several babies were born. It was a sad, sick time after we landed; in St. John we had to live in tents, the Government gave them to us and rations too. It was just at the first snow then, and the melting snow and rain would soak up into our beds as we lay. Mother got so chilled with rheumatism that she was never very well afterwards. . . .

It was two months from the day we left our home at Concord till we reached St. Ann's.

We were brought as far as Maugerville in a schooner, but we had to get the rest of the way, twelve miles, [nineteen kilometres] walking or any way we could, because the schooner could not get past the Oromocto shoals. . . .

At last we got to our land, pitched our tent and the boat went back for more.

When the boat got back to Oromocto the schooner was gone and had landed the last of the passengers.

There was a poor widow with four children waiting to come, but none of the men had the courage to put her aboard the boat, or even go aboard themselves, though we had a right to the use of it for another day, for it was paid for, and that poor woman had to sleep in a barn till the ice covered the river, and then some of the neighbours took a handsled and hauled her up to St. Ann's, twelve miles [nineteen kilometres]. There were no roads then you see, and the river was the only way of travelling.

We lived in a tent at St. Ann's till father got a log house raised. He went up through our lot till he found a nice fresh spring of water, he stooped down and pulled away the fallen leaves that were thick over it, and tasted it; it was very good; so there he built his house. We all had rations given us by the Government, flour and butter and pork; and tools were given to the men, too.

One morning when we waked we found the snow lying deep on the ground all round us, and then father came wading through it and told us the house was ready and not to stop to light a fire then and not mind the weather, but follow his tracks through the trees, for the trees were so many we soon lost sight of him going up the hill; it was snowing fast, and oh, so cold. Father carried a chest and we all took something and followed him up the hill through the trees.

It was not long before we heard him pounding, and oh, what joy to see our gable end.

There was no floor laid, no window, no chimney, no door, but we had a roof at last.

A good fire was blazing on the hearth, and mother had a big loaf of bread with us, and she boiled a kettle of water and put a good piece of butter in a pewter bowl, and we toasted the bread and all sat round the bowl to eat our breakfast that morning, and mother said, "Thank God, we are no longer in dread of having shots fired through our house. This is the sweetest meal I've tasted for many a day."

It was not long before father got a good floor down of split cedar, and a floor overhead to make a bedroom, and a chimney built. . . .

We soon got things planted the first spring, for they would grow so easy, one bushel [0.36 m³] of wheat yielded 30, the ground was all new you see. We had brought wheat and beans and seeds with us, and we could sell anything we had for money down.

Many people wanted the things we had, and father was always getting jobs of work from the gentry that soon followed the Loyalists.

1785-6.   There were the Chief Justice and the Governor and Parson Cooke and his family, and other ladies too, and we sold them cream and butter; they were glad to get the things and we were glad to sell, for it kept us in money to buy groceries.

I went to school the first winter up in St. Ann's on snow shoes. The next winter I hauled my brother on a handsled. This is why. My brother John had chopped his toe off when cutting wood with father; he was a big boy then. Our house was not much more than a hut, only one room, and little Ira then was just waddling alone, and was always meddling (as children will) and used to touch his brother's lame bandaged toe, and so father said if I could haul John to school he could give me another quarter's schooling, and I did. But, oh, it was hard work through the deep snow, and once it was so heavy that the poor boy got his toe froze before we reached the school. . . . There was no church or clergyman at St. Ann's when we first came (1783) and only two houses, one where Government House was and one where what is now the Church Green. All the space between, which is now the town, was covered with raspberry bushes, and my brother John and I used to run down there as hard as we could, when we had time, to pick berries, and we were proud when we got a pint to take to mother, for she had been used to plenty of fruit afore she came here. All the trees at the Point, as it was called, that is the flat piece of ground where Fredericton stands, had been cut down and the place settled by Scotch people long before, but the Indians had killed them all and burnt up their houses, and when we came it was all grown up with raspberries and such like. Father had the first cow that was in the place. He bought it for 10 guineas of the old inhabitants down at Maugerville (they mostly moved away when the Loyalists came, but not all). The cow was so poor and starved looking when he bought her that she could hardly walk home. . . .

. . . there was no stoves then (1786). Parson Cooke was coming over to baptize my little brother Ira that day and to dine with us; he lived over the river at St. Mary's; there were many people settled there. Loyalist soldiers had grants of land up the Naushwauk, and Madam Keswick and Douglas.

Parson Cooke held service in the King's Provision Warehouse, close by the Church Green, till the church was ready. They began building it pretty soon, in two years I think, and my brother John and I saw the first burying there ever was in the graveyard. It was a soldier, an officer, and we heard the drums beating while we were picking berries there and we ran to see it. In front of the King's Provision Warehouse there was always a sentry on guard walking up and down with his bayonet fixed. There was plenty of Indians coming to sell furs in those days. I've counted forty canoes going up the river all at one time. They used to come ashore to sell their furs to Peter Fraser, and folks say he used to cheat them; he would put his fist on the scale and say it weighed a pound and turn the scale in his favour.

One day when I was all alone in the house, except the baby, I saw a big Indian coming up the hill to the door; I was terribly afraid at first, for I knew he would perhaps stop all day and eat up everything in the house, so I ran to the cradle and catched up the baby and wrapped him in a quilt and went to the door just as the Indian got there, so I said, "Have you had the smallpox?" hushing the baby all the while, and he darted away as if he had been shot, and we had no Indians around all that summer; they all went away directly. They are afraid of smallpox, for Indians mostly die if they get it.

May 23, 1795. One day Parson Cooke came over to a funeral, it was in May, at freshet time, and the water was high and the wind began to blow and we wanted him to stop till next day, but he said they would be waiting for him, so he and his son, a big boy, started to paddle over home.

But next day someone saw a straw hat floating, his son's hat, and then the canoe bottom up, so we knew they were drowned, and it was more than a week before they found the bodies floating down the river. Oh, it was a terrible grief, we all loved him so. There's many a one named Cooke after him.

1. Why was the Ingraham family forced to move away from New York?

2. Where did they settle? How did they get to their new home? What help were they given by the British?

3. What would you say was the greatest hardship faced by the Ingraham family in their new homeland?

4. What were some of the problems and dangers of pioneer life as seen in this story?

Among the large number of Loyalists who settled in Nova Scotia was a group of Black Loyalists. They had been slaves in the Thirteen Colonies and had escaped to the British side during the Revolutionary War. About ten per cent of the Loyalists who came to Nova Scotia were Black. Two such Loyalists were Boston and Violet King.

The Story of Boston King, a Black Loyalist

Boston King was sixteen when the war broke out and had been apprenticed by his master to a carpenter. The carpenter was a cruel man, who often beat and tortured him.

King had heard that the British were offering freedom to slaves who ran away from their masters to join the British. At the first opportunity he ran away and came to the British side.

After the war had ended over two thousand former slaves were in the British camp. A Proclamation was issued that all slaves who had taken refuge in the British lines should be free. Boston King noted that this

> filled us with joy and gratitude. Soon after, ships were fitted out, and furnished with every necessary for conveying us to Nova Scotia. We arrived at Burch Town in the month of August, where we all landed safely. Every family had a lot of land and we exerted all our strength in order to build comfortable huts before the cold weather set in.

Burch Town was only nine and a half kilometres from Shelburne, the largest Loyalist settlement in Nova Scotia. Unfortunately the land in the region was quite poor and rocky. The Black Loyalists had the worst land of all. For years, the British gave the Loyalists free rations. When these were cut off, many people starved. Boston King recalls his experience:

> About this time the country was visited with a dreadful famine, which not only prevailed at Burchtown, but likewise at Chebucto, Annapolis, Digby, and other places. Many of the poor people were compelled to sell their best gowns for five pounds of flour, in order to support life. When they had parted with all their clothes, even to their blankets, several of them fell down dead in the streets, thro' hunger. Some killed and eat their dogs and cats; and poverty and distress prevailed on every side; so that to my great grief I was obliged to leave Burchtown, because I could get no employment. I travelled from place to place, to procure the necessaries of life, but in vain. At last I came to Shelwin [Shelburne] on the 20th of January. After walking from one street to the other, I met with Capt. Selex, and he engaged me to make him a chest. I rejoiced at the offer, and returning home, set about it immediately. I worked all night, and by eight o'clock next morning finished the chest, which I carried to the Captain's house, thro' the snow which was three feet deep. But to my great

disappointment he rejected it. However, he gave me directions to make another. On my way home, being pinched with hunger and cold, I fell down several times, thro' weakness, and expected to die upon the spot. But even in this situation, I found my mind resigned to the divine will, and rejoiced in the midst of tribulation; for the Lord delivered me from all murmurings and discontent, altho' I had but one pint of Indian meal left for the support of myself and my wife. Having finished another chest, I took it to my employer the next day; but being afraid he would serve me as he had done before, I took a saw along with me in order to sell it. On the way, I prayed that the Lord would give a prosperous journey, and was answered to the joy of my heart, for Capt. Selex paid me for the chest in Indian-corn; and the other chest I sold for 2s 6d and the saw for 3s 9d altho' it cost me a guinea; yet I was exceedingly thankful to procure a reprieve from the dreadful anguish of perishing from famine. . . .

The next winter, the same man gave King more work, and things improved.

On October 24, we left Pope's harbour and came to Halifax, where we were paid off, each man receiving £15 for his wages; and my master gave me two barrels of fish [two hundred and eighty-eight litres] agreeable to his promise. When I returned home, I was enabled to clothe my wife and myself; and my Winter's store consisted of one barrel of flour, [about eighty-eight kilograms] three bushels of corn, [about one-tenth of a cubic metre] nine gallons of treacle, [forty litres] 20 bushels of potatoes [about .7 m³] which my wife had set in my absence, and the two barrels of fish; so that this was the best Winter I ever saw in Burchtown.

In 1791, the British set up a company, the Sierra Leone Company, to return former slaves to Africa. Almost one thousand Blacks from Nova Scotia agreed to go back. Among them were Boston and Violet King. In Sierra Leone, King began a new career as schoolteacher and preacher. He never returned to Canada.

1. Why did Boston King join the British army?
2. Where did he and other Black Loyalists settle?
3. What difficulties did they face in trying to establish themselves in their new homeland?
4. Why do you think Boston King and so many other Blacks decided to return to Africa?

Early Shelburne

Shelburne—A Loyalist Community One of the first Loyalist communities in the Maritimes was Shelburne, Nova Scotia. Founded in 1783, the settlement was at first called Port Roseway. The site was selected because it had a fine harbour and seemed to offer a good location for trade, farming, and fishing. In the beginning Shelburne promised to become one of the great ports of North America.

By 1784, the population of Shelburne was about fifteen thousand. In the whole of North America only three cities, Philadelphia, New York, and Boston, were larger.

Many of the Loyalists who settled in Shelburne were professionals—lawyers, merchants, and business people. They knew very little about farming and fishing, and preferred to live in town, where they built beautiful large houses.

Soon Shelburne began to decline. Lack of good farm land and suitable industries meant few jobs were available. For a few years the British provided the necessary supplies to keep the town going. When this help was cut off, the people slowly began to move away. In 1829, the population numbered only 2697. Today the population is about 5000.

One of the important results of this wave of immigration was the creation of a new province in Canada. In 1784, under pressure from the thousands of Loyalists who had migrated from the Thirteen Colonies, Canada's third province, New Brunswick, was created. The new province had a western border reaching from the St. Croix River to Quebec and an eastern border with Nova

Scotia at the Isthmus of Chignecto. The Loyalists were energetic and hard-working people, and New Brunswick shortly joined Nova Scotia as a prosperous and productive province.

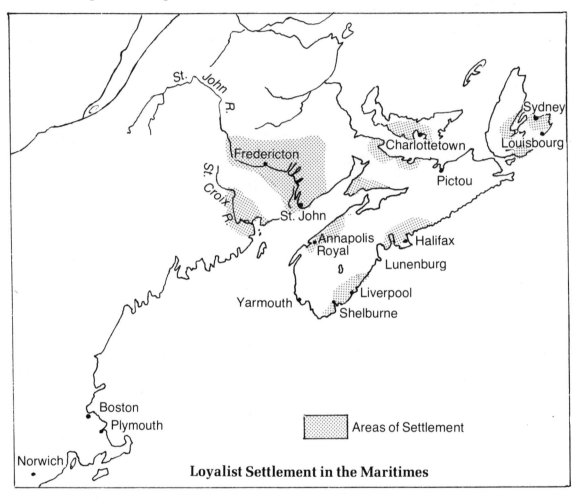

Loyalist Settlement in the Maritimes

Loyalists in Upper Canada

The Quebec Act of 1774 extended the borders of Quebec far to the west, into what is today Ontario. This opened a huge area of fertile land to future settlement. After the American Revolution many Loyalists migrated to the old Province of Quebec. However, the greater number of pioneers found their way to the new lands west of the Ottawa River.

It was only natural that the first Loyalist settlements in these lands, soon to be called Upper Canada, would be near the Great Lakes or along a navigable river.

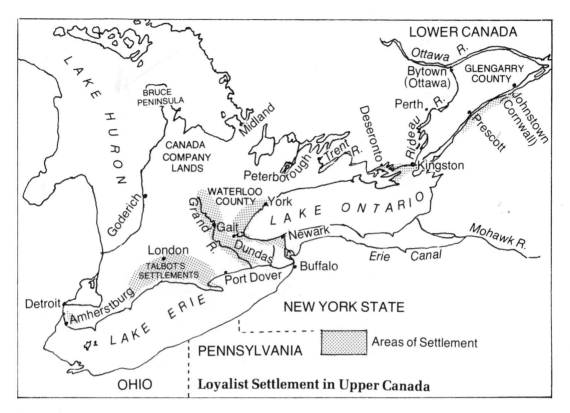

Loyalist Settlement in Upper Canada

1. Read the following accounts of Loyalist settlements in Upper Canada before 1812 with an outline map of modern Ontario beside you. Try to find the location and size of the settlements.
2. Judging by the following accounts, which of the locations described appeared to be the most prosperous by 1812?
3. Which of the areas described would you have chosen to live in if you had been a Loyalist immigrant? Why?

In the lower part of this province, the settlements do not extend back or north from the river St. Lawrence. Above Kingston, the settlements extend from Lake Ontario, 50 miles [80 km]. Above the head of the bay [of Quinte] on the lake shore, for about 100 miles, [160 km] the settlements do not extend more than 6 miles [9.6 km] from the lake. North from York, the settlements extend farther back, particularly on what is called Yonge-Street, which runs a due north course to Lake Simcoe. On both sides of this street, the farms are thick and well improved, the soil being very good, although the climate is not so favourable as it is farther to the southwest. From York, west, along the lake shore, there are but small settlements on the shore for 20 miles [.32 km]; after which, what is called Dundas-Street, 4 miles [6.4 km] from the shore, is thickly settled on both sides for twenty miles. . . . Farther south around the head of Lake Ontario, or more particularly Burlington bay, the settlements are thick, extending west 16 miles [25.6 km]. About 40 miles [64 km] up the Grand River is a thick settlement of Dutch, in Brant's township. Still to the east, as the road leads to Niagara, the settlements are thick near the shore of Lake Ontario.

Loyalists camping on the trip up the St. Lawrence, 1784.

After one gets 30 miles [48 km] east of the head of Burlington bay, and 20 from Niagara, the settlements of an old date are made, and pretty thick, all the way across from lake to lake, which is more than thirty miles. From the thick settlement west of the head of lake Ontario, towards the London district, the inhabitants are thin for 20 miles, through the tract of land belonging to the six nations of Indians. . . .

Niagara It is a beautiful and prospective place, being surrounded on two sides by water, the lake on the north, and the Niagara river on the east, and which affords a fine harbour for shipping.

Fort George of this place stands about half a mile [.8 km] from the mouth of this river. . . .

Indian Loyalists

Whereas His Majesty having been pleased to direct that in Consideration of the early Attachment to His Cause manifested by the Mohawk Indians, & of the Loss of their Settlement they thereby sustained that a Convenient Tract of Land under His Protection should be chosen as a Safe & Comfortable Retreat for them & others of the Six Nations who have either lost their Settlements within the Territory of the American States, or wish to retire from them to the British—I have, at the earnest Desire of many of these His Majesty's faithfull Allies purchased a Tract of Land, from the Indians situated between the Lakes Ontario, Erie & Huron and I do hereby in His Majesty's name authorize and permit the said Mohawk Nation, and such other of the Six Nation Indians as wish to settle in that Quarter to take Possession of, & Settle upon the Banks of the River commonly called Ours [Ouse] or Grand River, running into Lake Erie, allotting to them for that Purpose Six Miles deep from each Side of the River beginning at Lake Erie, & extending in that Proportion to the Head of the said River, which them & their Posterity are to enjoy for ever.

Given Under my Hand & Seal &c &c

25th Oct 1784

(Signed) Fred: Haldimand

Thayeadanegea, Joseph Brant, the Mohawk Chief. By G. Romney. From a print in the Public Archives of Canada.

Thayeadanegea was Joseph Brant's Indian name. Brant led the Indian Loyalists to the settlement on the Grand River. What Ontario city is named after him?

A Census of the Six Nations on the Grand River, 1785

	Persons
Mohawks	448
Onondagas Council fire	174
d° Bear's foot's party	51
Senecas	47
. . . Onondagas from the West	20
Upper Cayugas	198
Upper Tootalies [Tutelos]	55
Oghguagas [Mohicans]	113
Delaware Aaron's party	48
Oghguaga Joseph's party	49
Tuscaroras	129
Lower Cayugas	183
St. Regis	16
Montours	15
Creeks & Cherokees	53
Lower Tootalies	19
Delawares	183
Senecas from the West	31
Nanticokes	11
	1843

Although the Loyalists preferred the Maritime provinces, a large number came to Upper Canada. Note the different groups who chose to live there, and their main settlements. The names of the modern communities are also indicated.

Groups	Settlements
Pennsylvania Dutch and Mennonites (German)	Grand River (Kitchener-Waterloo)
Iroquois	Grand River (Brantford)
Scots	Bay of Quinte Glengarry County
English	Kingston, York (Toronto) Niagara

1. Locate these places on a map of present-day Ontario.
2. If you live in one of these communities, try to learn what proportion of the population of these modern communities has the same origins as the first settlers.

Land Distribution   The Loyalist settlers in the Province of Quebec were given free land in the following portions:

To every Master of a Family, One Hundred Acres, [forty hectares] and Fifty Acres [twenty hectares] for each person of which his Family shall consist.

To every single Man Fifty Acres.

To every Non-Commissioned Officer of Our Forces Two hundred Acres [eighty hectares].

To every private Man One Hundred Acres.

And for every Person in their Family Fifty Acres.

In addition to the free land, the British government gave a great deal of encouragement and help in other forms to the Loyalists:

Each Man and Boy above Ten Years of Age	Coats	1
	Waistcoats	1
	Breeches	1 Pair
	Hat	1
	Shirts (or 3-1/2 yards [2.15 m] Linen)	1
	Blankets	1
	Shoe Soles	1 Pair
	Leggings	1 Pair
	Stockings	1 Pair
Women or Girls above Ten Years of Age	Woolen Cloth	2 Yards
	Linen	4 D° [ditto]
	Stockings	1 Pair
	Blanket	1 D°
	Shoe Soles	1 D°
Children Under Ten Years of Age	Woolen Cloth	1
	Linen	2 D°
	Blanket (between 2)	1
	Stockings	1 Pair
	Shoe Soles	1 D°

N.B. Camp Equipage Issued a Tent for Every Five Persons with a Camp Kettle for each tent.

---

1. *Compare these aids with those given to settlers in the Maritimes.*   *Which group do you think was given more help?*

The settlers had little chance to inspect their new homes and selection of good land or bad was based on luck.

The free land in Upper Canada attracted not only Loyalists, but others in America such as servants and other workers who did not have enough money to buy their own farms there. Many of these immigrants from the south no doubt claimed to be Loyalists only to get free land. Since it was almost impossible to prove who was or was not a Loyalist, the British government gave land to all comers. In the year 1783 alone, over one million hectares of land were parcelled out to settlers in Upper Canada. By 1791, though the population was still quite small, the government decided a new province should be created. The differences between the new English-speaking settlers and the old French *habitants* created some problems. Each side was accustomed to its own vastly different systems of laws, religion, and government. In view of these differences, the Constitutional Act of 1791 was passed, dividing the old Province of Quebec into Upper Canada (Ontario) and Lower Canada (Quebec), each with a separate government. The first Lieutenant-Governor of the new province was to be John Graves Simcoe.

The Great Migration

The Loyalist migration gave a new character to British North America. Can you think of all the changes which the Loyalists brought? The next important event was the Great Migration of the first half of the nineteenth century. Between 1815 and 1850 over eight hundred thousand people emigrated to British North America, tripling the size of the original population.

From what lands did these people come?
Why did they choose Canada for their new homeland?

In 1815, peace returned to Europe after more than twenty years of war with Napoleon. British soldiers returned home to find no jobs. Labour troubles, poverty, and a shortage of land at home caused many to look to Canada.

In the years that followed, other factors encouraged British immigration to Canada. The population of the British Isles increased at a sharp rate, adding to the large number of those already unemployed. It was the duty of the community, and especially the churches, to look after such people. Special homes were set up for them. However, this was an expensive burden and many communities tried to solve their problems by encouraging the poor to take up land in Canada.

Natural disasters, such as the crop failures of the 1840s which wiped out the potato harvests in Ireland, also forced large numbers to migrate. At the same time the system of transportation and communication was improving. More and faster ships were crossing the Atlantic, making the voyage to Canada less dangerous than it had been. Also, letters such as the one below, from relatives in Canada praising the country, were arriving in England, Ireland, and Scotland.

I really do bless God every day I rise, that he was ever pleased, in the course of his providence, to send me and my family to this place Lanark County, Upper Canada. Were you here and seeing the improvements that are going on among us, you would not believe that we were once Glasgow weavers!

Urge my brothers to come out if ever they wish to free themselves from bondage . . . this is the land of independence to the industrious—the soil will repay the labourer for the sweat of his brow.

The natural temptation to follow was fed in the beginning by the generous policy of Britain. Until 1825 the government of Upper Canada agreed to provide immigrants from the British Isles with free transportation, supplies, tools, food, and land. Naturally, this was a very expensive policy, and after 1825 it was stopped. While it lasted, thousands of immigrants made their way to Upper Canada. After 1825 many were attracted by advertisements placed in newspapers by land companies promising cheap land and prosperity in Canada.

A settler's hut. This is a very romantic picture of frontier life. Why might farming be difficult in a place like this?

Most settlers paid their own way to British North America. When they arrived, they found that most of the good government land was no longer available. Much of this land was reserved for churches and schools; desirable land around already settled areas was hard to obtain.

Because of this, newcomers to Canada turned more and more to land companies for help. Several land companies in Upper Canada with large tracts of land for sale helped in the settling of new immigrants.

Here is a typical offer of help to immigrants from a land company:

> But to those who mean to purchase lands from the Company, all care upon the subject of travelling expenses is obviated by a liberal and proper arrangement, which is published for the information of emigrants, as follows:—
>
> The Company's agents, on the arrival of emigrants at Quebec or Montreal, will, for the season of 1832, convey them, *free of expense*, To York, or the head of lake Ontario, which is in the vicinity of their choicest lands, *provided the emigrants pay a first instalment in London, Quebec, or Montreal,* of two shillings an acre, [five shillings a hectare] upon not less than one hundred acres, [forty hectares] and the Company's agents, in all parts of the Upper Province, will give such emigrants every information and assistance in their power. . . .

1. *Compare the selling techniques used in this advertisement to those which appear in today's newspapers. Make up an advertisement to attract settlers to Canada today.*

The Talbot Settlement   One of the earliest and largest of the land companies was started by Colonel Thomas Talbot. By studying how this company worked, you should get a better idea of how land companies in general operated in Upper Canada at this time.

Colonel Talbot, an Irishman, had come to Canada in 1791 and served as secretary to Lieutenant-Governor John Graves Simcoe. Shortly after, he returned to England, but not before he had an opportunity to visit the land along the north shore of Lake Erie. He was impressed by the quality of the soil and realized the potential of the area. When he returned to Canada he petitioned for, and in 1803 received, a grant of two thousand hectares along the shore of Lake Erie in present-day Elgin County.

In return for the grant Talbot promised to bring settlers to the area. The government in turn agreed to give him sixty hectares for every settler he was able to place on a twenty hectare farm in the township.

To each settler Talbot gave twenty hectares of land free. In addition, each was allowed to buy another sixty hectares for about $7.50 per hectare. Before the settler received a clear title to his land from Talbot, he had to meet certain stiff requirements. Some of these were:

—build a house six metres by four and a half
—live on the land at least five years
—cultivate four hectares within ten years

COLONEL THOMAS TALBOT
FORTE ET FIDELE
Born Ireland 1771. Secretary to Lt. Gov. Simcoe 1792-4. Settled on Lake Erie 1801 & colonized district. Died London U.C. 1853. Buried Tyrconnel Ont.

From Water Colour Portrait by J.D. Wandesforde. In Library, University of Western Ontario, London, Ont.

Chair used by Colonel Talbot. In Library of University of Western Ontario, London.

Sketch of Talbot's Residence Port Talbot
From "The Diary of Mrs. Simcoe."

—build a road along half of his frontage
—cut down all the trees on a strip thirty metres wide in front of his property.

In addition, Talbot insisted that saw mills, grist mills, and good roads be built in his settlement. Because of these requirements, few settlers came at first. In fact, it was six years before the first settler came to the Talbot settlement. However, by 1831 Talbot could look back and say:

I was the first person who exacted the performance of settlement duties, and actual residence on the land located, which at that time was considered most arbitrary on my part, but the consequence now is that the settlers I forced to comply with my system are most gratified and sensible of the advantage they could not otherwise for a length of time have derived by the accomplishment of good roads, and I have not any hesitation in stating that there is not another settlement in North America which can, for its age and extent, exhibit so compact and profitably settled a portion of the new world as the Talbot settlement . . . My population amounts to 40 000 souls.

1. *Do you agree with Colonel Talbot's methods and rules? If you had a land grant in a country as undeveloped as Canada in the 1830s, and wished to parcel it out to settlers, what rules and regulations would you set up?*

By 1837 the Talbot settlement had fifty thousand settlers and about two hundred and twenty thousand hectares of land. It was one of the most successful settlements in Upper Canada.

Thomas Talbot

Colonel Thomas Talbot, born in Ireland in 1771, was a man of unusual character and temperament. His first act after receiving his land grant in 1803 was to build a large wooden house, which he called Castle Malahide after his home in Ireland. Colonel Talbot never married, and lived in this house with only one or two servants for most of his remaining fifty years.

He was often rude and cruel to those who wished to purchase land in his Settlement. Talbot would interview prospective settlers in a room in Malahide Castle. If he disliked someone, he would sell him one of the worst lots in his settlement, far away from roads and people. Sometimes he would not sell the person any land at all.

On one occasion, a Scottish Highlander whom Talbot had insulted picked the Colonel up, carried him outside, threw him on the ground and held him there until the Colonel agreed to give him a good lot. After this incident Colonel Talbot carried on all interviews through a wooden window while the prospective settler waited outside. Now if the Colonel disliked a person, he would shut the window in his face and loose the dogs on him. Because of such methods the Colonel was greatly disliked by many of his settlers.

For most of his life Colonel Talbot was quite lonely and unhappy. He went back to England for a brief time, but returned to Canada and died in London, Ontario in 1853.

Pioneer Life in English Canada

Hardships The English pioneers in Canada did not have to face the same hardships and dangers as the early French settlers. The Indian threat had been removed, and roads had improved greatly, allowing easier communication between settlements. However, pioneering in the wilderness was never easy, and the pioneers of the Maritimes and Upper Canada had their own problems to face.

On Board an Immigrant Ship in the Thirties.

For those coming from overseas, their troubles started even before they arrived. Sea voyages were still unpleasant and even dangerous. The voyage could last as long as three months and ships were often overcrowded. As a result, the passengers, as one person wrote:

> ... suffered considerably from a shortage of food and water. The berthing arrangements alone were enough to demoralize them, for we learn that, "besides two tiers of berths on the sides, the vessel was filled with a row of berths down the centre, between which and the side berths there was only a passage of about three feet [about one metre]. The passengers were thus obliged to eat in their berths. In one were a man, his wife, his sister, and five children; in another were six full-grown young women, whilst that above them contained five men, and the next eight men". . . .

Another passenger noted:

> Our water for some time past has been very bad. When it was drawn
> out of the casks it was no clearer than that of a dirty kennel after a
> heavy shower of rain; so that its appearance alone was sufficient to
> sicken one. But its dirty appearance was not its worst quality. It had
> such a rancid smell that to be in the same neighborhood was enough
> to turn one's stomach; judge then what its taste must have been. . . .

Lack of fresh food and water often led to illness and death. One mother
sadly reported:

> We had the misfortune to lose both our little boys; Edward died 29th
> April, and William 5th May; the younger died with bowel complaint,
> the other with rash, fever and sore throat. We were very much hurt to
> have them buried in a watery grave; we mourned their loss; night and
> day they were not out of our minds. We had a minister on board, who
> prayed with us twice a day; he was a great comfort to us, on account
> of losing our poor little children. . . . There were six children and one
> woman died in the vessel.

The most difficult time for all settlers was usually the first two years, while
they were trying to build houses and clear enough land to grow the crops
needed for their food. One who lived through such times as a boy on the frontier recalls the experience:

> . . . The whole country was a forested wilderness which had to be
> subdued by the axe and toil.
> For a time we led a regular Robinson Crusoe life and with a few
> poles and brushwood, formed our tents on the Indian plan.
> As the clearances enlarged, we were supplied with some agricul-
> tural implements, for we brought nothing with us but a few seeds
> prepared by the careful forethought of the women.
> My father who had naturally a mechanical turn, amused himself
> of an evening in making spinning wheels, a loom, and a variety of
> useful things for farming purposes. Time passed and having grown
> some flax and obtained some sheep, my mother set to work to prepare
> the same for some clothes in which we were greatly in need of.
> She had not any thread, so my father, which doubtless he had
> learned from the Indians, stripped off the Bass Wood Bark, saturated
> it in water like Flax, and obtained a fine strong and useful thread.
> Necessity has no law. Consequently it was immaterial to us how the
> clothes were made, as long as the material held together. We none of
> us had any shoes or stockings, winter or summer, as those we brought

with us were soon worn out. At length my father tanned some leather, and I recollect the first pair of shoes he made which fell to my lot, I greased and putting them too near the fire, on returning to my grief found that my shoes were all shrivelled up, so that I could never wear them. I was twelve months before I obtained another pair, so many daily occurrences of life having to be attended to. . . .

The most trying period of our lives, was the year 1788 called the year of scarcity. . . .

All the crops failed . . . for several days we were without food, except that the various roots we procured and boiled down to nourish us. We noticed what roots the pigs eat; and by that means avoided anything that had any poisonous qualities. . . .

. . . Our poor dog was killed to allay the pangs of hunger, the very idea brought on sickness to some, but others devoured the flesh quite ravenous.

Clearing Land, about 1830.

Once they had received their grants of land, the settlers faced the backbreaking task of clearing them. How would you set about clearing a large section of forest for farmland? Here is one farmer's description:

After the trees have been felled, the most suitable kinds are split into rails for fences, and the remainder, being cut into logs twelve feet [three metres, sixty centimetres] long, and hauled together into large piles, and burnt. The land cleared in this manner is sown with wheat, and harrowed two or three times, and in general an abundant crop rewards the toils of the owner.

After the felling, dividing, and burning the timber have been accomplished, the stumps still remain, disfiguring the fields, and impeding the effectual operation of the plough and harrow. The immediate removal of the roots of the trees is impracticable and they are therefore always allowed to fall into decay, which state they are generally reduced in the space of eight or nine years. Pine stumps however seem scarcely susceptible of decomposition, as they frequently show no symptoms of it after half a century has elapsed. . . .

To those used to the comforts of city life, the houses of the pioneers must have been quite a shock. The log cabins were usually about 6 m long, 5 m wide and from 3 to 3.5 m high. Often they were built in a few days, with little care being taken to put in floors, chimneys, or windows. Some had only a door as an opening. The smoke from cooking found its way out through large gaps between the logs of the wall.Of course, mosquitoes, flies, and other insects also found their way in. One can imagine how cold such a cabin must have been in the winter.

A home in the woods. How is the house built? What problems might its inhabitants have in wet weather or in winter?

A settler reports on early pioneer houses:

Sometimes the shanty has a window, sometimes only an open doorway, which admits the light and lets out the smoke. A rude chimney, which is often nothing better than an opening cut in one of the top logs above the hearth, a few boards fastened in a square form, serves as the vent for the smoke; the only precaution against the fire catching the log walls behind the hearth being a few large stones placed in a half circular form, or more commonly a bank of clay raised against the wall.

Nothing can be more comfortless than some of these shanties, reeking with smoke and dirt, the common receptacle for children, pigs, and fowls. But I have given you the dark side of the picture; I am happy to say all the shanties on the squatters' [settlers'] ground were not like these; on the contrary, by far the larger proportion were inhabited by tidy folks, and had one, or even two small windows, and a clay chimney regularly built up through the roof; some were even roughly floored, and possessed similar comforts with the small loghouses.

You will, perhaps, think it strange when I assure you that many respectable settlers, with their wives and families, persons delicately nurtured, and accustomed to every comfort before they came hither, have been contented to inhabit a hut of this kind during the first or second year of their settlement in the woods.

Wednesday, January 23. This is the very coldest day we have had. . . . The thermometer was twenty below zero, [−29° C] with a strong wind. It blew very hard during the night; the mercury stood only three degrees above zero [−16° C] in our room whilst we were dressing. At noon it rose to five, [−15° C] and once we contrived to raise it to eight, [−13° C] which is the utmost a good fire has been able to do for it. . . . Much of to-day has been spent in keeping ourselves warm, by which I do not mean standing or sitting over the fires, but going about piling wood upon them, and also with paste and brown paper seeking to keep out the cold wind. . . . When Aunt Alice and I were pasting up the wind-holes, my mother reproved us, saying it was ridiculous for people to come to Canada and not be able to bear a breath of air.

New Towns   Slowly, communities grew and took shape. The land was good, and crops were plentiful. Towns grew. Here is a list of some of the largest towns of Upper Canada in 1845:

Toronto	— 19 706
Hamilton	— 6 475
Bytown (Ottawa)	— 7 000
London	— 3 500
Kingston	— 6 123
St. Catharines	— 3 500
Berlin (Kitchener)	— 400
Windsor	— 3 624

Find these cities on a map of modern-day Ontario. What is their present population? List the cities in order of size for 1845, and for today. Which cities seem to have grown most?

As towns grew, there were new opportunities for skilled workers. Here are some newspaper want ads for 1816:

WANTED

IMMEDIATELY, (in the Spectator Office) TWO JOURNEYMEN Printers VIZ:—A PRESSMAN and a COMPOSITOR—liberal wages will be given. . . . St. David's, U.C., Oct. 4, 1816.

WANTED

A miller of an established character, such a one by applying to the Subscriber at GRIMSBY MILLS, (40 Mile Creek) will meet with good encouragement.

Likewise a Blacksmith who is ac-quainted with Mill Work, will find a good place.—Men with families will be preferred.

Grimsby, October 4, 1816. WM. CROOKS

WANTED

TWO JOURNEYMEN, At the BOOT and SHOE-MAKING business, of steady habit to whom liberal wages will be given. For particulars apply to the Subscriber in Harton at the Cross Roads near Terreberry's Tavern.

October 4, 1816.   ERASTUS ELDERKIN

The social, educational and religious needs of the pioneers were also looked after.

Education Education was still expensive. At first the government did not provide any money for schools and only the rich could send their children to school. After 1816 the government provided tax money for schools and even the poor could now educate their children. The stress in public schools was on the "Three Rs"—Reading, Writing, and Arithmetic. Here is a description of a typical lesson of those days:

> Mr. Judd's method of teaching was characterized by the spelling which was a large element in the exercises, being conducted in chorus, the good spellers leading, and the learners following, and all at the top of their voices, thus: l-e-g-e-r, leger; d-e, legerde; m-a-i-n; legerdemain. "The noise was as the sound of many waters", and could be heard for a great distance around. It suited the teacher well

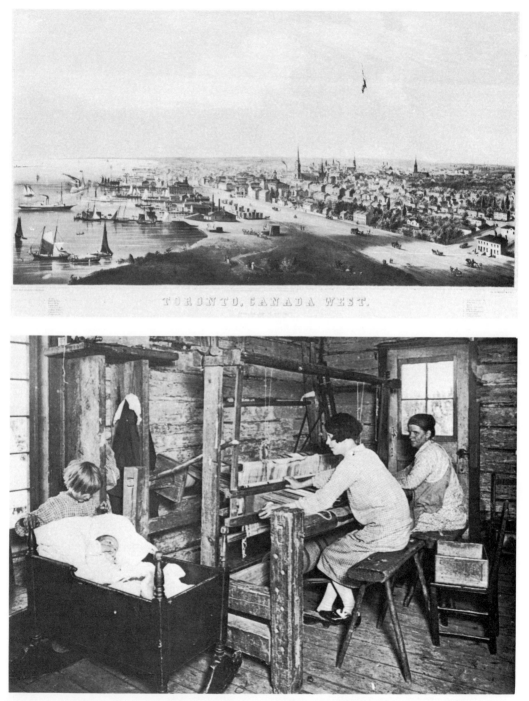

At first the materials for making clothes were imported from England. In time these materials were made in homes and factories across Canada. Looms such as the one in this picture were the most commonly used machines.

enough, for he was quite deaf, and it was fun for the children, and a great deal of this sort of drill made them ready spellers of, at least, all the words in the textbook.

The Schools were then open for six months of the year. I went to School for five half years. It was a log School House with a big fireplace in it, and seats all round the wall. The first time I went to School, it was in a square room. Some one called the Master out one day, and he shut the door after him. As soon as he was out, one of the Scholars raised a dancing tune, and then all of the Scholars got up and commenced going through a Highland dance. In the midst of this, the door opened, and in rushed the School Master with a big gad and lashed them all round, myself included. . . . Everyone spoke Gaelic, most of them could speak nothing else but that.

1. *How is a modern classroom different from the one described above?*

2. *Why do you think school was only open for six months in pioneer days?*

Religion Townspeople had built churches from the very early days. But farmers had to travel many kilometres to attend services on Sunday. The roads were either very bad or non-existent, so a trip to church was an all-day affair. Those settlers who lived far from town could not go to church at all. The Methodists sent circuit riders to serve the religious needs of these pioneers. Here is an account by Reverend Anson Green of one of his weekly visits in 1824:

. . . My path was a winding Indian trail, where no wheel carriage had ever passed. I was obliged to jump my horse over logs, ride him through deep mud-holes and bridgeless streams, guided sometimes by marked trees. When I got a short distance beyond Peterboro' I entered a clearing with two or three log cabins in view. In one of these lived a godly old Yorkshire woman, who received me joyfully. Her house was covered with hollow logs, halved, and so arranged as to shelter its inmates from rain and snow. The room was about fifteen by twenty feet [four and a half by six metres] in size, and it served for our kitchen, bed-room, parlour, dining-room, and church. Here I preached to a congregation of eight souls, and was happy. O how these people in the bush value the Gospel, and love the messengers who deliver it to them. On Wednesday returned to the town-line, and found my way to the house of Mr. Morrow, in Cavan, and preached to the best congregation, I found in these woods. . . . Thursday, preached at Mr. Sheckleton's, and on Friday at Mr. Thompson's, in Monaghan. . . .

Presbyterian Prayer-Meeting.

St. Thomas, Ont., Anglican Church—Erected 1824.

Stamford, Ont., Anglican Church—St. John the Evangelist; erected 1825.

Entertainment   While life in the back woods was hard, the early settlers had many occasions for fun!

July 4—Captain Wickham and all his family were in the greatest possible bustle the whole of the morning, in making preparations for their company ... the people began to arrive, consisting of young farmers, dressed in coats of glossy blue cloth, with broad white buttons, and rosy damsels in white calendered gowns, somewhat rumpled by having been packed too close in their carts during the journey. Some came in these carriages, and others on foot, till a large room below was quite full, and they all began to dance.

The fiddler sat on a chair placed upon a large table, playing country dances, and roaring out the figure. There was not an old person in the room to direct the flock, which was noisy and riotous beyond measure.

A Village Dance in 1840.

As in every generation, young people found new ways of getting into mischief.

... When the settlement was formed, money was plentiful, and with some of our youths who were not kept to hard labour, frolic was the order of the day, and sometimes even of the night. Take the following as an instance. On the morning of the 26th of March, 1818, it was found that all the signs in the village had changed their places ... a tavern sign was fixed over a shop, and the shop sign over the tavern. The sign from the stage-house was fixed over the Superintendent's office, and a merchant's sign attached to the residence of the Catholic priest.

In the towns social events were very elaborate. Here is how the King's Birthday was celebrated in 1807:

> On Wednesday, the 3rd, . . . a numerous and splendid assemblage of ladies from various and distant parts of the district were presented to Mrs. Gore. . . .
>
> The ball commenced at 8 o'clock [20:00] in the Council House, which was fitted up and lighted in an elegant manner, with an orchestra of the charming band of the 41st Regiment. A temporary building was also erected, eighty feet [twenty-four metres] in length and of sufficient width for two sets of tables to accommodate 200 persons at supper, and the building was connected with the dancing-room by a covered way.
>
> Mrs. Gore and the Honorable Robert Hamilton led off the first dance, and about fifty couples of spirited dancers occupied the floor till one o'clock, [01:00] when they retired into the supper-rooms where a most sumptuous entertainment, served up with true English elegance, was provided.

Barn-raising "bees" were also a popular way of getting together. What other important role would they serve?

> [1834] Monday, 21st:—Very rainy. Poor prospects for tomorrow's work; two hands at the village bringing over a supply of whiskey, etc., the other two making the pike poles for raising the frame, cleaning and preparing the shanty for the accommodation of the people coming from a distance. . . .
>
> Tuesday, 22nd:—A bad rainy morning; however, as people came forward we commenced toward 9 o'clock [09:00] to put the bents [upright sections forming main framework] of the building together. . . . It was with difficulty we got them persuaded to stay and persevere tomorrow; however, I sent for a fiddler and cajoled and flattered them as well as I could. . . .
>
> Wednesday, 23rd:—Began to put up the frame with thirty men or thereabouts; found the bents so heavy that at first we feared a failure, but, after everyone got themselves fairly put to their mettle, it went up and so did all the others before night. . . . We also got the wall plates up to the beams ready for putting into their places in the morning. While the men were at supper this evening a half-playful wrestling scuffle occurred. . . . Joseph St. German was thrown down in the kitchen, and melancholy to tell, he received some mortal injury, and in the course of seven or eight minutes expired, to the horror and regret of everyone. . . .

Thursday, 24th:—Sent a warrant to the constable to call a jury by daylight; they assembled about half-past 11 o'clock [11:30] and proceeded to investigate the unhappy occurrence of last night, and found a verdict of manslaughter against Ronald McDonald. . . . They have used a barrel of pork [about ninety kilograms] and one of flour [about eighty-eight kilograms] with fifteen gallons [sixty-seven and a half litres] of whiskey, besides tea and sugar, etc. One of the hands made a coffin for St. German, and he was removed immediately after the inquest by his friends.

1. *Who provided entertainment and refreshments at a bee?*

2. *How was the barn built?*

3. *What misfortune occurred during this bee? How did it happen?*

Travel Travel in early pioneer times was dangerous. Today we must have good roads to travel at the high speeds we like. Otherwise our vehicles would soon fall apart. Early roads in Canada, however, were at first nothing more than trails cut through the woods. At some points, such as swampy places, logs were laid side by side to form the "corduroy roads" which made stagecoach travel possible. The stages had no springs. Imagine riding a pioneer stage over log roads!

Here are some descriptions of stage travel in early Canada:

But, beyond Hamilton . . . we reached a swamp, which had to be crossed on a road made of trees cut into lengths and laid side by side, their ends resting in the trunks of others placed lengthwise. . . . This was my first experience of "corduroy roads", but we had several more stretches of them before we got to our journey's end. I have long ago learned all the varieties of badness of which roads are capable, and

Corduroy road in South Porcupine, Ont. Corduroy roads were still being built as late as 1911.

question whether "corduroy" is entitled to the first rank. There is a
kind made of thick planks, laid side by side, which when they get old
and broken, may bid fair for the palm. I have seen a stout, elderly
lady, when the coach was at a good trot, bumped fairly against the
roof by a sudden hole and the shock against the plank at the other
side. But, indeed, "corduroy" is dreadful. When we came to it I tried
everything to save my poor bones—sitting on my hands, or raising
my body on them—but it was of little use; on we went, thump,
thump, thumping against one log after another, and this, in the last
part of our journey with the bare boards of an open wagon for seats
. . . But we got through without an actual upset or breakdown, which
is more than a friend of mine could say, for the coach in which he was
went into so deep a mud-hole at one part of the road, that it fairly
overturned, throwing the passengers on the top of one another inside,
and leaving them no way of exit, when they came to themselves, but
to crawl out through the window.

1. *Aside from the uncomfortable ride,
    what other problems might face the
    traveller on a long trip?*
2. *Some early observers remarked
    that travel was often more pleasant*
    *in winter than in summer. Can you
    suggest reasons for this? What
    drawbacks might there be to winter
    travel?*

Some of the pioneers' worst problems could not be solved by hard work. These were isolation, loneliness, and discouragement. We can guess at the problems, and the solutions that were sometimes tried, in the following advice to immigrants:

> . . . every young farmer or labourer going out (who can pay for the passage of two) to take an active young wife with him. . . .
>
> Unmarried women, who have no fortunes, and are active, and industrious, without much pride or vanity, and who relish a quiet and retired life . . . have an opportunity of being well married. . . .
>
> . . . as the settlers must scramble about in all weathers . . . stout flannels and coarse cloths . . . must not mind fashion; the best coat and breeches are those that can come farthest through the brush with fewest holes in them . . . there is not a better article for the purpose than Scotch blanket . . . called plaiding.
>
> . . . religious and loyal prints—coloured Scriptural subjects with texts attached, home scenery of school and village churches. Portraits of Her Majesty, Prince Albert and the royal children, Wellington and Nelson, views of Windsor Castle, the House of Parliament, our cathedrals. . . .
>
> Above all things do not take your decanter or your corkscrew. . . . You are going to a country where you may literally swim in whisky or gin, and pretty nearly in brandy and rum. But resolve never to taste either. Drinking is the great vice of the country.

Another settler warns a prospective immigrant:

> In the first place I must tell you what you will miss here. You will miss society of which you are fond; at least you will find no one of your own age with whom you would like to associate much, and anything in a literary or scientific way in a still rarer occurrence; but you will meet with some very agreeable, well informed young men, some of whom I know you will like, and a quiet rubber or a game of chess with occasional varieties will not be wanting.
>
> Then I am afraid of our hot summers (the thermometer 95 [35° C] in the shade last Saturday) and our cold winters, minus 17 [−27° C] at Peterboro. Only one thing more strikes me with regard to you; it is a matter of slight importance in itself but it recurs every day—viz. eating. Next year things will be much improved in this respect. But do what you will, for a year or two you will have often to dine on salt pork. These will be your trials. . . .

Slowly, however, the forest was cleared, rich farms grew, and pioneer families prospered. Visitors from more settled countries would still remark on the discomfort of pioneer farms. A great deal of work remained to be done. A great deal of patience was still needed. But when visitors were reminded how much had been done under such harsh conditions with only rough tools and equipment, they could not help but be amazed. Ann Langton, visiting her brother's home in Upper Canada in 1837, remarked:

> At last, however, after all delays and disappointments, our long journey is accomplished. John looked very proud when he handed his mother into his little mansion. His arrangements for our accommodation are very snug. What most strikes me is a greater degree of roughness in farming, buildings, gardens, fences and especially roads, than I had expected. But when one looks at the wild woods around, and thinks that from such a wilderness the present state of things has been brought out by a few hands, and how much there is for those few hands to be constantly doing, one's surprise vanishes, and one rather wonders that so much has been done, than that so much remains to be done.

Log house in the bush. How long do you think settlers have been here? What work still remains to be done?

Word Study

American Revolution	Lieutenant-Governor	Tories
Breeches	Lower Canada	United Empire Loyalists
Castle Malahide	Posting	Upper Canada
Grist Mill	Shanty	Year of Scarcity
Land Company	Tar and feather	

Things To Do   1. Using the descriptions and pictures in this chapter, try to build a model of a pioneer cabin. Matchsticks, toothpicks, popsicle sticks, or even twigs make fine materials for this purpose. Use them for the outside of the model. The frame can be cut out of cardboard, and the sticks then glued on.

2. Find out what kinds of trees grow in Ontario today, and their location. On an outline map of Ontario, show what types of trees were most common in the early farming communities.

3. There were very few roads in early Upper Canada and even these were often in very bad shape. Over wet and swampy areas the government build corduroy roads. How were such roads built? What effect would they have on stage and other methods of transportation?

4. Make a diagram of a typical sixty hectare homestead lot after three years of occupation. Show the location of the road, cabin, cleared area, and forest area in the homestead. Show also what crops might have been grown on this farm.

5. If your library has books on ships throughout the ages, find some information on the ships that carried immigrants to Canada during the Great Migration. This information should include:

   (a) the size of the ship;
   (b) the length of the voyage;
   (c) the number of passengers carried;
   (d) the dangers to passengers during the voyage.

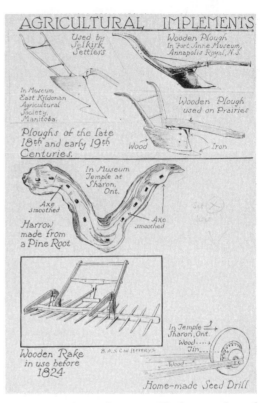

6. Many Canadians still share a bond of loyalty to Britain and the British Commonwealth. Some have formed clubs and organizations to preserve this loyalty. One such club which began in Loyalist times, is the Imperial Order Daughters of the Empire. With the help of your teacher, librarian, and telephone directory, try to locate other organizations of this type in Canada.

7. In years past, Canada has fought beside Great Britain in several great wars. Find out more about Canada's involvement in the Boer War and World War I. Do you think the Loyalist tradition was behind Canada's participation in these wars? Do you think the Loyalist tradition is as strong today?

4
Settlement of the West

Toronto, December 16, 1974. A group of two hundred people met in a cold barn just north of Toronto last night to discuss an unusual adventure. They were all hoping to become part of a group planning to take up homestead land in Alberta. Canadian Wagon Train is an organization which plans to lead sixty people from Toronto to northern Alberta. They hope to make the trip much as the first settlers to the West did—in fifteen covered wagons.

These modern-day pioneers have applied to lease several thousand hectares of land in the Peace River area of Alberta. The group plans to leave in April, and reach their destination four months later. They hope to average thirty-two kilometres a day travelling along the Trans-Canada Highway.

It will not be easy. The space-age pioneers will face many of the same problems the first pioneers did almost a century ago. The site is about 880 km northeast of Edmonton, and 80 km from the nearest town. It has no roads, no electricity or running water. The settler's first task will be to make their own homes, with winter soon approaching. Winters in northern Alberta are often bitter, and temperatures at times drop to 40 or 50 degrees below zero.

A local homesteader also notes that clearing the land will be a long, hard task. "It took me ten years to clear forty hectares," he notes.

Among the would-be pioneers are people who are willing to give up careers for this chance at homesteading. These include sales people, electricians, printers, movie actors, and their families. Why are they giving up a comfortable life for an uncertain future? Here are some answers:

—"I like a clean environment. It's a perfect place to raise a family."
—"I want to get back to the land and get something we can say is ours."
—"I hate city life. I hate the noise and the smog."
—"I just want to get away from all the hustle and bustle."
—"I'd like to raise a small dairy herd and maybe beef cattle."

The call of the West is still strong today.

The West in 1867

It was 1867, the year of Confederation in Canada. Bells rang, fireworks exploded and bands marched. The new nation consisted of only four provinces—Ontario, Quebec, New Brunswick, and Nova Scotia. Its population too was small—3 300 000 people—and 75% of it lived in Ontario and Quebec. Most people still lived and worked on their farms. However, there was a bustling city life also. The Province of Quebec boasted Montreal, a lively city of

100 000, and Quebec City, a stately capital of 60 000. Ontario too had Toronto, a rapidly growing city of 50 000.

In the West, Indians and their half-brothers the Métis still hunted buffalo on horseback. At a time when Montreal had gaslights on its streets, and passengers could ride the train between Montreal and Toronto six days a week, Edmonton was described this way:

> The establishment at Edmonton boasts of a windmill, a black-smith's forge and carpenter's shop. The boats required for the annual voyage to York Factory in Hudson Bay are built and mended here. . . Wheat grows luxuriantly. . . . There are about 30 families living in the Fort. . . .

Hudson Bay Fort Edmonton.

Canada's West was still a frontier. The Indian and Métis population was small and scattered. By the time of Confederation much of the good farming land of Ontario and Quebec had been taken up. For newcomers and those who dreamed of owning their own farmlands, the West with its six and a half million square kilometres of open land seemed their best hope.

The Hudson's Bay Company   But would the West be opened up to farming set-tlements? In the beginning there was much doubt. At the time of Confederation the West was not part of Canada. Much of it was the property of the Hudson's Bay Company, granted by Royal Charter by King Charles II of England in 1670. This area was called Rupert's Land; it included a huge part of modern-day Canada. The charter gave the Company ownership and all rights of trade in the lands washed by rivers flowing into Hudson's Bay. One look at a map of this network of rivers and lakes will show clearly how very large this land grant was.

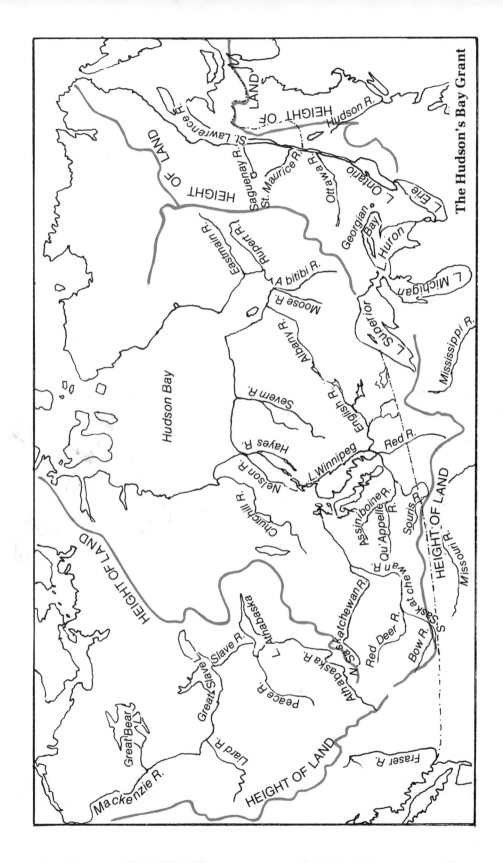

The Hudson's Bay Grant

The Company was interested mainly in the fur trade, for furs were still in great demand in Europe. Beaver, marten, muskrat, otter, bear, fox, and lynx were the most popular types of fur. The Company was naturally opposed to any policy of settlement. Can you think of reasons why? What would happen to the Company's sources of furs if farming communities developed in its territory?

David Thompson in the Athabaska Pass, 1810.

The North West Company   In that part of the West not controlled by the Hudson's Bay Company, another organization, the North West Company, was busy at work. It too was interested in the fur trade. In its efforts to find new sources of furs it sent out explorers from its headquarters in Upper Canada far to the west. It was men of the North West Company such as Alexander Mackenzie, Simon Fraser, and David Thompson who opened up the Canadian West all the way to the Pacific. Under incredibly hard conditions they explored unknown lands and charted canoe routes. It is from the diaries of these men that we get some of our first glimpses of the Canadian West.

> The whole of this country may be pastoral, but except in a few places, cannot become agricultural. Even the fine Turtle Hill, gently rising, for several miles, with its Springs and Brooks of fine Water has very little wood fit for the Farmer. The principal is Aspen which soon decays: with small Oaks and Ash. The grass of these plains is so often on fire, by accident or design, and the bark of the Trees so often scorched, that their growth is contracted, or they become dry; and the whole of the great Plains are subject to these fires during the Summer and Autumn before the Snow lies on the ground. These great Plains appear to be given by Providence to the Red Men for ever, as the wilds and sands of Africa are given to the Arabians.
>
> *Alexander Mackenzie*

In 1821 the two rivals, the North West Company and the Hudson's Bay Company were united under the name of the Hudson's Bay Company. The new organization could now claim control as far as the Pacific to the west, Labrador to the east, the Arctic shore to the north, and the forty-ninth parallel to the south. In 1849 it was granted by the British government the rights of colonization for Vancouver Island. The Company's rights in this area were to be renewed every twenty-one years.

By the year of Confederation, many Canadians were concerned about the future of the West. Would the Hudson's Bay Company permit settlement in its territory? Was the land even suitable for settlement?

The Red River Settlement   Both questions had been partially answered by the settlement at Red River. A young Scottish nobleman, Thomas Douglas, the fifth Earl of Selkirk, was concerned with the plight of the poor in Scotland and Ireland, and resolved to help them. He felt that the only future for these starving families was immigration to Canada. As we have seen, however, good land in Upper Canada and the Maritimes soon became scarce. The solution appeared to be the West.

Selkirk bought shares in the Hudson's Bay Company and became a partner. Then, in 1811, he received a grant of three hundred thousand square kilometres from the Company to establish a settlement. At the site where the Red and the Assiniboine Rivers meet, and where the present-day city of Winnipeg stands, Selkirk began his colony. In 1812, the first settlers from Scotland arrived. By the next year other Scottish Highlanders found their way to the Red River settlement. Eventually the settlement extended as far south as the Pembina River in present-day North Dakota. It included in its numbers Scots, Irish, Welsh, and English.

Selkirk had little prior knowledge of the West, and of its climate and soil. He had however, read Mackenzie's *Journal*. How might Mackenzie's description of Red River have influenced Selkirk?

> . . . the Red River runs in a Southern direction to near the head waters of the Mississippi. On this are two trading establishments. The country on either side is but partially supplied with wood, and consists of plains covered with herds of the buffalo and the elk, especially on the Western side. On the Eastern side are lakes and rivers, and the whole country is well wooded, level, abounding in beaver, bears, moose-deer, fallow-deer, &c. &c. . . . There is not, perhaps, a finer country in the world for the residence of [the Native People] than that which occupies the space between this river and Lake Superior. It abounds in every thing necessary to the wants and comforts of such a people. Fish, venison, and fowl, with wild rice, are in great plenty.

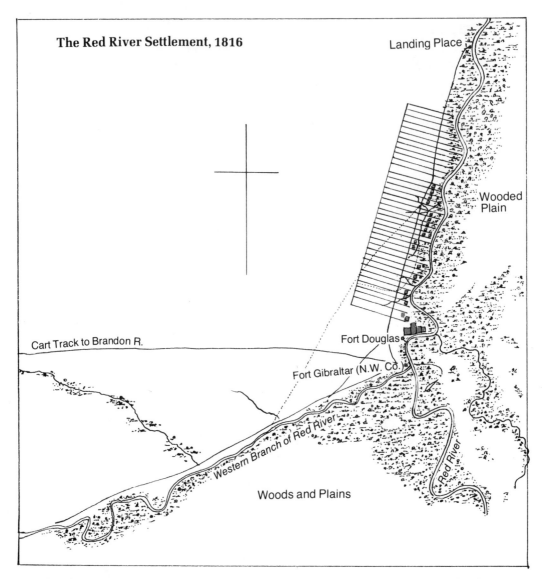

The first few years were very difficult for the settlers. They lacked proper tools to break the sod and harvest the crops, and were unfamiliar with the conditions of the area. They were caught totally unprepared for the plagues of grasshoppers, floods, and early frost which swept away most of their crops in those first few years.

Their greatest problem, however, was the North West Company. The Company realized that the Selkirk settlement posed a threat to its business. A glance at the map shows that the settlement was centrally located between the source of furs to the west, and the export centres in eastern Canada. The Nor'Westers, as the traders of the North West Company were called, believed that the settlement had been planted on purpose by the rival Hudson's Bay Company to destroy them.

They took action in 1815, by trampling the crops and burning the homes of the settlers. More than one hundred and thirty settlers were carried off to Fort William, the Company headquarters in Upper Canada. In 1816 the violence became much worse. In June of that year a battle broke out between the settlers and a group of Métis at Seven Oaks, located today in the heart of Winnipeg. At the end of the fight, twenty-one settlers lay dead.

The fight at Seven Oaks, 1816.

Here is an account of the battle by James Pritchard, one of the settlers who fought in it:

> Upon observing that they were so numerous, we had extended our line, and got more into the open plain; as they advanced, we retreated; but they divided themselves into two parties, and surrounded us again in the shape of a half-moon. . . .
>
> From not seeing the firing begin, I cannot say from whom it first came; but immediately upon hearing the first shot, I turned and saw Lieut. Holte struggling. (Several persons present at the affair, such as a blacksmith named Heden, and McKay, a settler, distinctly state that the first shot fired was from the Bois-brulés and that by it Lieut. Holte fell). . . .
>
> A fire was kept up for several minutes after the first shot, and I saw a number wounded; indeed, in a few minutes almost all our people were either killed or wounded. I saw Sinclair and Bruin fall, either wounded or killed; and a Mr. McLean, a little in front defending himself, but by a second shot I saw him fall. . . .

Their intention clearly was to pass the Fort. I saw no carts with them. I saw about five of the settlers prisoners in the Camp at Frog Plain. Grant said to me further: "You see we have had but one of our people killed, and how little quarter we have given you. Now, if Fort Douglas is not given up with all the public property instantly and without resistance men, women and child will be put to death." He said the attack would be made upon it that night, and if a single shot were fired, that would be a signal for the indiscriminate destruction of every soul. . . .

1. Why did the fight begin?

2. Who fired the first shot? Is there proof of this?

3. Was the skirmish fight planned by the Métis?

As you try to answer the above questions, read the following two letters from members of the North West Company and consider their attitude toward the settlers:

> . . . your posts should be strengthened with men and extra supplies of goods, and measures should be taken for a vigorous opposition. . . . We forbear to suggest the particular details of this opposition, as you will be better able to judge of them than we are, but the opposition ought to be general and followed up at almost any expense. . . . The object in view is well worth making sacrifice for. . . . The Hudson's Bay Company . . . by their grant to Lord Selkirk . . . are striking at the very root of . . . [your] Fur Trade. In short, no means should be left untried to thwart Selkirk's schemes.

> . . . we will do our best to defend what we consider our rights in the interior. Something serious will undoubtedly take place. Nothing but the complete downfall of the colony will satisfy some by fair or foul means. A most desirable object, if it can be accomplished; so here is at them with all my heart and energy.

Meanwhile, help was on the way for the frightened settlers. Selkirk hired about one hundred former soldiers and brought them to Red River. The presence of these men discouraged any further fighting.

These incidents and the legal problems which followed cost Selkirk a great deal of money and ruined his health. He returned to England in 1817 and died three years later.

The Red River Colony, however, endured. At first it was not as successful as Selkirk hoped it would be, but it did become the first permanent settlement in Canada's West. The present century has brought Selkirk's vision to reality. The

West has become a food producer not only for Canada, but for many parts of the world.

This success, however, was still well in the future. In 1850 prospects looked much dimmer. If even the fertile valley of the Red River faced so many obstacles to its survival, what were the prospects for other, less attractive, parts of the West?

By the year of Confederation the question of the settlement of the West had become very important. The Hudson's Bay Company wished to protect its fur interests and to discourage settlement. Opposing the Company's policy were immigrants and poor people who hoped to own their own land in the West. The politicians too wished to encourage settlement, for they hoped that the West would then become part of Canada. This would greatly add to the power and wealth of the new nation. Many Canadians who longed for a strong nation, stretching from sea to sea, also favoured settlement. They were afraid that if Canadians did not settle the West, the Americans to the south, hungry for land, soon would.

In 1867, shortly after Confederation, Canada began negotiations with the Hudson's Bay Company to purchase Rupert's Land. In 1869 the Company agreed to sell its lands. It received £300 000 in payment, and also one-twentieth of the fertile lands, as well as blocks of land around its trading posts. In return, Canada now possessed a vast new land for future settlement.

Wagon train crosses the Prairies as Indian and Métis hunters look on. What might the hunters be thinking as they watch the wagons bringing an end to their way of life?

The Settlement of the Canadian West

It was the common feeling among those in government that the development of the West was the key to Canada's future. It would provide open farmlands to attract immigrants. It would add greatly to Canada's economic strength. It would also provide Canada with an unbroken link of settled communities from Nova Scotia to British Columbia. This would protect the West and prevent it from being taken over by the United States.

With this in mind, John A. Macdonald, Canada's first Prime Minister, began certain policies to encourage settlement. The first was to build a railway to link East and West. Building such a railway, at the time the longest in the world, was a large task for such a small country. It would be very expensive, it would take a long time to complete, and there would be great difficulties involved. In fact, the last spike of this railway, the Canadian Pacific, was not driven until 1885.

The second policy was to offer free land. As soon as the Canadian government purchased Rupert's Land, it immediately sent out surveyors to draw up plans for townships and homesteads.

The Canadian government followed the American system of giving out land in the West. It divided the prairie west into townships made up of 36 one-mile

A Township Survey

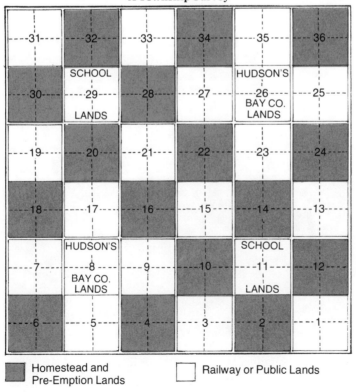

Homestead and Pre-Emption Lands   Railway or Public Lands

squares (2.6 km²). Each square consisted of 640 acres (256 ha). A homestead in turn consisted of 160 acres (64 ha) or one-quarter of a square. Such homesteads were commonly known as quarter sections.

In 1872, the Canadian government passed the Dominion Lands Act providing a free homestead of 160 acres (64 ha) to any male over the age of 18, or any widow. It also set aside land in each township to be used as grazing land. In return the settlers had to agree to live on the land for three years; during this time they had to put up a home and break at least 10 acres (4 ha) of soil each year. Settlers could also buy nearby quarter-sections at public auctions. Here is part of the Homestead Regulations of 1908:

Homestead Regulations
September 1, 1908

Any quarter-section vacant and available of Dominion land in Manitoba, Saskatchewan or Alberta, excepting 8 and 26, may be homesteaded by any person the sole head of a family, or any male over eighteen years of age and is British subject, or declares intention to become a British subject, on payment of an entry fee of ten dollars.

A widow having minor children of her own dependent on her for support is permitted to make homestead entry as the sole head of a family.

Entry must be made in person, either at the land office for the District or at the office of a Sub-Agent authorized to transact business in the District, except in the case of a person who may make entry for a father, mother, son, daughter, brother or sister, when duly authorized by the prescribed form which may be had from your nearest Government Agent.

A homesteader may perform residence duties by living in habitable house on homestead for six months in each of three years.

A homesteader may perform the required six months' residence duties by living on farming land owned solely by him, not less than eighty (80) acres [32 ha] in extent, in the vicinity of his homestead. Joint ownership in land will not meet this requirement.

Six months' time is allowed after entry before beginning residence.

A homesteader residing on homestead is required to break 30 acres [12 ha] of the homestead (of which 20 [8 ha] must be cropped) before applying for patent. A reasonable proportion of cultivation duties must be done during each year.

When the duties are performed under regulations permitting residence in vicinity, 50 acres [20 ha] must be broken (of which 30 [12 ha] must be cropped).

Of course, under this system many people were able to acquire large areas of land. Farmers lucky enough to have four or five sons over the age of eighteen could file for a homestead for each son. Other farmers who had sons younger than eighteen would sometimes also file for homesteads. Since no birth certificates were required in those days, this trick was usually very successful.

1. *You have decided to apply for a homestead in the West. As yet, you do not know where you wish to settle. It would be useful to have some information about the West to help you make your decision. What facts would be of help to you? Certainly some knowledge of the climate, soils, and vegetation of the West would be useful.*

2. *Examine the following evidence closely. Which area of the West would be most appealing to you as a possible site for a homestead?*

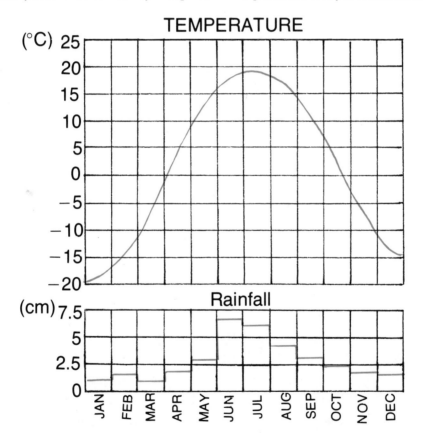

1. Here is a chart showing the yearly rainfall and temperature range of Saskatoon. With the help of an encyclopedia or a geography book, do a similar chart of Calgary, Edmonton, Medicine Hat, Regina, and Winnipeg. What conclusions can you draw about the climate of the Prairies?

2. Study the soil and climate charts and decide how the land could best be used. What types of farming would be most successful?

3. Compare your choices with those shown in the map of Prairie farming which follows.

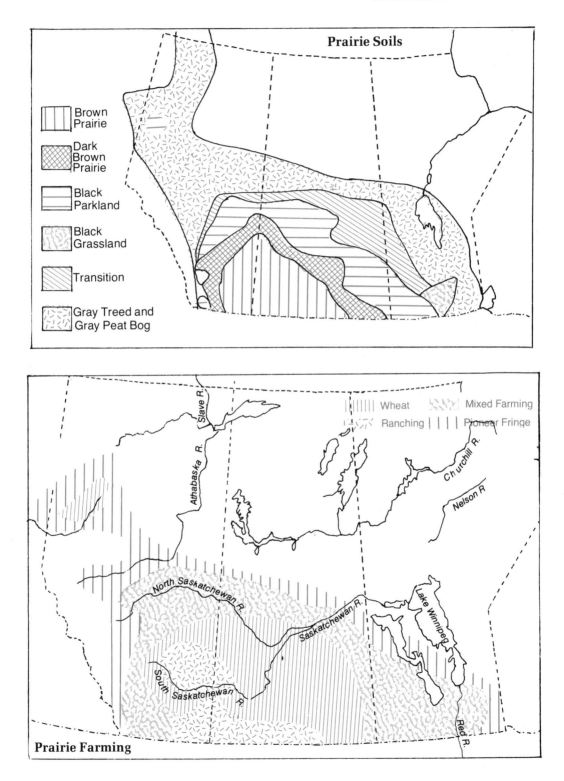

Prairie Soils

Brown Prairie

Dark Brown Prairie

Black Parkland

Black Grassland

Transition

Gray Treed and Gray Peat Bog

Wheat | Mixed Farming

Ranching | Pioneer Fringe

Slave R.

Athabaska R.

Churchill R.

Nelson R.

North Saskatchewan R.

Saskatchewan R.

South Saskatchewan R.

Lake Winnipeg

Red R.

Prairie Farming

Early Problems In 1871, the entire population of the Prairie Provinces was only 73 228, including Indians and Métis. When the government put its settlement policy into effect, it hoped that a flood of settlers would rush into the West to take advantage of the generous offer. Yet 10 years later, the population of the West stood at only slightly more than 100 000. Between 1874 and 1877 a total of 3067 homestead entries had been registered. These were certainly disappointing figures.

   The two main stumbling blocks to settlement were quickly pointed out. The first was lack of transportation. To get to their homesteads in the West, settlers had to make the journey by all means imaginable. Here is one description of such a trip. Compare the trip taken by these early settlers with that planned by the group described at the beginning of this chapter.

> We came up the great Lakes from Collingwood to Duluth by steamer *Frances Smith*, distance 1000 miles, [1600 km] from Duluth to Moorhead on the Red River by railway 212 miles [339 km]; and from Moorhead to Winnipeg by steamer 500 miles [800 km]. In Winnipeg we were joined by David McDougall and Rev. H. M. Manning and wife. Before leaving Winnipeg we had to buy our year's supply of provisions, also horses, oxen, buckboards and Hudson Bay Carts to haul our families and freight.
>
> David McDougall (Free Trader) had come to Winnipeg to purchase supplies for his store at Morley. He acted as guide and Captain to the whole party.
>
> When we were all ready we pulled out from Winnipeg in our long journey across the great Prairie to the Rocky Mountains. All single rigs, (one horse and buckboard), (one ox and cart) were used. Each ox hauled about 900 lbs [405 kg] and travelled from 10 to 15 miles [16 to 24 km] per day. We camped every night (No travelling on Sundays) forded all rivers and streams, except the South Saskatchewan, near Batoche. Here we swam the horses and oxen and had our families and freight taken over on a big scow operated by Gabriel Dumont. After we left the Saskatchewan, we met a lone Scotchman travelling from Edmonton to Winnipeg with an ox and cart and bound for Scotland on a holiday trip. (You'll find a Scotchman everywhere.)
>
> . . . some of our party left for Edmonton; the remainder of the party came on to Morley the end of our journey where we arrived on the 21st day of October, 104 from the time we left home in Ontario.

1. *On an outline map of western Canada, indicate the different means*   *by which settlers arrived in the West.*

Settlers with Red River carts stop for a meal. Red River carts were built with no metal parts. As they rolled across the Prairies the squealing wheels could be heard at long distances. Even the strongest nerves were sometimes worn to a frazzle.

A second problem was the money required to equip a homestead. Although the land itself was free, a great number of other things were required to actually run the farm. While prices of 1870 may not seem high to us today, we should remember that the average wage in those days was perhaps two or three dollars a day.

The first requirement of a family settling on its new homestead was, of course, a house. A good portion of prairie land, however, was barren of trees, and lumber was very expensive. As a result, a new type of building, the "soddy", appeared in the West. The soddy had four sod walls. The roof was also made of sod, supported by poplar poles. There was no actual floor, simply a hard layer of packed dirt.

Some settlers preferred to have their soddy without windows, for these only let in unwanted light and cold. The sod itself would simply be plowed from the prairie in large strips which were cut into "bricks" and placed on top of one another. An average "sod brick" would be thirty centimetres wide by seventy-five centimetres long. With the help of a neighbour, the soddy might take only one or two days to construct. The entire cost of such a house, including the door, hinges, latches, and perhaps a window, would be between three and four dollars. By the turn of the century there were over a million such houses in the West.

Settler's first shack. Some settlers used to say that when it rained for two days outside it was sure to rain three days inside. What materials were used in this house?

Before reading the next account, try to make your own list of the things one might need to take along to a homestead. How does it compare with this list, suggested in 1882?

Intending settlers having horses, cattle and implements, will do right by bringing them along with them; but those not having live-stock can purchase outfits at Winnipeg; or, if not caring to encumber themselves with farming implements, can purchase them at Battle-ford. The prices at Winnipeg are: Double wagons, $65 to $75; Red River carts, $10 to $15; Iron-Bound carts, $30 to $35; Buckboards $50 to $75; Wagon harness, $30 to $40; Cart harness, $6 to $10; Single harness, $20 to $30; Canadian teams, $250 to $400; Native ponies, $50 to $80; Yoke of oxen, $150 to $175; Camping outfit: a good tent, tin stove, frying pan, tin cups, axes, spades, hammer, brace and bits, or auger, drawing knife, saw, nails, assortment of wagon bolts, logging chain, hobbles and ropes for horses, a shot gun, powder and shot, as game is plentiful. Provisions: flour, bacon, beans, dried apples, sugar, tea, baking powder, etc. Route: take train from Winnipeg to Brandon or to the end of the C.P.R. Wagons drawn by Canadian horses—the load should not exceed fifteen hundred pounds [six hundred and seventy-five kilograms]. Good oxen in carts—from five hundred to eight hundred pounds [two hundred and twenty-five to three hundred and sixty kilograms]. The best time to travel is in early spring. A fair average rate per day is for oxen 15 miles, [24 km] for horses 15 to 25 miles [25 to 40 km].

1. How much money would be
   required to outfit even the most
   inexpensive expedition?

2. How long would the trip from Winnipeg to Calgary take?

A third problem concerned the crops. Although the land was rich and fertile, the wheat production of the Prairie West was surprisingly low. The chief drawback seemed to be the weather. Late springs and early falls made for a short growing season, especially for the type of wheat grown at that time. In 1891 Canada's entire wheat export was only seventy-two thousand cubic metres.

The solution came in two stages. The first actually began in 1842. In the fall of that year, David Fife, an Ontario farmer, planted some samples of wheat he had received from a friend. Only three plants survived the winter. He saved these three and in the fall harvested the first crop of what would be called Red Fife. This hardy wheat first spread to the United States and later to the Canadian West. It was ideally suited to the climate of the Prairies and by 1900 few other types of wheat were grown there.

The second improvement was made in 1904. In that year, Sir Charles Saunders, a Canadian wheat expert, succeeded in crossing Red Fife wheat with other types gathered from all over the world. The new wheat was called Marquis, and it ripened eight days earlier than Red Fife. This eliminated the constant risk to wheat of early frost in the Prairies. By 1930 over eighty per cent of western Canadian wheat was of the Marquis variety.

The First Wave of Settlers

The improvement of the wheat crop and the completion of the C.P.R. across the West in 1885 made the task of settlement a little easier. By 1891 the population of the West had grown to over two hundred and fifty thousand. At first most of this increase was due to immigration from eastern Canada and the U.S. By 1880, however, people had begun arriving from Germany, Scandinavia, and eastern Europe. Here is a description of the life of one such homesteader in the years 1893 to 1903:

> I came to Calgary from Germany in October, 1893, with empty pockets, and when the first spring arrived I was sixty dollars in debt. I lived in Calgary for three years, earning enough money to buy a few head of cattle, which I gave out on shares. I cannot say that this was a success, as parties did not look after them properly, so I made up my mind to get a farm of my own, and I must say I did not like Canada very much until then.
>
> I homesteaded a quarter section and bought another quarter section for which I could only make a small payment and gave a

mortgage for the balance, which I paid as it became due. I started with five cows and three small horses. My farm was in a bad state of cultivation, the man I bought the farm from advised me not to do any farming at all as it would not pay, but it was no wonder it would not pay: four years in succession grain had been sown on the stubble on the same piece of ground, and as I bought the place in the beginning of May, I could only plow a little, the balance I sowed on the old stubble for the fifth year. The grain came up well, but soon rose bushes and weeds covered all of it; the grain at that time was about five inches [twelve and a half centimetres] high, the weeds ten inches [twenty-five centimetres]. I set the mower to work and cut the whole clean to the ground. My neighbors were laughing at my proceeding, but when I threshed I got fifty bushels of oats to the Acre [seven cubic metres to the hectare]. Since then I have farmed every year from one hundred to one hundred and twenty acres [forty to forty-eight hectares] and had never any less than seventy bushels of oats to the acre [10 cubic metres to the hectare].

I have so far only spoken of oats, but do not mean that this is the only crop grown here; in fact, I have seen splendid fields of spring wheat yielding fifty bushels No. 1 to the acre; also barley has proven a great crop, as it has yielded between forty to fifty bushels to the acre. The best of all this country is good for is fall wheat. I have watched my neighbors for the last four years raising fall wheat, and came to the conclusion that this is the crop for the future. This fall I have sown forty acres [sixteen hectares] and have made preparations to sow three hundred acres [one hundred and twenty hectares] next fall. This may sound big, but I will only show my confidence in wheat growing. I may state that my farm today consists of six hundred and forty acres [two hundred and fifty-six hectares] of land, with buildings worth six thousand dollars. I keep now, over one hundred head of cattle, thirty head of mostly Clyde horses. I intended to sell this place, and asked fifteen thousand dollars. I was offered fourteen thousand by Mr. Henderson, of Sarnia, Ont., but would not let it go. Besides this farm, I own another six hundred and forty acres of land and considerable town property, and feel satisfied with my earnings for the last ten years.

Most immigrants settled on homesteads, but town life in the West was also becoming lively and attractive. Winnipeg was the largest western city, as it was the point from which all homesteaders began their voyage west. Here is a description of Winnipeg in the 1880s:

. . . Of course the city was pretty rapid, with lots to drink and plenty to gamble and horse racing galore and similar sports were the rage. With dances, operas, swagger champagne suppers, and late hours, it was one continuous merry round. But gay life in Winnipeg was grossly exaggerated, because it was a comparatively small place, running speedily ahead of other places of even larger size in its daily round of gaiety. Hideous crime itself . . . was totally unknown. There was scarcely even a murder or a shooting scrap and very few scandals. . . . The police regulations were usually strictly enforced, and, while the bars were kept open until all hours of the night, the liquor was of a good quality, and there were fewer drunken people staggering on the streets than could be seen in other places which made greater pretensions of a monopoly of all the virtues. The police records prove this. So while it was called wicked, it held no real genuine carnival of crime. It was simply a wide open frontier outpost of civilization.

Inside an immigrant home. Not all immigrants picked up homesteads in the West. Many remained in cities and had to work very hard just to survive. Sometimes a whole family lived in a single small room which served as kitchen, living room, and bedroom. This picture is of an immigrant slum house in Winnipeg. To make ends meet, the women usually took in laundry or mended clothes.

Despite the improvements, the growth of the West continued to be very discouraging to the Canadian government. In 1896, homestead applications reached their lowest point in many years. It was then that Sir Wilfrid Laurier, the Prime Minister of Canada, took action. He appointed Clifford Sifton, a Westerner, as Minister of the Interior in charge of immigration. Over the next fifteen years, Sifton organized the biggest campaign in Canadian history to attract settlers. He began sending out pamphlets to Europe and the United States, encouraging immigration to Canada.

COMMENCING A PRAIRIE FARM IN MANITOBA

A PRAIRIE FARM IN MANITOBA AFTER THREE YEARS

Poster showing the kind of progress made on a Western homestead after three years' work. What kind of shelter did the settlers have the first year? From what you know of the work required to clear a farm, and the kinds of houses built, do you think this poster is realistic? What would be the purpose of circulating it?

Homestead land in the United States was quickly running out. In order to give everyone an equal chance at the available lots, land rushes were held. In wagons, on horseback, and in carts, thousands of people charged from a set starting point to be the first to get to the free land. Whenever land rushes were held, such as the Oklahoma rush of 1901, the Canadian government set up tents advertising free land to the north. Americans not fortunate enough to find land in the U.S. West began to think about Canada.

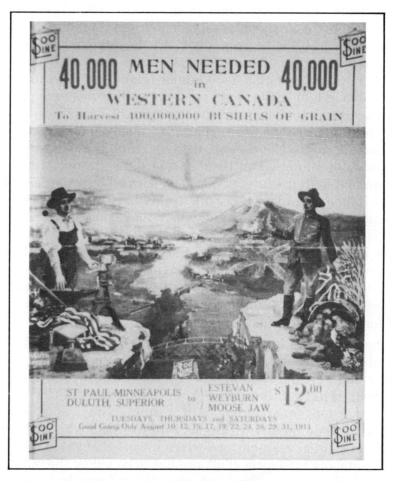

Other methods were also used. Sifton describes his own policies:

> . . . In those days settlers were sought from three sources; one was the United States. The American settlers did not need sifting; they were of the finest quality and the most desirable settlers. In Great Britain we confined our efforts very largely to the North of England and Scotland, and for the purpose of sifting the settlers we doubled the bonuses to the agents in the North of England, and cut them down as

much as possible in the South. The result was that we got a fairly steady stream of people from the North of England and from Scotland and they were the very best settlers in the world. I do not wish to suggest that we did not get many very excellent people from the more southerly portions of England, but they were people who came on their own initiative largely, which was the best possible guarantee of success.

Our work was largely done in the North. Then, came the continent—where the great emigration center was Hamburg. Steamships go there to load up with people who are desirous of leaving Europe. The situation is a peculiar one. If one should examine twenty people who turn up at Hamburg to emigrate he might find one escaped murderer, three or four wasters and ne'er-do-wells, some very poor shopkeepers, artisans or laborers and there might be one or two stout, hardy peasants in sheep-skin coats. Obviously the peasants are the men that are wanted here. Now, with regard to these twenty men, no one knows anything about them except the shipping agents. These men are sent in from outlying local agencies all over Europe. They arrive at Hamburg and the booking agents have their names and full descriptions of who they are and where they come from. No one else has this information.

We made an arrangement with the booking agencies in Hamburg, under which they winnowed out this flood of people, picked out the agriculturalists and peasants and sent them to Canada, sending nobody else. We paid, I think, $5 per head for the farmer and $2 per head for the other members of the family. . . .

When I speak of quality I have in mind, I think, something that is quite different from what is in the mind of the average writer or speaker upon the question of Immigration. I think a stalwart peasant in a sheep-skin coat, born on the soil, whose forefathers have been farmers for ten generations, with a stout wife and a half-dozen children, is good quality. A Trades Union artisan who will not work more than eight hours a day and will not work that long if he can help it, will not work on a farm at all and has to be fed by the public when work is slack is, in my judgment, quantity and very bad quality. I am indifferent as to whether or not he is British born. It matters not what his nationality is; such men are not wanted in Canada and the more of them we get the more trouble we shall have. . . .

1. *According to Sifton, from which countries did the finest settlers come?*

2. *What type of man was Sifton seeking?*

3. *Why were artisans not desired?*

Here is an example of land advertising, a Canadian government pamphlet of 1909:

So successful were these methods that almost ninety thousand Americans came to Canada in the period 1899-1901. Between 1897-1914, the number reached one million. Some Canadians were alarmed at such a large influx and newspapers in the East warned of an "American invasion".

The Law Moves West

A hundred years ago there was no law in western Canada. In the vast prairie grasslands between Manitoba and the Rockies there were hardly more than 30 000 people, most of them Indians living on the rapidly diminishing buffalo herds. Save for a few honest settlers and missionaries the white men were ruffians; sharp traders pushing whisky among the Indians, horse-thieves and outlaws from Montana—all the elements for an era as vicious and violent as the American Wild West.

Canada's story was different due in part to a band of young men who were steadfast and persevering almost beyond belief. The Canadian Mounties have become a legend. . . . No police force in the world commands greater respect and admiration.

The beginning of the Force was an epic thousand-mile [sixteen hundred kilometres] march across the unmarked plains by 318 scarlet-coated horsemen, none of whom had seen the territory before. Part of their assignment was to find a gang of Montana renegades who had massacred a band of innocent Assiniboine Indians in the Cypress Hills. To those drunken horse traders, killing an Indian was sport; they murdered all but a few terrified women and left the chief's head impaled on a post. The grisly episode brought an outcry from missionaries and honest traders, and hastened the organization of the North West Mounted Police.

The Mounties' destination was Fort Whoop-Up . . . on the Oldman River about eight miles upstream from today's Lethbridge. Their orders were to round up the killers, suppress the whisky traffic, protect the Indians and collect customs duties along the newly-marked international boundary.

But they did something more significant. The opening of the American West was marked by bitter and bloody Indian wars. In Canada, during the first five years of NWMP administration, not one Indian or policeman died at the hand of the other.

With a combination of integrity, courtesy and raw nerve this unique company of men upheld the law, won the respect of the Indians and made agricultural settlement possible. Their heritage is a saga that can still be read in the old forts and cairns that mark their adventures in Western Canada. It all began at Lower Fort Garry, the Stone Fort that still stands on the west bank of the Red River, 20 miles [32 km] north of Winnipeg. The fort was built by George Simpson, governor of the Hudson's Bay Company in 1831. The Big House where Simpson lived still stands; so do two stone three-storey warehouses.

It was to this fort that the first small band of recruits came on Oct. 22, 1873. Here was the real birthplace of the North West Mounted Police—here, on November 3, 1873, the Oath of Office was administered to 150 men. . . .

. . . On June 7, 1874 the NWMP arranged in three troops of 50 men, left the Stone Fort and rode 63 miles [100 km] south to Fort Dufferin, the departure point for their march west . . . it was a convenient place for the Force to await the return of Commissioner George Arthur French, who was bringing 150 new men from Toronto. . . .

The newcomers arrived on June 19 and pitched their tents near the Boundary Commission quarters. A few hours later there was a terrific thunderstorm and the horses stampeded. Troop Sergeant Sam Steele, who became superintendent in 1883, wrote: 'A thunderbolt fell . . . Terrified, the animals broke their fastenings. The six men on guard were trampled . . . the maddened beasts overturned huge wagons . . . dashed through a row of tents. Crazed with fright, the majority were 30 to 50 miles [48 to 80 km] into Dakota before compelled by sheer exhaustion to halt.' All the horses were recovered, but the Force lost several precious days.

In the late afternoon of July 8, bugles sounded and six shining divisions cantered into place. The great trek was about to begin. . . .

The going was heavy. A diary record for July 13, the fifth day, notes: Marched at 5 a.m. [05:00]. Many delays owing to parts and wagons breaking down. Travelled till eight in the evening. Distance from Dufferin 59 mi. [94 km]

French return to Dufferin with 'D' troop in December, leaving the other five scattered across the plains. He reported to Ottawa. 'These men gave little cause for complaint . . . working at high pressure during four months from daylight to dark. Horses failing and dying never stopped them. . . . We left with the thermometer at 95 to 100 degrees, returned with the thermometer at -20 to -30 [-28 to $-34°$ C] having marched 1959 miles [3134 km] without a single loss of life or limb. . . .

. . . On June 30, 1882 the site of the present city of Regina—then called Pile o' Bones—was chosen as the capital of the Northwest Territories. A week or so later Commissioner A. G. Irvine received orders to erect the NWMP headquarters there also.

For 38 years Regina was the base of this growing Force and it is still a major training centre. In 1920 headquarters was moved to Ottawa and the Force's name changed to Royal Canadian Mounted Police. . . .

'Only a poet could do justice to the site,' recorded a young constable after 'F' division pitched its tents one August day in 1875 in the angle between the Bow and the Elbow rivers, where the city of Calgary now stands.

Although it began as a police post and was named by Macleod, all that marks Fort Calgary today is a boulder at the corner of Sixth Street and Ninth Avenue SE.

One of the most exciting episodes in the police story was played out here. In 1879 the Sarcees—a branch of the Blackfoot confederacy—were destitute, as the Sioux had been at Wood Mountain. Goaded by hunger, 400 Indians descended on the fort demanding meat. The commanding officer, C. E. Denny, was away at Fort Macleod; four Mounties held the post. One rode furiously to get Denny, and the inspector and 10 police galloped back. Fortunately no blood had been shed. Denny went straight to the chief. 'Go to Macleod,' he said. 'You'll get beef there.' But the Indians stayed.

Two days later Denny delivered an ultimatum: 'Move tomorrow by this time or I'll move you,' he ordered.

At the specified hour Inspector Denny and a sergeant, flanked by 13 armed police, walked into the camp. The constables stood in a quiet line while Denny and his assistant calmly took down teepees. The Indians raved but Denny kept steadily on. He said nothing and no shots were fired, but slowly the Indians began to load up. By noon the entire tribe was on the march.

Only Denny's coolness and, in his own words, 'bluff and the grace of God' had prevented a massacre. . . .

One of the most heart-breaking episodes in the history of the Canadian West took place at Wood Mountain, a one-time Boundary Commission post that Commissioner French bought along with the depot, two corrals and eight tons [seven tonnes] of hay for the horses for $100 in 1874.

Wood Mountain was in Cree and Assiniboine country but it was the Sioux who made it famous. In 1876 Chief Sitting Bull's braves from Montana annihilated Custer's army and many Indians fled north. By December, nearly 3000 were camped near the post.

Inspector James Walsh confronted them: 'Only if they obeyed the Great White Mother's laws could they stay.' His attitude was friendly but firm and during the winter Sioux and police learned mutual respect.

A year later Sitting Bull himself arrived with more Indians. His first encounter with Walsh was dramatic. 'Yesterday,' the chief said, 'I was fleeing from the white man, cursing them . . . The White

Forehead Chief walks into my lodge alone and unarmed. He gives me the hand of peace.' That night Inspector Walsh slept peacefully in the Sioux camp.

By 1880 the buffalo had almost disappeared. Ottawa, its hands full caring for starving Crees and Assiniboines, refused to take on the Sioux. The United States had agreed to accept them back, but Sitting Bull refused to go.

The Mounties did what they could for the refugees. Walsh wrote: 'The conduct of these destitute people would reflect credit on the most civilized community.' He continually urged their return south. Finally hunger accomplished what words couldn't. A broken Sitting Bull sent this message ahead. 'Once I was strong and brave. (Now) my women are sick and my children freezing. My arrows are broken and I have thrown my warpaint to the winds.' He returned to the U.S. in 1881, became involved in another uprising and was killed in an attempted arrest in 1890. . . .

The earliest of the NWMP posts is Fort Macleod, built in 1874, 33 miles [51 km] northwest of Lethbridge. It is only 21 miles [34 km] from the site of Whoop-Up, the destination of the Mounties' long march. Whoop-Up was reached on October 18, 1874. . . .

This was Blackfoot country, a four-tribe confederacy ruled by Chief Crowfoot. Macleod's task was to enforce the law . . . establishing firm and cordial relations by consistent fair-dealing.

During the winter of 1876-77 Macleod, now commissioner, was instructed to negotiate terms for a Government-Blackfoot Treaty. It was signed Sept. 22. At the ceremonies Crowfoot praised the Force in these words: 'If the police had not come to this country, where would we be now? Bad men and whisky were killing us. The Mounted Police have protected us as the feathers of a bird protect it from the frosts of winter. I will sign.'

People Who Came

By far the greatest number of settlers were from England and the rest of Europe. This group included the first really large number of immigrants to come to Canada from non-English-speaking countries. It was also this wave of immigrants which would help sketch the outlines for our cultural mosaic of today. The West benefited most by this migration, but every province in Canada gained new settlers.

In order to achieve this goal Sifton worked very hard. His agents were at work everywhere in Europe. To poor peasants in Europe the offer of free land was hard to resist. To a religious group called the Mennonites, Sifton even promised their own schools in Canada, and also freedom from military service.

The Mennonites do not believe in war or violence as solutions to problems. They try to live by the words of the Bible. Why might they be attracted by Sifton's offer?

The response was astounding. Settlers came from Germany, Russia, the Ukraine, Poland, Italy, Austria-Hungary—over a million people from more than thirty different countries. Certain religious groups also made their way to the West at this time, such as the Doukhobors, Mennonites, and Jews from Russia.

English Immigrants, Quebec, P.Q., c. 1911.

Doukhobor women pulling a plough, Thunder Hill Colony (Man.) 1899. Without horses or cattle, very little could be done. When new villages were built, horses were used to haul logs. Often, to let the animals rest, human beings would hitch themselves to the plough.

Sikh workers c. 1900. Many immigrants came to Canada from non-European countries. Sometimes it was possible to tell where immigrants came from by their clothing. What is the homeland of the people in this picture?

Russian Jews and Poles. *From photographs in the Public Archives of Canada.*

The Ukrainians Among the most significant groups of settlers to migrate to the West were the Ukrainians. Between 1891 and 1914, about one hundred and eighty thousand people from the Ukraine came to Canada. Why did they come?

In the nineteenth century, the Ukraine was divided between two empires, those of Russia and of Austria-Hungary. Under foreign rule, many Ukrainians were subjected to political and economic discrimination. At the same time, several parts of the Ukraine suffered from overpopulation and scarcity of land. It seemed the only way to escape poverty was to emigrate. In the 1890s Canada was offering sixty-four hectares of farm land for only $10.00. This offered great hope to those who loved to farm, but were too poor to own their own land in the Ukraine.

The Ukrainian immigrants tended to settle in the northern parts of Manitoba, Saskatchewan, and Alberta. Here the land was wooded, and reminded them of the land back home. The flat prairie land to the south was not as attractive to them.

As farming people, the Ukrainians did not face as many difficulties as other immigrants with no farming background. Their experience proved very beneficial for Canada. The Ukrainian settlers alone were able to farm over four hundred thousand hectares of land.

The Ukraine also contributed to the development of Canada's famous Marquis wheat. Three Ukrainian wheat strains, Red Fife, Turkey Red, and Kabanka, were the ancestors of Marquis and other Canadian wheats.

Like other settlers in the West, the first Ukrainian immigrants suffered great hardships. The winter temperatures in the prairies were colder than they had ever known and the summer heat at times was unbearable. Swarms of mosquitoes and black flies, poor soil, lack of money, supplies, and medical care, and finally, loneliness, made survival very difficult.

Yet more and more Ukrainians flocked to the West. Naturally, as strangers in a foreign land they wished to be among their own kind. The result was a series of Ukrainian bloc settlements. The map below shows how these bloc settlements were clustered in Alberta. Note how many of the names are of Ukrainian origin.

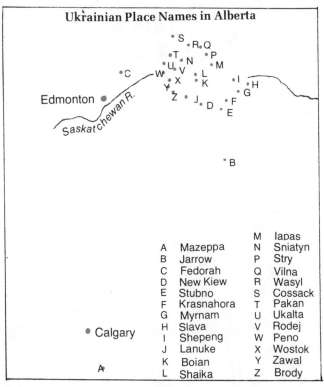

Ukrainian Place Names in Alberta

A	Mazeppa	M	Iapas
B	Jarrow	N	Sniatyn
C	Fedorah	P	Stry
D	New Kiew	Q	Vilna
E	Stubno	R	Wasyl
F	Krasnahora	S	Cossack
G	Myrnam	T	Pakan
H	Slava	U	Ukalta
I	Shepeng	V	Rodej
J	Lanuke	W	Peno
K	Boian	X	Wostok
L	Shaika	Y	Zawal
		Z	Brody

Andrzej Petelski family, Benito, Man., c. 1931.

The bloc settlements let Ukrainians continue to practice their own language, religion, and social customs. This helped to produce a truly Ukrainian Canadian identity. The bloc settlements were described in this way by one observer:

> Each settlement is a little Ukraine in which anything of a foreign nature rarely intervenes to mar the even tenor of their ways. For miles one may ride and see nothing but thatch-roof houses . . . hear nothing but Ukrainian from the adult members of the settlements; feel nothing but a sense of strangeness which even time has not altered for Anglo-Saxons long resident in the districts. "We are the foreigners here," one said to us, and the remark serves to emphasize the solidarity and oneness of the rural Ukrainian colonies in the Canadian West.

One visitor described a Ukrainian farm in this way:

> The main building was a combination home-barn structure that housed all the farm stock, cattle, hogs and chickens in one end, with a large room in the other for the family. . . . At one end of the room there was one of those large home-built continental stoves, that had a small fireplace but an extensive platform surrounding it on which the family slept. At the other end of the room there was a large table. . . . The building was of logs, plastered inside and out with the usual mixture of clay and straw, and the same material furnished the floor. Overall the building was topped with a thatched roof.

The Prairie Population

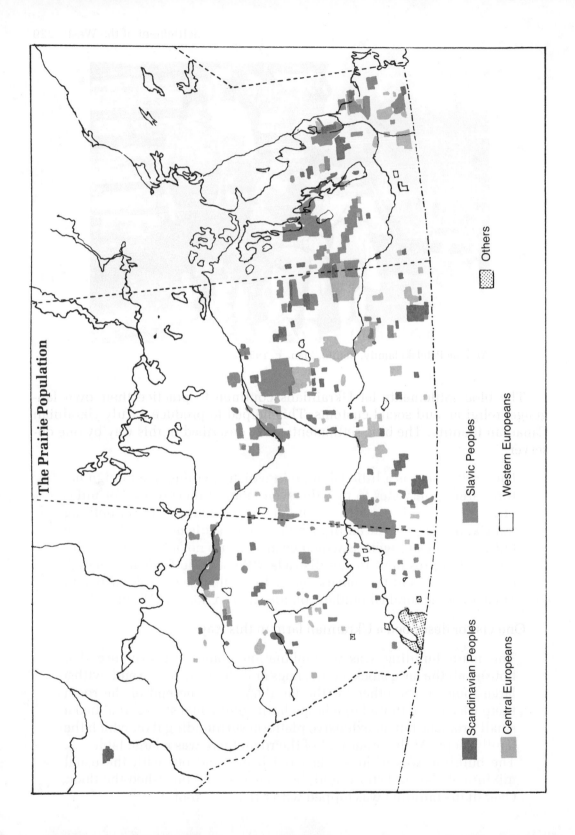

Scandinavian Peoples

Central Europeans

Slavic Peoples

Western Europeans

Others

1. *Can you detect any pattern to the settlement of the West according to this map?*

2. *Which ethnic groups came to the West in largest numbers? Rank them according to size.*

This wave of non-English peoples caused prejudice to surface in some parts of Canada. Typical of this attitude was the following speech by a Rev. W. D. Reid:

> Canada today faces the greatest immigration problem that has ever confronted any nation. . . . Of the Anglo-Saxon we are not in the least afraid, but when we consider that last year over twenty-one per cent of all the incomers to Canada were non-Anglo-Saxon, who can not speak our language, have no sympathy with our ideals, and are foreigners in every sense of the term, then we begin to understand what a task is ours as a nation. One man out of every five who lands on our shores is a foreigner. He comes here with a foreign tongue, foreign ideals, foreign religion, . . . with centuries of ignorance and oppression behind him, often bringing with him problems that the best statesmen of Europe have failed to solve. . . .
>
> . . . A very large percentage of them are absolutely illiterate. From northern Italy only fourteen out of every hundred . . . can either read or write. From southern Italy fifty-six out of every hundred are illiterate. The illiteracy of the Russian Jew runs about twenty-three per cent, and he is perhaps the hardest of all to assimilate. He is industrious, hard-working and sober, but from the viewpoint of national digestion is like Jonah of old, still indigestible.
>
> All authorities agree that intemperance is the great curse of the Slav wherever you find him. In a land like Canada, where we shall have to fight for our very existence, surely, if we are wise in this crisis, we will abolish liquor from our land altogether and give this foreigner a chance, when he comes to his new environment.

1. *What problems caused by immigration does the speaker foresee for Canada's future?*

2. *Do you remember what prejudice is? Do you think this writer is prejudiced? Why might English Canadians feel this way toward immigrants? Is this feeling still present today?*

3. *Write a reply to Rev. Reid, giving your thoughts about the immigrants. Compare your letter with the following. It is Sifton's defense of the Doukhobors:*

> . . . First respecting the Doukhobors, there is nothing in reality in the charge that special advantages have been given to the Doukhobors. As stated the cost of getting these people to Canada was $7.47 per head. British immigrants cost us vastly more than that; although

we do not pay that amount as a bonus the entire expenses of the propaganda in Great Britain have to be taken into consideration. These are the cheapest immigrants that ever came to Canada in large numbers. As to special privileges; the feed, grain, stock and agricultural implements that were furnished were furnished by their friends and not by the Government, except in some trifling cases, and whatever was advanced has been paid back. A reserve was made and a certain time allowed for the performance of homestead duties and payment of fees on condition of the people taking up their residence there and doing substantial improvements. There is not one of these inducements that would not be given in the case of any large body of desirable settlers from any other part of the world. The cry against the Doukhobors and Galacians [Ukrainians] is the most absolutely ignorant and absurd thing that I have ever known in political life. There is simply no question in regard to the advantage of these people, and I do not think there is anyone in the North-west who is so stupid as not to know it—even the Editor of the Telegram.

The policy adopted of exciting racial prejudice is the most contemptible possible policy because it is one that does not depend upon reason. . . .

1. What arguments does Sifton have in defence of the Doukhobors?
2. Why, in his opinion, has there been opposition to this group?
3. Find out more about the Doukhobors. What is their position in Canada today?

Homestead Life

Since much of this immigration took place at the beginning of our present century, it is probably natural to think that settlers had a much easier time of it than the pioneers before them. We should remember that many of the inventions of transportation, communications, and farming equipment are very recent. Those who took up homesteads in the West at this time had to battle poor roads, bad communications, harsh weather, and crop failures much as people a century before them did. Although it is true that the railway was in operation by 1900, new settlers in the West still had a very difficult time. Let us follow the growth of Jack Stokoe's homestead over a ten-year period.

Stettler, Alta
31/5/09

Dear Father,

... I have filed on NW 1/4 24-33-2 W4 and the NE 1/4 23-33-2 and am waiting for my receipts from Calgary.

I have bought a team of oxen, 6 years old weighing 1800 each, a wagon and plow, tent, stove, cooking outfit, hardware, etc. and am going out to my land as soon as I can get away. I want to get a few acres broken for crop next Spring if I can. Very few people I notice get any land plowed first year as they are generally hauling lumber and putting up buildings etc. when they first go out and the plowing season is over before they are ready. They generally have to haul oats and hay 30 or 40 miles and pay exorbitant prices for it at that. ... I also bought a tent 10 × 12 (3 ft. wall) for $10 so as to save the necessity of buying and hauling lumber and building material till after plowing season when I will have more time and better roads.

... When I got out to 5 I found the land comparatively no good, too rough and hilly so I went on through 4 and 3 which were the same. Of course the railway survey goes right through so the land will be taken up some day. It wasn't till I got into 2 that I struck some fine land sloping down from the hills so I picked out the best sections and figured I was 140 miles out by trail. I struck for Stettler and made it in 4-1/2 days walking right through every day from breakfast till supper (8 or 9 o'clock) without dinner. I hadn't time to stop at midday the trail was fierce for walking and the last two days it rained to beat four of a kind. I was just 1/2 a day slower than a team of horses. When I was out in 2 I was miles from anybody and I went from breakfast one morning till 4:30 next afternoon (32 hours) without anything to eat and I slept on the prairie with nothing extra over me but a raincoat. I had to get up at 3:30 in the morning and start walking, it was too cold and damp to sleep. ... I walked well over 300 miles as I was running all over looking at land. ... The land out in my Township is almost all taken up already. I had some trouble getting land after my long walk. Some people were ahead of me filing at Calgary. But I got a good place. ... By the time I get out there I will have some neighbours I guess. ...

Yours affectionately,
Jack

Dear Father,

I am on my homestead at last. I put up my tent yesterday afternoon and got everything nicely under cover when it commenced to rain—it is raining yet, coming down to beat four of a kind. The tent stands it all right only nothing must be allowed to touch the sides or it draws water in. That is one drawback to a tent: another is, there are no nails to hang things on. Apart from these two drawbacks a tent is a first rate thing to live in, it is eminently healthy and well lighted and ventilated. I have four pairs of blankets and a good quilt, so I am pretty well off as regards shelter. . . .

. . . I will have lots of neighbours soon. Mr. and Mrs. Weber will be residing here in two weeks time. They farmed 800 acres in Dakota and are very well off, they will work a large outfit. . . .

I had a great time getting out here. I left Stettler on Monday night about 5 o'clock and pulled a few miles out of town before dark. I led the way with my bull team. . . . But the weather got unbearably hot and the bulls would pant and loll their tongues just like a couple of dogs so I realized there was nothing else for it but to . . . travel the cattle at night. . . .

. . . I found that oxen travelled much more easily at night, they don't get out of breath so much nor did the flies bother them. They averaged 2 miles an hour travelling at night and 1-1/2 during the day. . . .

I set up my new stove yesterday, it seems to be all right, although I haven't tried the oven yet. If I get one load of wood home it will do till fall. . . .

This rain will make the plow go easy. I will start in right away as soon as I get back from the bush: it is a pity I can't get a little bit of fuel closer, to last me till plowing is done.

Yours affectionately,
Jack

8/8/09

. . . I got 10 acres broken before I lost my oxen and it has been too dry to plow since I got them again. 10 acres is enough for just now in case the CPR is not through as soon as expected. . . . There was a small bluff of poplars West of here which I thought I would have for fuel so I struck off at 8 o'clock last Friday morning and was back at night with a big load; it was 13 miles each way and the wood was all standing and had to be chopped. I went back on Monday and cleared the bluff out and have quite a lot of fuel home now. I made a hayrack out of the poles and am using it now.

I commenced to dig a well and went down 12 feet through solid clay and then it got too deep for me to pitch out of so I quit and sent to the store for a pulley wheel which arrived last night so I will rig up shear legs and dig the rest of the way into a bucket and haul it up. I kept it 5 feet wide to give me room to work. I expect to hit water at 20 feet. I have a shallow well 5 feet deep that will do me a while but it will be no good after frost comes, it will freeze solid. . . .

There will be quite a few people out here this fall, at present there are six homesteaders here and a lot of land is taken up upon which entry must be made this fall or it will open for cancellation. In fact there are only one or two sections left open around here that are any good. . . .

Wilhelmina, Macklin P.O.
Sask.
8/10/10

Dear Father,

I am at home again for a day or two. I have been out working at Robinson's building a stable. I put in a week cutting flax for him too, and I have also made a trip to the bush. I intend starting out on Monday again for another load of wood: I will probably be away till Wednesday evening. I am only at home once in a while these days. . . .

I traded off my oxen for another horse away back in June, I still have the pony and have been working him with the other two horses right along. There is one of my neighbours out here wanting to buy him so I may sell. I have earned $85.00 this last few weeks with my horses, a thing I could never have done with oxen. . . .

Robinson has 85 names on his list now for whom he hauls the mail: when I came in here last spring he had only 22 names.

My shack is 12 × 16 with an 8 × 8 cellar 6 ft. deep. I will send you a photograph of it when I get it tidied up. I haven't got the dirt hauled away yet that came out of the cellar. The stable is 14 × 20 and will hold 5 head of stock (I only have 3 at present.)

Give my regards to all.

Yours affectionately,
Jack

Wilhelmina P.O., Alta
10/12/11

Dear Father,

. . . There is quite a large population here this Winter and things are humming. There is a dance about every Friday night and card parties, etc. galore. We intend having a Social between Xmas and New Year to help pay for the school house organ.

I am busy digging another well for Robinson, the storekeeper. . . . I am now 24 feet down and getting a dollar a foot. . . . I have hauled quite a number of loads of freight from Macklin this fall. I got four loads out in two weeks and made $65.00 out of it.

. . . The school work keeps me busy just now, I am preparing the assessment roll and sending out tax notices, etc. at present. . . . The tax this year to raise revenue to carry us through till next December will be 7 cents per acre. . . .

Yours affectionately,
Jack

---

1. What problems did Jack Stokoe have in choosing his homestead?
2. What do you think were his greatest difficulties in the first few years?
3. What evidence is there that Jack's homestead was prosperous?
4. Can you find any evidence of social life in the West at this time?

The Result of the Struggle

Immigration finally slowed down with the outbreak of the Great War in 1914. How successful had Sifton's policies been? The results can be measured in these statistics:

Number of Homestead Entries, 1874-1930

Year	Number of Entries	Year	Number of Entries	Year	Number of Entries
1874	1 376	1893	4 067	1912	39 151
1875	499	1894	3 209	1913	33 699
1876	347	1895	2 394	1914	31 829
1877	845	1896	1 857	1915	24 088
1878	1788	1897	2 384	1916	17 030
1879	4068	1898	4 848	1917	11 199
1880	2074	1899	6 689	1918	8 319
1881	2753	1900	7 426	1919	4 227
1882	7483	1901	8 167	1920	6 732
1883	6063	1902	14 633	1921	5 389
1884	3753	1903	31 383	1922	7 349
1885	1858	1904	26 073	1923	5 343
1886	2657	1905	30 891	1924	3 843
1887	2036	1906	41 869	1925	3 653
1888	2655	1907	21 647	1926	4 685
1889	4416	1908	30 424	1927	5 760
1890	2955	1909	39 081	1928	7 233
1891	3523	1910	41 568	1929	16 157
1892	4840	1911	44 479	1930	17 504

Population of the Prairies

Year	Manitoba	Saskatchewan	Alberta	Total
1871	25 288	48 000		73 228
1891	152 506	98 967		251 473
1901	255 211	91 279	73 022	419 502
1911	461 394	492 432	374 295	1 328 121
1921	610 118	757 510	588 454	1 956 082
1931	700 139	921 785	731 605	2 353 529

The high point of the long, slow, often difficult period of settling of the West came in 1905. In that year Alberta and Saskatchewan joined Confederation as new provinces. Canada was now truly a nation from coast to coast. It was also now a nation with more than two cultures. The new immigrants brought along different cultures and many chose to preserve customs and traditions of their homelands. The new nation was well on the road to developing its own identity. An important part of the Canadian identity would be its mosaic of cultures.

Word Study

Galicians	Marquis Wheat	men in sheepskin coats
quarter-section	Doukhobors	C.P.R.
sod bricks	Mennonites	soddies
Red Fife		

Things to Do 1. The Canadian Wagon Train left Toronto on April 1, 1975, bound for the Peace River district of Alberta. Newspapers carried almost daily stories of the trip. Check back issues of your local newspaper to discover what happened. What difficulties did the wagon train meet? Would a wagon train in 1875 have had similar problems?

2. At its completion in 1885, the Canadian Pacific Railway was the longest railroad in the world. It was also very significant in determining the pattern of settlement in the West. The railroad cut down on the time, costs, and hazards of travel west.

   With the aid of your teacher and librarian, gather information on some of the men who helped build the C.P.R. Some of the most important individuals were Sir Hugh Allan, William Van Horne, and Donald Smith. Two books which will be very useful for your research are The National Dream and The Last Spike by Pierre Berton.

3. Should the C.P.R. have been built? Set up a debate on the C.P.R. from the point of view of:
—a settler
—an Indian
—the North West Mounted Police
—a conservationist
—a taxpayer in the East
—a manufacturer in British Columbia

4. Compare pioneer life in the West in the 1880s with that of New France in 1700 and Upper Canada in 1800. Think about transportation, entertainment, climate, makeup of ethnic groups, enemies, suitability of soil, patterns of settlement.

5. In the past wheat was the West's main product. Today, the West provides most of Canada's oil, natural gas, and beef. Within a few years these resources may be depleted. What efforts have been made by the Federal and Provincial Governments of Canada to develop new resources in the West?

5
Immigration Today

You have seen the words "bilingualism" and "biculturalism" earlier in this unit. A word Canadians are hearing more often today is "multiculturalism". This is the idea that each ethnic group in Canada should be encouraged to keep and develop its own heritage. It recognizes the fact that Canada is a "cultural mosaic". Have you ever seen a mosaic? It is a picture made up of hundreds of pieces of coloured stone. All the pieces are part of the same picture, yet each retains its separate quality. In the same way Canada's society is made up of many groups. It is Canada's policy to allow each group to retain its identity.

The U.S. has been described as a "melting pot". How is a "mosaic" different from a "melting pot"?

As you have seen in this unit, Canada was settled by people with many different cultures. Many Canadians describe themselves with two terms. Jane is an "English Canadian", Henri is a "French Canadian", Hans is a "German Canadian", Maria is an "Italian Canadian". Today, most of us use these terms with no prejudice. Yet it was not long ago that an immigrant might be told, "Stop talking in that dirty foreign language. This is an English-speaking country." In schools, immigrant children were often ridiculed and made to feel ashamed because of their customs and manners.

The policy of multiculturalism recognizes that Canada was built and continues to grow by the contributions of people with many different heritages. Newcomers should be encouraged to keep elements of the culture of their homelands and share them with other Canadians. Certainly, in order to feel 'at home' in Canada immigrants will want to learn English or French and adjust to many of our customs and ways. This is not always easy. Imagine how you might feel if your family chose to move to another country where the language and customs were very different from those you know. The government of Pierre Trudeau summed up its policy on multiculturalism in this way:

It's a matter of freedom really. We can't tell people coming to this country to adapt to the culture of the Scots or the English or the Irish. We can't tell the blacks to become white or the white to adopt the Indian or Inuit culture . . . multiculturalism simply recognizes that fact.

In this chapter we will be looking at immigration today.

—Where have the immigrants come from?
—How many have chosen Canada as their home?
—Where are the immigrants settling?
—What problems are they facing in adjusting to a new way of life?
—What is the future immigration policy in Canada?

The Importance of Immigration   Canada is still growing through immigration. Since 1867, the year of Confederation, over ten million immigrants have made Canada their home. Four million have come since 1945. It is hard to imagine what Canada would be like today without the large-scale immigration of the past.

The effect it has had on the economic, social, and political life of Canada has been tremendous. Canada today is one of the world's leading industrial nations. It is also one of the world's largest food producers. The standard of living of its citizens is among the very highest in the world. Of course, this great prosperity is largely due to the wealth in land and natural resources of this country. Yet without the hard work of settlers from the time of Champlain until the present, this wealth might still be untapped.

The patterns of immigration in the past, and the importance immigration will have on Canada's future, are easily seen in the charts and statistics which follow.

For many years the economy of the West was based on wheat and cattle. This photograph shows a new industry, which will be very important in the future, for all of Canada. Where have large oil deposits been discovered in the West?

Immigration since 1867

Since its discovery, Canada has attracted immigrants from many lands. The number of newcomers has been rising since Confederation. However the rate of immigration has not been steady. Examine the following statistics carefully:

Immigration to Canada by Calendar Year, 1852-1971

1852	29 307	1882	112 458	1912	375 756	1942	7 576
1853	29 464	1883	133 624	1913	400 870	1943	8 504
1854	37 263	1884	103 824	1914	150 484	1944	12 801
1855	25 296	1885	79 169	1915	36 665	1945	22 722
1856	22 544	1886	69 152	1916	55 914	1946	71 719
1857	33 854	1887	84 526	1917	72 910	1947	64 127
1858	12 339	1888	88 766	1918	41 845	1948	125 414
1859	6 300	1889	91 600	1919	107 698	1949	95 217
1860	6 276	1890	75 067	1920	138 824	1950	73 912
1861	13 589	1891	82 165	1921	91 728	1951	194 391
1862	18 294	1892	30 996	1922	64 224	1952	164 498
1863	21 000	1893	29 633	1923	133 729	1953	168 868
1864	24 779	1894	20 829	1924	124 164	1954	154 227
1865	18 958	1895	18 790	1925	84 907	1955	109 946
1866	11 427	1896	16 835	1926	135 982	1956	164 857
1867	10 666	1897	21 716	1927	158 886	1957	282 164
1868	12 765	1898	31 900	1928	166 783	1958	124 851
1869	18 630	1899	44 543	1929	164 993	1959	106 928
1870	24 706	1900	41 681	1930	104 806	1960	104 111
1871	27 773	1901	55 747	1931	27 530	1961	71 689
1872	36 578	1902	89 102	1932	20 591	1962	74 586
1873	50 050	1903	138 660	1933	14 382	1963	93 151
1874	39 373	1904	131 252	1934	12 476	1964	112 606
1875	27 382	1905	141 465	1935	11 277	1965	146 758
1876	25 633	1906	211 653	1936	11 643	1966	194 743
1877	27 082	1907	272 409	1937	15 101	1967	222 876
1878	29 807	1908	143 326	1938	17 244	1968	183 974
1879	40 492	1909	173 694	1939	16 994	1969	161 531
1880	38 505	1910	286 839	1940	11 324	1970	147 713
1881	47 991	1911	331 288	1941	9 329	1971	121 900

1. *Using these figures, make a graph showing the pattern of immigration between the years 1867 and 1971.*
2. *In what year did immigration reach its highest peak in Canada? What year was the low point?*
3. *What periods seem to have had most immigration? What periods* had least? Find out what policies or events might explain these differences. Did people immigrate in these periods because of conditions in Canada or in their own countries?
4. *Has immigration increased or decreased in the past five years?*

Sources of Immigration   In the period since the end of World War II in 1945, and especially since 1951, immigration to Canada has boomed. Between 1945 and 1974, almost four million immigrants have made their way here. Where have they come from? The following table gives a partial answer:

Country of Birth of Post-War Immigrants, 1946-71

Country of Birth	1946-55	1956-68	1969	1970	1971	1946-71
Albania	..	287	21	14	8	330
Algeria	..	2 854	196	169	124	3 343
Argentina	97	2 490	377	234	205	3 403
Australia	6 388	24 668	2 628	2 515	1 542	37 741
Austria	21 167	15 005	598	494	360	37 624
Belgium	15 078	14 732	769	485	363	31 427
Bermuda	..	835	122	85	98	1 140
Brazil	102	2 038	320	273	217	2 950
Britain	338 561	468 998	28 790	23 688	14 230	874 267
Bulgaria	..	704	78	107	95	984
Canada	8 948	11 251	1 134	1 140	1 222	23 695
Ceylon	..	1 109	215	212	253	1 789
China	15 423	29 622	5 185	3 397	3 694	57 321
Czechoslovakia	17 091	15 571	5 029	1 703	585	39 979
Denmark	6 359	22 277	650	486	342	30 114
Egypt	..	15 223	1 839	1 273	999	19 334
Estonia	..	1 081	51	28	17	1 177
Finland	4 824	11 482	772	694	452	18 224
France	24 422	44 950	3 612	2 958	2 059	78 001
Germany Fed. Rep.	122 743	130 767	4 208	3 220	2 082	263 020
Greece	14 897	75 623	7 106	6 440	4 822	108 888
Hong Kong	..	10 555	3 354	2 250	2 581	18 740
Hungary	16 542	51 235	1 132	1 023	847	70 779
Iceland	..	288	69	52	18	427
India	4 381	25 289	6 736	7 089	6 301	49 796
Iran	..	1 085	130	168	227	1 610
Ireland, Republic	15 041	27 133	1 627	1 410	954	46 165
Israel	1 080	6 375	558	585	417	9 015
Italy	133 225	311 514	10 685	8 659	5 937	470 020
Japan	423	3 724	750	821	830	6 548
Latvia	13 416	1 809	40	29	44	15 338
Lebanon	..	6 104	831	899	739	8 573
Lithuania	11 654	1 216	55	34	31	12 990
Luxembourg	..	656	22	13	2	693

Country of Birth	1946-55	1956-68	1969	1970	1971	1946-71
Malta	..	8 195	381	307	242	9 125
Mexico	556	1 711	349	437	354	3 407
Morocco	..	8 522	616	514	284	9 936
Netherlands, The	107 790	56 598	2 412	1 843	1 262	169 905
New Zealand	2 346	7 395	895	947	640	12 223
Norway	6 047	6 174	321	252	149	12 943
Pakistan	..	3 676	885	1 010	961	6 532
Philippines	..	10 904	3 138	3 305	4 213	21 560
Poland	101 433	34 987	1 563	1 403	1 527	140 913
Portugal	..	67 413	7 917	8 594	9 776	93 700
Romania	13 143	7 146	453	488	377	21 607
St. Pierre & Mique-lon	..	300	18	15	22	355
Saudi Arabia	..	63	9	11	11	94
Spain	..	12 904	998	913	620	15 435
Sweden	..	4 417	316	290	337	5 360
Switzerland	7 139	15 557	1 606	1 576	843	26 721
Syria	..	1 829	392	316	277	2 814
Tunisia	..	1 261	144	108	83	1 596
Turkey	..	7 104	671	491	442	8 708
South Africa	..	9 133	819	829	774	11 555
U.S.S.R.	23 458	9 223	394	406	349	33 830
United States	70 739	139 124	19 258	20 859	20 723	270 703
Yugoslavia	24 055	51 570	5 462	6 892	3 547	91 526
Africa, n.e.s.*	4 375	6 301	2 339	1 124	1 199	15 338
Asia, n.e.s.	3 678	12 031	2 268	3 619	3 726	25 322
Central America	226	641	168	219	187	1 441
Europe, n.e.s.	36 572	247	34	14	14	36 881
South America	3 219	12 323	3 461	3 999	4 176	27 178
West Indies	5 169	43 795	13 803	13 286	11 202	87 255
Other Countries	20 512	4 200	752	999	886	27 349
TOTAL	1 222 319	1 883 294	161 531	147 713	121 900	3 536 757

* country not specified

1. Which country has sent Canada the most immigrants since 1945?
2. Rank the next four countries in order. Are you surprised by your findings?
3. Note the trend of immigration from these five countries over the last three years. In what direction is this trend going?

Destination of Immigrants This great influx of immigrants has accounted for about one-third of Canada's population growth since 1945. However, not all areas of Canada have benefited equally from this immigration. Ontario in particular seems to have been the province most attractive to immigrants during this period.

Planned Destination of Post-War Immigrants, 1940-71

Province	1946-55	1956-68	1969	1970	1971	1946-71
Newfoundland	2 565	6 881	832	630	819	11 727
Prince Edward Island	2 490	1 402	182	185	172	4 431
Nova Scotia	23 495	20 847	2 167	2 007	1 812	50 328
New Brunswick	12 827	12 714	1 239	1 070	1 038	28 888
Quebec	240 432	399 533	28 230	23 261	19 222	710 678
Ontario	636 033	996 819	86 588	80 732	64 357	1 864 529
Manitoba	62 343	67 940	6 380	5 826	5 301	147 790
Saskatchewan	36 881	32 255	2 492	1 709	1 426	74 763
Alberta	95 343	120 045	11 274	10 405	8 653	245 720
British Columbia	109 347	219 164	21 953	21 683	18 917	391 064
Yukon and N.W.T.	563	1 811	194	205	183	2 956
Unspecified	. .	3 883	. .	. .	. .	3 883
TOTAL	1 222 319	1 883 294	161 531	147 713	121 900	3 536 757

1. Rank the provinces in order of the destination of immigrants.
2. Can you explain why so many have chosen Ontario?
3. Do you detect any changes in the intended destination of immigrants in Canada in recent years?
4. What effects do you think this trend will have on the Province of Ontario? On the other provinces?
5. Do you think this pattern of immigration is desirable? Should Canada try to spread the immigrant population evenly across the country?

The pattern of settlement of these post-war immigrants shows a notable change from that of immigrants at the turn of the century. At that time, a great number chose to settle in the West. Today almost eighty per cent of immigrants to Canada head for the large cities. The Metropolitan Toronto area, for example, has been the destination of about one-quarter of all post-war immigrants to Canada. Why has this change taken place?

One reason, of course, is that the Government is no longer offering free land in the West. Other reasons may become clear when we read this table:

Intended Occupational Groups of Post-War Immigrants, 1946-71

Occupational Groups	1946-55	1956-68	1969	1970	1971	1946-71
DESTINED TO LABOUR FORCE						
Managerial	4 213	18 606	2 566	3 095	3 464	31 944
Professional	44 526	184 232	26 883	22 412	16 307	294 360
Clerical	46 788	120 046	12 222	12 143	9 909	201 108
Transportation Trades	14 331	14 694	710	632	599	30 966
Communication Trades	1 001	4 912	222	211	141	6 487
Commercial Sales Workers	25 257	32 412	2 744	2 599	2 107	65 119
Financial Sales Workers	474	2 927	543	431	379	4 754
Service and Recreation Workers	69 447	122 526	9 060	7 852	6 387	215 272
Farmers	138 195	54 473	2 283	2 129	2 160	199 240
Construction Trades	52 516	87 116	5 964	6 001	4 005	155 902
Fishers, Trappers, Loggers	12 928	2 979	132	111	87	16 237
Miners	10 029	5 955	389	272	237	16 882
Manufacturing and Mechanical Trades	148 095	217 596	17 479	16 005	12 161	411 336
Labourers	58 743	100 364	2 018	1 614	1 324	164 063
Others	9 255	5 617	1 134	2 216	2 015	20 237
TOTAL	635 798	974 755	84 349	77 723	61 282	1 833 907
NON-WORKERS						
Spouses	252 347	351 646	27 389	25 361	21 333	678 076
Children	289 298	474 386	38 754	34 493	29 684	866 615
Others	44 876	82 507	11 039	10 136	9 601	158 159
TOTAL	586 521	908 539	77 182	69 990	60 618	1 702 850
GRAND TOTAL	1 222 319	1 883 294	161 531	147 713	121 900	3 536 757

1. In which occupational category do the greatest number of immigrants belong?
2. Rank the next four largest occupational categories of immigrants.
3. Which of these occupations would require the worker to live in a city? Which away from the cities?
4. What percentage of immigrants would have to settle in the cities in order to pursue their occupations?
5. Compare the figures for 1945-1968 with those for 1969-1971. Is the trend of the last three years towards or away from city-based jobs?

Immigration Laws

Another reason for this pattern of settlement lies in Canada's immigration laws. On October 1, 1967, a new set of immigration laws came into effect. Immigrants may now come to Canada under any one of three different categories:

1. *Sponsored Dependents* These may include the husbands or wives of immigrants already in Canada, as well as children under the age of twenty-one if they are in good health and of good character.

2. *Nominated Relatives* This category includes children over the age of twenty-one, married sons or daughters under the age of twenty-one, parents and grandparents under the age of sixty, brothers, sisters, nephews, nieces, aunts, and uncles (but not cousins). Most immigrants probably come to Canada through this system.

3. *Independent Applicants* People in this category have no one to sponsor them from Canada. For them, entering Canada is more difficult. These applicants must meet certain standards: of education; job skills; age; health; good character; knowledge of French or English; relatives in Canada; a job already waiting for them; and job opportunities in their area of destination.

The Point System   Suppose you want to immigrate to Canada. You must score *at least* fifty points on this one-hundred-point "test" for permission to come.

Item	Maximum Points
Education and Training	20 (1 point for each successful year of formal education or occupational training.)
Personal Assessment	15 (The official interviewing you decides this.)
Occupational Demand	15 (Does Canada *need* your particular skill?)
Occupational Skill	10 (10 points if you are a professional, down to 1 point, if you are an unskilled labourer.)
Age	10 (All 10 points if you are under 35; 1 point off for each year over 35.)
Definite Job Arranged	10 (All or nothing; 10 if yes, 0 if you have no job waiting for you.)
Knowledge of French and English	10 (5 points if you know only French or only English.)
Relative in Canada	5
Employment Opportunities	5

A score of fifty points or more does *not* guarantee that you will be able to enter Canada. Officials in charge of immigration may refuse permission, for their own reasons. You may not be told these reasons.

Could you get into Canada? Could your parents?

From a Canadian Government Booklet

How to Become a Canadian Citizen

Listed below are the qualifications required and the procedures to be followed by an alien seeking naturalization in Canada:

Qualifications: You must:

a. gain admission to this country for permanent residence
b. live here for five years after admission
c. be able to speak either English or French
d. show that you are of good character
e. have a knowledge of the responsibilities and privileges of citizenship
f. intend to live here permanently
g. be ready to comply with the oath of allegiance.

Now let us look at these qualifications a little more closely to see exactly how they apply to you.

Admission: People who come to Canada with the idea of living here permanently apply to the immigration authorities for the status of *landed immigrant.* This means that they have been admitted to the country for permanent residence. Many others come here for some temporary purpose, perhaps to follow a course of study, to stay with friends, or to represent a business firm. They are admitted as *non-immigrants.* . . .

Residence: You must have lived in Canada for at least five years before you can apply for citizenship. A period of *continuous* residence is not required if you can show you have lived in the country for a total of five years during the eight years immediately before you make application. A further requirement is that you must have lived in Canada for 12 of the 18 months immediately before your application. . . . The period of residence starts from the time you obtain *landed immigrant* status. . . . There are in addition the two following exceptions to this rule:

a. Any period that you have spent abroad in the service of the federal

or a provincial government, or as the wife of someone who is serving a Canadian government abroad, will count as residence in Canada.
b. If you are the wife of a Canadian citizen you can qualify after only *12 months* residence in this country.

Language: The law states that you must have an adequate knowledge of either English or French, and this is something which the Court will be asked to decide when you appear before it for a hearing. ... The law provides some exceptions to the rule that an applicant must speak English or French before becoming a citizen and the following people can qualify without doing so:
a. The wife, husband, widow or widower of a Canadian citizen.
b. Anyone 40 years of age or more at the time of admission as a landed immigrant who has since lived here continuously for more than 10 years.
c. Anyone less than 40 years of age at time of admission as a landed immigrant who has since lived here continuously for more than 20 years.

Character: You will be required to satisfy the Court that you are a person of good character. Members of the community may testify on your behalf by giving you letters of reference or appearing before the Court to support your application. Your employer, your bank manager, your business associates, religious and community leaders—indeed, any reputable citizen—would be suitable. If an applicant has been convicted of a criminal offence the Court would also wish to know the details of the case although there is no reason to think that this would automatically disqualify him.

Knowledge: You will be expected to have some knowledge of Canada and of the responsibilities and privileges of Canadian citizenship. ... Some elementary knowledge of Canadian geography and history, the economic life of our country and its political system will equip an applicant very well.

Permanent Residence: You must intend to make your home in Canada. This does not mean that you cannot go abroad temporarily or to accept employment but you are expected to maintain a close association with this country and to return here in due course, looking upon it as your permanent home.

Oath of Allegiance: You must be willing to swear an oath of allegiance or to make an affirmation in the following terms:

"I .... swear that I will be faithful and bear true allegiance to Her Majesty Queen Elizabeth the Second, her Heirs and Successors according to law, and that I will faithfully observe the laws of Canada and fulfil my duties as a Canadian citizen. So help me God." ...

Procedures: There are only three steps to become a Canadian citizen. You must:

a. apply for citizenship.

b. appear before a Court for a hearing.

c. attend a Court ceremony of presentation.

Application: There are a few simple rules to remember in making your application. They are:

a. You must *yourself* make application for citizenship. A husband, for example, cannot apply on behalf of his wife. There is one exception to this rule which allows the responsible parent to apply on behalf of a minor child—one under the age of 21. The term "responsible parent" is interpreted as meaning the father, unless the mother has legal custody of the child or is, in fact, the guardian. ...

Hearing: When your application has been posted for the regulation period the Court which has jurisdiction in your area will inform you, well in advance, of the date appointed for your hearing. ...

Presentation: When your application is approved, the Department of the Secretary of State will forward to the Court your Certificate of Citizenship, and the Court will fix a date for its presentation to you at a public ceremony .... You will be required to swear or affirm the oath of allegiance in open Court, having previously signed a statement renouncing any former allegiance, and the Presiding Officer will present your Certificate and congratulate you upon becoming a citizen of Canada.

---

1. *Why do you think certain age requirements are listed?*
2. *What do you think is meant by "good character"?*
3. *Do you think there should be other qualifications for immigrants to Canada? If so, which ones?*

Since so many people coming to Canada are sponsored by relatives, it is easy to see why certain settlement patterns develop. Most post-war immigrants have chosen the city as their home. It is only natural that the new immigrants will want to live near their relatives and friends. This means that the trend towards the city is likely to continue in the future.

Immigrants' Problems

In the past, immigrants to Canada had to face a great number of hardships. Most of these, as we have seen, were related to the environment. They had to cope with social problems too. The problems faced by today's immigrants are quite different. In the beginning of this unit, we suggested some of them: learning a language; trying to adjust to a different future; finding a job without being fluent in English or French, or having enough training; and sometimes having to deal with prejudice against their race or religion or culture. Many immigrant groups have formed their own communities. This trend is evident in Metropolitan Toronto. Before World War II about three-quarters of Toronto's population was of English background. Today the English still form the largest single group, but now they form only about forty per cent of the total. Other groups, mostly Italian, German, Jewish, and French, are now large proportions of the population as well.

1. *If your area has a mixture of ethnic groups, find out where each of them has settled.*
2. *If you have a friend or relative who has recently emigrated to Canada, ask how he or she chose a place to live.*

Within a community of people from the old homeland, new immigrants can feel at home and find help in making the adjustments they will have to make in their new country. Among the reasons new immigrants might give for settling in such an area are:

— staying with their sponsors, who are often members of the family and who have taken responsibility for their well-being
— being among others who speak the same language
— being near relatives and friends, especially as many new Canadians come from cultures where close family ties are very important
— being close to their jobs
— having access to cheap housing.

Once new immigrants have learnt English or French and are used to "Canadian" ways, they often move out of these neighbourhoods.

You have probably heard the expression "generation gap". What does it mean? Imagine how much wider the gap could be between parents raised in a culture with very strict traditional standards of behaviour, and their children, who are growing up in the 1970s in Canada.

Here is a case study which shows this problem.

Maria Spiliatopoulos is the fifteen-year-old daughter of Greek immigrants. Six years ago Maria and her family came to Toronto from Athens and since that time she has had no problems making friends. Her parents' friends are almost all Greek, but most of Maria's friends are English-speaking. It is natural for her to want to share the activities they enjoy. These include going to school dances and movies with boys.

Maria's parents think she is too young to be going out with boys. They believe giving teenagers too much freedom without some parental control is the cause of much of today's youth problem. In Greece girls were expected to help around the house after school, and dating was permitted only when they were ready for marriage.

Maria's older brother, Theodore, who has a full-time job, still lives at home. He is expected to contribute his pay to the family income. He then gets an allowance to pay for his clothing and other expenses.

Maria understands her parents' ideas, but she believes that now they are in Canada, they should try to adopt Canadian attitudes. Maria is afraid that she might lose her friends if she does not conform to their way of doing things. It seems to her that her parents want to continue living in the old ways and do not want to change. These differences have been causing arguments at home between Maria and her parents, and their relationship lately has been very tense.

Three generations of a Greek family in Halifax, Nova Scotia.

1. *Why do you think Maria has adopted Canadian customs more quickly than her parents?*
2. *In what way do Maria and her brother have less freedom than other Canadian teenagers?*
3. *Do you think more is expected of Maria and Theodore than your parents might expect of you?*
4. *Maria's parents do not speak English very well. Maria seems to be concerned, perhaps even embarrassed, by this. Why do you think she feels this way? Is this a common feeling among immigrant children whom you know?*
5. *Is the role of the family among immigrant groups different from that among other Canadians? If so, in what ways?*

The Future

A recent poll showed that two of every three Canadians feel that Canada does not need any more immigrants. The majority felt that:

— The job situation is very serious. Immigrants would only take jobs away from other Canadians.
— Our population is already large enough. Canada has enough trouble housing its present population and providing welfare for many.

A very small part of this group said they simply didn't like foreigners. About one Canadian in four feels that Canada should continue to encourage immigration. They feel that immigrants have contributed to Canada's development of its natural resources. They also believe immigrants bring new and valuable ideas and skills. As well, with Canada's declining birth rate, its population can continue to grow only through immigration. What is your opinion on this issue? Should Canada allow more immigrants?

On February 3, 1975, Canada's Immigration Minister announced a new policy for immigration. Over the next few years, this will be one of the most important questions facing Canadians.

The Minister outlined four options on immigration:

1. Canada can continue with its present system with points given for family ties, education, and job prospects.
2. It can set up a global quota. This means that only a certain number of immigrants will be allowed, but that Canada will take people from all over the world.
3. It can set up a quota system for each country.
4. It can make the number of immigrants dependent on the number of jobs available.

The choice facing Canadians "is nothing less than the future of Canada's size, population and growth". What would be your choice?

Conclusion

Canada continues to attract immigrants of different backgrounds. The rate is sometimes boosted by refugees escaping political or religious troubles at home. (Immigration requirements are often less strict for victims of such troubles.) In 1957 over 30 000 Hungarians came to Canada when the Soviet Union invaded their country. Nearly 10 000 came in 1968 when the Soviet Union invaded Czechoslovakia. In 1971, 240 refugees came from Tibet. In 1972, nearly 5000 Asians found their way to Canada when they were driven out of Uganda. In 1973 hundreds of Chileans were granted a home in Canada following political problems in their country.

Our mosaic pattern of different cultures has made us in many ways unique. The skills, knowledge, and hard work of immigrants over the centuries have developed Canada's farmlands and built our cities. Immigrant groups have enriched us with new styles in music, clothing, food, and entertainment. We have all benefited by the chance to learn more about many different cultures—most of which are far older than Canada. In Ottawa on February 24, 1974, Canada's Minister for External Affairs spoke of the importance of minorities in building Canada:

> There is as I see it a . . . process of change and maturing in our society. There was a time when it was commonplace for the second generation to scoff at parents whose accents and whose customs identified their origins. It is my experience . . . that we have come—not all the way—but some distance from these narrow attitudes . . . .
>
> As you and I are shaping the new Canada, we are learning about Canada. . . . So far as I can observe, the 22 million other inhabitants of this country are going through the same school. We are all learning to be Canadians whether we have recently emigrated from Italy or Scotland, whether our we are the sons and daughters of immigrants or whether our ancestors came to New France or were United Empire Loyalists. And we are all teaching one another.
>
> Canada will continue united and continue to be more than the sum of its parts as long as our varied elements keep our minds and our hearts open to this learning process.

Word Study

alien	landed immigrant	oath of allegiance
ethnic group	naturalization	post-war immigrants
generation gap	nominated relatives	sponsored dependents
independent applicants	mosaic	

Things to Do 1. Debate the resolution: that Canada needs more immigrants to build this country.

2. The problems our early settlers had were very different from those faced by today's immigrants. Prepare a list of the hardships, and natural advantages the early settlers met. Make a similar list for today's immigrants. Which group do you think is better off?

3. Write a short skit based on the situation of Maria and Theodore. Begin by having Maria's parents discover she has a boyfriend, and Theodore announce he is moving away from home.

4. Conduct a poll in your neighbourhood. Find out what ethnic groups live there. Talk to members of different ethnic groups and find out why they came to Canada. What problems did they have in adjusting to a new way of life?

5. Find out what services are available to members of ethnic groups in your community. Some of the services you might look for are: ethnic newspapers; grocery stores; movie theatres; sports facilities; churches; and television and radio programs.

6. You have heard Canada described as a "cultural mosaic," where members of minority groups can retain their traditions and values. Interview an immigrant friend and his or her family. Find out how much of their original culture they still retain. You might discuss language, food, dress, music, sports, and other forms of entertainment. How much of their cultural heritage does the younger generation retain?

7. The Province of Quebec has recently passed Bill 22. This Bill makes French the only language of education for immigrants to the province who do not speak English. In the past, many immigrants preferred to have their children educated in English.

Why do you think the government of Quebec passed this Bill? How would you feel about this law if you were an immigrant? What effects do you think this will have on immigration for the Province of Quebec? For the rest of Canada?

Unit 4
Shaping the Canadian Character

Farmers!
BEWARE!
The enemies of the King and the People,—of the
CONSTITUTION,
AND
SIR FRANCIS HEAD,
ARE, DAY AND NIGHT, SPREADING
LIES.

They say Sir Francis Head is recalled,—Sir Francis Head is NOT recalled, but is supported by the King and His Ministers.
They say Tithes are to be claimed in Upper Canada,—Tithes shall NOT be claimed in Upper Canada says a permanent Act of Parliament,
FARMERS
Believe not a word these Agitators say, but think for yourselves, and SUPPORT SIR FRANCIS HEAD, the friend of Constitutional Reform.

New names to
Canadian history
More are coming.
Will you be there?
ENLIST!

1
Introduction

Recently an American nightclub entertainer had herself buried alive in a casket for several days along with her pet snake. All that was provided was a single light bulb and an air vent. Of course, the entire incident was a promotional stunt, aimed at advertising her show. Yet only a certain type of person could manage such a stunt. Imagine yourself for a moment enclosed in such a container. What would be your reaction? Or imagine yourself on top of Toronto's new CN Tower. Again what would be your feeling looking out from a five hundred and forty metre tower? Many people are afraid of heights; others are afraid of the dark, or lightning, or snakes. Almost everyone is afraid of something. Would you be able to make an honest list of the things of which you are afraid? Try!

Do you know why you are afraid of some things and not others? That may be a very difficult question to answer. Some people's fear of the dark may be traced back to being left alone in a dark room as infants. Some may be afraid of heights because of frightening scenes they have seen in movies. Regardless of the reasons, what you dislike as well as what you like is part of your personality. The word "personality" is a hard word to define. Have you ever heard statements such as "Mary has a great personality" or "Bill has a dull personality"? You have probably used the word "personality" often yourself.

What does the word mean? Sociologists define it as the sum total of all the qualities which make up an individual human being. These include physical characteristics such as:

—height
—weight
—skin colour
—eye colour
—hair colour
—shape of mouth, nose, etc.

They also include habits and attitudes such as:

—smoking
—eating a large breakfast
—liking housework
—enjoying sports
—generosity
—shyness or boldness
—acting impulsively, or after much thinking.

Of course, we cannot choose the physical qualities we inherit from our parents. Other parts of our personality—habits and attitudes—may be the result of our environment. Our environment includes the natural surroundings, the neighbourhood we live in, the kinds of friends we have, the types of TV shows we watch. The qualities a person is born with can tell us a lot about that person's potential. The environment may determine whether he or she will achieve that potential. For example, Shirley may be born with all the physical qualities to become a great athlete. However, if she does not eat proper foods she may not reach her physical potential. Also she may have friends who are not interested in sports, but prefer doing science experiments instead. They may help turn Shirley's interests away from sports. Many of the habits and attitudes you have and develop are influenced by the interests of your parents, friends, and teachers.

The decisions you make now can be very important in shaping the kind of person you will be in the future. You probably run into dozens of situations each day where you must make decisions. They may appear to you to be small and unimportant, but they can be basic to moulding your personality. If you have a homework assignment to do, will you put it off for today, or try to have your older sister do it for you? If either becomes a habit, it might shape your attitudes in the future. There will be times when major decisions can determine you whole future. Will you go to university or find a job after high school? What kind of job will you have as an adult? Once such decisions are made they are usually quite difficult to reverse.

As you can see, the ingredients which go into making up a personality are very complex. Weighing all these factors, do you think you are ready to write a short "personality profile" of yourself? Try it. In this "profile" include the events and individuals which you think helped form your personality.

In many respects, countries have "personalities" too. Often the same ingredients are at work forming the character of a country and of a person. Countries have physical qualities, which we call geographical features. These can include types of soils and natural resources, the presence of rivers, forests and mountains, types of climate, and the actual size of the country. To some extent these features can determine a country's potential.

Whether this potential will be reached depends often on outside factors. What sorts of "friends" does a particular country have? If they are more powerful, they can determine its course of action. Throughout its history, Canada has had one very powerful "friend", first Great Britain and then the United States, and each greatly influenced Canadian development.

The kind of nation Canada is today is also the product of decisions made by its leaders at crucial times in the past. If these decisions had been different, the historical events which shaped Canada might have turned out differently. As a result, Canada might not exist today, or at least would be very different. Many people think that because certain events happened in the past, they were bound to happen that way, that they were inevitable. Of course, nothing could be farther from the truth.

Compared to most other countries, Canada is very young, but there have been many events and decisions in its past which became turning points. In this unit, we will be looking closely at some of the important events, and people, who have helped to shape the Canadian personality. As you study the following chapters, examine the critical choices which were possible at important moments. What decisions would you have made in the same circumstances? How did these decisions affect the future of Canada? How would Canada today be a different country if these decisions had been different? These are the questions you should try to keep in mind as you study some of the events of the past which have moulded the Canadian nation.

The Plains of Abraham today.

2
The Battle for Quebec

Moments of crisis. Canada has faced many such moments in its history. To a very great extent, the Canada we know today is the product of decisions made at these critical times. Certainly, if the decisions made in difficult situations had been different, Canada would be a different country today.

In this chapter we will be studying one of the most important events in the history of Canada—the Battle for Quebec in 1759. Most readers are familiar with the outcome of the battle. Many also know the significance of the outcome. Canada changed hands, from French to English. But was this result inevitable? Could the outcome have been different? If France and not England had won the Battle of Quebec, what effect would this have had on the future of Canada?

Since the Battle of Quebec itself was so important, the decisions made by the opposing commanders are of great interest. In this chapter you will have an opportunity not only to see what decisions were made, but to stand in the commanders' places and make the decisions yourself.

Before you begin, try to answer the following questions:

1. Are you familiar with any of the events of the Battle of Quebec?
2. Which of the following names are familiar to you: Montcalm, Wolfe, Pitt, Vaudreuil, Bigot, Murray, Carleton, Cook?
3. Who commanded the French forces? Who commanded the British forces?

The Setting

It is late spring, 1759. For three years English and French armies have been locked in a great struggle for power in Europe and in North America. The war will last until 1763 and will be known in history as the Seven Years' War. It is the aim of William Pitt, the British Prime Minister since 1757, to drive French power from North America. He has designed a grand strategy —the war in Europe would be used as a diversion, while the real objective would be the capture of the French Empire in North America.

One large step toward this goal has already been taken. On June 26, 1758, the great French fortress at Louisbourg is captured by English forces under General Wolfe. The gateway to the St. Lawrence and the French capital at Quebec is now open.

The French are also aware that Quebec will be the next target. The city, however, is located on an ideal site, and as the British are soon to discover, is a very difficult prize to capture. A glance at the map will give an indication of the strong position of the fortress city.

The city guards New France from a point where the St. Charles River flows into the St. Lawrence. At this point the great river is only nine hundred metres wide. On a narrow shelf of land along both rivers sits the Lower Town, location of most of the homes, businesses, and of the dockyards. Above, on a great rock, sits the Upper Town and its fortress.

The city is well protected by water and cliffs on all sides except the west, where the Plains of Abraham stretch behind the city. This is the weak spot in Quebec's defenses. The Plains, however, are protected from invasion by kilometres of cliffs along the St. Lawrence and St. Charles. At some points the cliffs reach heights of over ninety metres. The French have worked to build fortifications to protect the city's land front. By 1759 these fortifications are still not finished and the city's land front remains open. Along the north shore there is only one site near Quebec which is suitable for landing. This is the Beauport shore just east of the St. Charles River.

The natural fortifications of Quebec are aided by the tricky and very dangerous currents of the St. Lawrence. The French, who have been navigating the river for one hundred and fifty years, still occasionally lose ships in these currents. They do not believe the English will be able to sail any large number of ships upriver above the city. Quebec seems able to withstand any invasion.

The Armies

The British Forces   The British army which prepares to invade Canada is of the highest quality. It is not large in numbers, consisting of only eighty-five hundred men. But it is very experienced and has very able leaders. One general later remarks that this army was commanded by "probably the finest body of English officers which has ever taken the field".

At the head of the army is Major-General James Wolfe. Only thirty-two, Wolfe has already shown skill and energy as a leader during the capture of Louisbourg the year before. Pitt has decided to place the important task of the Quebec campaign on Wolfe's young shoulders. Assisting Wolfe is a group of young officers, including Monckton, Murray, Townshend, and Carleton. Murray and Carleton will later become Governors of the Province of Quebec.

The task of sailing this army up the St. Lawrence is given to the Royal Navy. 49 ships will transport Wolfe and his soldiers. These will be followed by almost 150 supply ships. The great fleet is manned by over 13 000 sailors led by some famous officers, including Admiral Saunders and James Cook. Cook will become more famous later for his voyages of discovery in the Pacific.

The Theatre of Battle

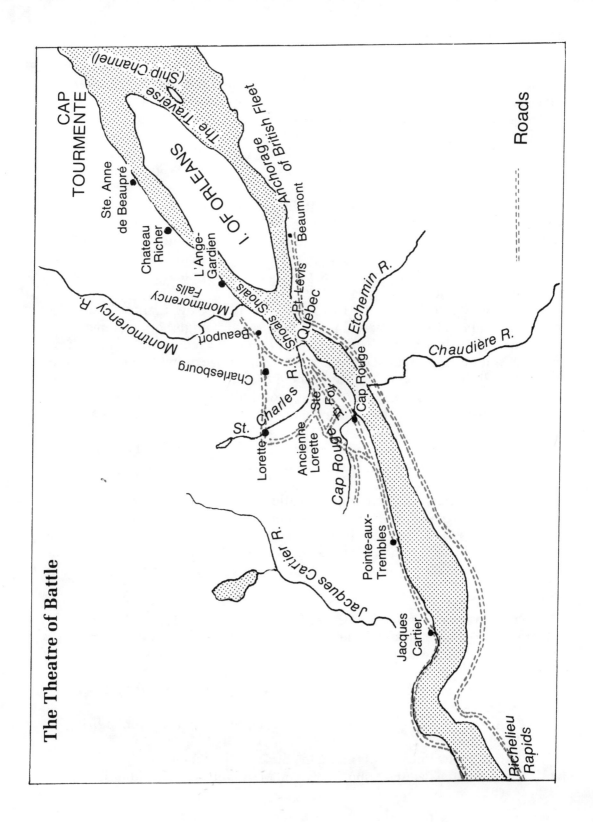

CAP TOURMENTE

Ste. Anne de Beaupré

Chateau Richer

L'Ange-Gardien

Montmorency Falls

Montmorency R.

Beauport

Charlesbourg

St. Charles R.

Lorette

Ancienne Lorette

Ste. Foy

Cap Rouge R.

Cap Rouge

Jacques Cartier R.

Pointe-aux-Trembles

Jacques Cartier

Richelieu Rapids

Chaudière R.

Etchemin R.

Pt. Levis

Quebec

Beaumont

Anchorage of British Fleet

(Shoals) Shoals

The Traverse (Ship Channel)

I. OF ORLEANS

Roads

The French Forces Opposing the invasion will be the regular army and the whole society of New France. At the prospect of the invasion of their country, thousands of French Canadians, including boys in their teens and old men in their eighties, rush to the defense of Quebec. Together with the regular army, a number of sailors, and perhaps 1500 Indian allies, these men make up a force of over 15 000. Considering that the population is no more than 60 000 this figure is astounding. Every able-bodied French Canadian male seems to be under arms.

This unit has less experience and training than the British army, but it can count on a solid defense, and determination in fighting on behalf of its homeland. It too is well led. At the head of the army is Louis-Joseph, Marquis de Montcalm-Gozon. At forty-seven he is much older than Wolfe and has also won some billiant victories in past years. Since 1756 Montcalm has been Major-General of the armies of New France.

Assisting Montcalm are the Governor-General of New France, Vaudreuil, and its *Intendant*, Bigot. Montcalm and Vaudreuil, though both talented, have not been able to get along in the past. This may prove costly to French efficiency and morale. Bigot is dishonest and cannot be counted on for any help. Later, he will be recalled to France to stand trial for fraud and theft. Montcalm does have two able assistants. One is the youthful Louis-Antoine de Bougainville, who, like Cook, will become a famous explorer. The other is a competent soldier, the Chevalier de Lévis.

Quebec has almost no naval defences. French leaders do not believe the English will be able to navigate above Quebec with a large fleet and so do not fear a naval invasion.

As the opening stages of the great battle develop, you will be asked to face the problems of the generals and make their decisions. Keep before you at all times the maps of Quebec and its surroundings. They will help you to see the problems, and the answers, more clearly. Think each choice out slowly and carefully. Remember, the future of Canada depends on your decisions.

The Battle for Quebec

The Preparations Even before the fall of Louisbourg in 1758, Montcalm had been expecting an attack on Quebec. He has therefore set about developing a plan for the defense of the city. Several alternatives are open to him. What should he do?

1. Try to meet the British farther downstream, before they reach Quebec?
2. Attempt to fortify the south shore at Point Lévis to prevent a British landing opposite Quebec?
3. Fortify the line of cliffs along the St. Lawrence above Quebec?
4. Fortify the Beauport shore between Montmorency Falls and the St. Charles River?

What would your choice be?

1. Attack the British downstream. This might be a good choice if the French had a strong navy. However, they can probably count on no more than 5 ships for such an attack. Also, as you should have detected from the maps, just 48 km downstream from Quebec the river opens up to a width of almost 19 km. A naval battle here would give the British a great advantage. Choose again!

2. Fortify the south shore. A wise selection. This would prevent the British from obtaining a good landing site directly across from Quebec. Unfortunately, the French do not see things your way. This is an oversight which will cost them dearly during the British invasion. Choose again.

3. Fortify the line above Quebec. A good choice. This would prevent the British from landing their troops upstream and so prevent them from reaching Quebec's weak spot, the Plains of Abraham. However, the French consider the cliffs a natural barrier to attack. Also you have forgotten that they do not think the English will be able to navigate a large fleet through the narrow tricky channels upstream. They feel there is little need to fortify this area. Go back and choose again.

4. Fortify the Beauport shore. You have a keen eye for military detail, for this is indeed the decision Montcalm makes. East of Montmorency the cliffs rise steeply above the St. Lawrence. However, the area from this point to the St. Charles River, as we have seen, is an ideal landing spot. If the British gained the shore it would put great pressure on Quebec. The French fortify the entire 10 km stretch of Beauport shoreline. They also fortify the western bank of the St. Charles River, further protection against British access to the Plains of Abraham. This action by Montcalm makes a British landing on the north shore almost impossible for over 48 km around Quebec.

The British Arrive   By June 21, 1759, word has reached Quebec that the great British fleet has begun to move upstream. Six days later Wolfe's army lands on the south shore of the Isle d'Orléans, within sight of Quebec. To the great surprise of the French, not a single vessel has been lost. The great seamanship of Saunders and Cook has brought Wolfe's army to the gates of Quebec.

Montcalm in the meantime has shifted his supply base to Batiscan, eighty kilometres upstream. This will give the French army a line of retreat if Quebec should fall. It also means that Quebec is to be supplied from a dangerously distant base.

Wolfe, for his part, has scouted the Quebec defenses. He has been able to gain valuable information about the city from Major Patrick Mackellar.

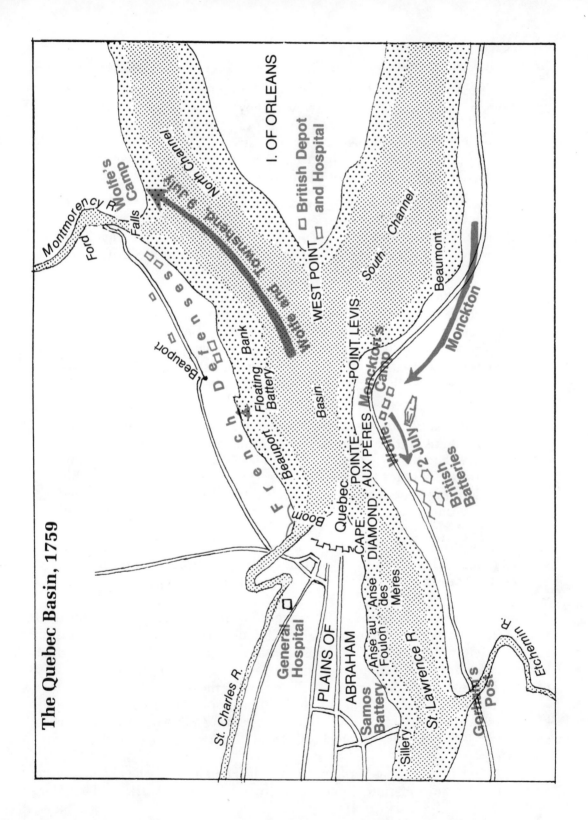

The Quebec Basin, 1759

Mackellar had spent some time in Quebec in 1756 as a prisoner of the French and had learned a good deal of the strengths and weaknesses of the city. From these reports, and from what he can see, Wolfe is very impressed by the French position. He realizes the campaign may be a long one.

After he has established himself on the south shore of the St. Lawrence, Wolfe must decide on a plan of attack. He considers three options:

1. A direct attack on the Beauport shore.
2. Land an army west of the town.
3. Land east of Beauport and try to evict the French.

What should Wolfe do?

1. Attack the Beauport shore. This is an inviting prospect, for success here would almost guarantee a speedy British victory. Wolfe however realizes that the shore is heavily fortified and an attack might spell disaster for his army. It is still too early to take such risks. For the time being, Wolfe rejects this plan. Go back and choose again.

2. Land west of the town. A good choice. The French have not fortified this area heavily. A landing will give Wolfe easy access to the Plains of Abraham. The cliffs, however, provide a serious obstacle. He cannot land his army quickly, and if the French detect his plan they will cut his army to pieces. Your plan might work, but it is still early in the campaign, and Wolfe does not want to take any chances yet. Try again.

3. Land east of Beauport. This is Wolfe's decision. He feels that driving the French from Beauport is his best chance, but he does not yet dare a frontal attack. He sets up his headquarters east of the Montmorency River, near the Falls. From this point he is able to gain a view of the entire scene. In Wolfe's own words:

> The ground, to the eastward of the falls, seemed to be (as it really is) higher than that on the enemy's side, and to command it in a manner which might be made useful to us. There is besides a ford below the falls, which may be passed for some hours in the latter part of the ebb and beginning of the flood tide; and I had hopes that possibly means might be found of passing the river above, so as to fight M. Montcalm, upon terms of less disadvantage than directly attacking his entrenchments.

The French React   With Wolfe at Montmorency, Montcalm has new problems. The English navy threatens to land troops west of Quebec. Montcalm counters by placing Bougainville, with a mobile force of about 1000 men, to the west of the city. It will be Bougainville's task to follow the movements of the British navy and prevent a landing.

Along the Montmorency River opposite Wolfe's camp, Montcalm has stationed his Indian allies. In the heavily wooded area they are valuable fighters and will give the British many problems.

In the meantime Wolfe has a hard time trying to decide on a plan of attack. Lacking such a plan, he decides instead to bombard Quebec with his guns from the south shore. The British artillery does great damage in both the Upper and Lower town. One hundred and eighty of the city's finest houses, churches, and other buildings are destroyed. The French are now paying for their failure to defend Point Lévis.

With the British camp set up at Montmorency and the guns firing on Quebec from the south shore, Montcalm must make a decision. He and his aide, Lévis, agree that four courses of action are available. What should Montcalm do?

1. Attack the British across the Montmorency?
2. Hold his position and wait for the British to make the first move?
3. Make a limited attack across the St. Lawrence and drive the British from the south shore?
4. Place most of his army along the Montmorency and await the British attack?

Your decision is:

1. *Attack the British across the Montmorency.* This is a possibility. However, what do you know of the British strength in this area? Nothing? Well, Montcalm is in almost the same position. The river can be forded at only three places. If Wolfe has these well guarded it could mean disaster for the French. Montcalm cannot afford the risk.

2. *Hold his position.* You think Montcalm should wait for Wolfe to make the first move? So does Montcalm. Unfortunately there is pressure from Vaudreuil and others in the city for some action. Montcalm must consider the damage that the British guns are doing to the city. He must take some action. Choose again.

3. *Try to drive the British from the south shore.* You are a gambler at heart. If you did not choose this originally because you thought it a dangerous move, at least you agree with the experts. However, this is what Montcalm decides to do. He decides on a night raid by sixteen hundred troops and Indians. Many of these troops are inexperienced; they have to cross rough bushland at night. The expedition is based on hope, and no general should base victory on such faint hopes. Surprisingly, the troops are able to land on the south shore without

arousing the British. However, the inexperienced troops soon panic, mistake their own men for the British, and begin to shoot at one another. Only the Indians keep calm. But when they see the chaos among the French they realize the attack is hopeless. The whole unit is forced back to Quebec. The bumbling of these soldiers is even more evident when we learn that the British first hear about the raid *five days later!*

4. *Reinforce the west bank of the Montmorency.* This is a tempting possibility. Wolfe must also cross by the same three fords and if he decides on this course of action the French would be waiting. However, if Montcalm weakens the St. Charles area by pulling his forces out, the British could land their own troops there and drive a wedge between the city and the main body of the French army. This would be disastrous for the French. Choose again.

The humiliating incident at the south bank makes Montcalm revert to his second plan. He decides that any new attack on the British will be hopeless. He will hold his position and wait for Wolfe's move. The only offensive action he will take now will be to occasionally send fire-rafts against the British fleet. These attempts end in failure too.

The British Strike   In the British camp Wolfe has problems of his own. He knows he must capture Quebec before the end of the summer, for he is not prepared for a fall and winter campaign. He cannot afford to wait Montcalm out, for time is on the French side. To this point, after a month at Quebec, Wolfe still has not taken any strong action. His army is becoming restless. Wolfe realizes he must strike soon, but in which direction?

In preparation, he sends parties upriver to scout for possible landings above Quebec, and to find the enemy's supply base. Wolfe is pleased that his navy controls the river, but his landing parties usually meet resistance from the French and Indians under Bougainville.

Near Montmorency, where his own forces are strongest, Wolfe adds heavy guns and plans to build rafts for a possible attack on the French defenses at Beauport.

As July draws to a close, Wolfe decides to strike. Three plans of action are open to him.

1. Attempt a landing west of Quebec.
2. Attempt a direct attack against the Lower Town.
3. Attack the French defenses at Beauport.

Your strategy is to:

1. *Land west of Quebec.* Actually Wolfe considers this plan until the

last moment. The resistance of the French above the city discourages him however; in Wolfe's own words:

> But what I feared most, was that if we should land between the town and the river Cape Rouge, the body first landed could not be reinforced before they were attacked by the enemy's whole army. . . . I thought once of attempting it at St. Michael's, about three miles [about five kilometres] above the town; but, perceiving that the enemy were . . . preparing against it, . . . it seemed so hazardous that I thought it best to desist.

2. *Attack the Lower Town.* Wolfe actually considers this line of action also. If successful, this plan would quickly end the war. However his artillery has been unable to knock out the guns of the Upper Town. With Quebec's fire-power still present any attempted landing could prove suicidal. On the whole, not a good choice. Try again.

3. *Attack the Beauport defenses.* A very risky piece of action if this is your choice. However this is precisely what Wolfe plans to do. If you had decided against this, you can at least take satisfaction in knowing you are right. Wolfe soon has cause to regret his decision. His plan is to attack Beauport by landing his forces on the beach, but from the beginning he runs into trouble. As he explains in a letter to Pitt:

> At a proper time of the tide, the signal was made, but in rowing towards the shore, many of the boats grounded upon a ledge, that runs off a considerable distance. This accident put us in great disorder . . .

The eager soldiers waded ashore in chest-high water, but in their eagerness they lost their discipline, and

> instead of forming themselves as they were directed, ran on impetuously towards the enemy's entrenchments in the utmost disorder and confusion, without waiting for the corps which were to sustain them and join in the attack.

A large number were killed in this attack, and as a final act of irony, even the weather seemed to turn against the British:

> . . . it was near night, a sudden storm came on, and the tide began to make; so that I thought it most advisable, not to persevere in so difficult an attack. . . .

The battle of Montmorency, as it is called, comes to an end. It is a costly defeat for the British, who lose four hundred and fifty men killed or wounded.

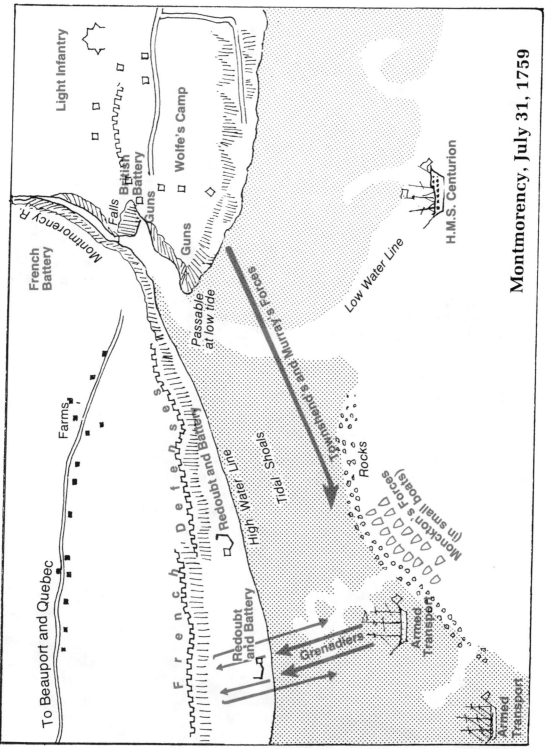

Montmorency, July 31, 1759

Light Infantry

Wolfe's Camp

British Battery

Guns

Guns

Falls

Guns

Montmorency R.

French Battery

Farms

To Beauport and Quebec

French Defenses

Redoubt and Battery

Redoubt and Battery

High Water Line

Tidal Shoals

Rocks

Passable at low tide

Townshend and Murray's Forces

Low Water Line

H.M.S. Centurion

Monckton's Forces (in small boats)

Grenadiers

Armed Transport

Armed Transport

It is costly also in terms of morale. Wolfe's officers had not liked the plan from the beginning. With defeat, they grow restless. They feel Wolfe is indecisive.

Wolfe, who has been quite ill for most of the campaign, is also discouraged. Lacking a solid plan of action, he must content himself with small skirmishes and the occasional raid on the French countryside.

The Final Assault   With the summer drawing to a close, and with his own health getting worse, Wolfe decides to ask the advice of his unhappy officers, Monckton, Townshend, and Murray. He still favours some form of attack along the Beauport defenses, but his officers think otherwise. They submit to him the only plan which has a chance of success:

> We are therefore of the opinion that the most probable method of striking an effectual blow, is to bring the troops to the South Shore, and to direct the Operations above the Town. When we establish ourselves on the North Shore, the French General must fight us on our own terms; We shall be betwixt him and his provisions, and betwixt him and their Army opposing General Amherst.
>
> If he gives us battle, and we defeat him, Quebec and probably all Canada will be ours, which is an advantage far beyond any we can expect by an attack on the Beauport side. . . .

1. Where did Wolfe's generals propose to attack the French?
2. What advantages did they see in this plan?
3. Why did they oppose the Beauport plan?

Wolfe agrees to the plan, and on September 1st moves his forces from Montmorency to the south shore. Landing the troops on the north shore will still be a problem, for Bougainville, whose forces have been strengthened to about three thousand, still patrols the area. Where to land? Wolfe spends the next ten days scouting the shoreline and rejecting several possibilities. At last he is ready. The place he has chosen is described by his Chief Engineer:

> The place is called [Anse au] Foulon . . . it must be observed that the bank which runs along the shore is very steep and woody and was thought so impracticable by the French themselves that they had then only a single picket to defend it. This picket which we supposed might be about 100 men, was encamped upon the bank near the top of a narrow path which runs up from the shore; this path broke by the enemy themselves, and barricaded . . . but about 200 yards [180 m] to the right there appeared to be a slope in the bank, which was thought might answer the purpose. These circumstances . . . seemed to promise a fair chance of success.

Wolfe's Cove, Quebec City.

This landing place, Anse au Foulon, is now known as Wolfe's Cove. About 02:00 on the morning of September 13, while part of the English fleet fakes an attack at Beauport, the main body of the British army is to land at the Cove. They are to float there on small boats under cover of night. This would not appear suspicious, for the French themselves had been bringing supplies to the city by boat past this point.

On this night, however, the French have cancelled their supply shipments. Luckily for the British, the French sentries have not been informed of this. When the first British boats are challenged by a sentry with "Qui Vive?" (Who goes there?), a quick-thinking British officer replies, in French, "La France". The boats are allowed to pass.

The British land successfully, make the fifty metre climb up the cliffs and surprise the few sentries, whom they quickly defeat. The whole plan is so much tinged with luck that modern experts do not consider it very sound. Nonetheless it is successful. By early morning the entire British army is drawn up on the Plains of Abraham, facing Quebec.

The Final Defence Montcalm, who has been keeping watch on the Beauport shore, must now make the final decision in the Battle of Quebec. The choices are quite simple. There are two options open to Montcalm. What should he do?

1. Stay in the fortifications of Quebec, wait for Bougainville to arrive and try to pin the British between them.
2. Meet Wolfe in the open.

You decide to

> 1. *Wait for Bougainville.* The French could have used you at Quebec in 1759. This would appear to be the wiser decision of the two. It is what Vaudreuil suggests. Perhaps the French would have lost the battle anyway, but certainly the presence of the second army on the field would have improved their chances. However, on the spur of the moment, Montcalm selects the second option.

> 2. *Meet Wolfe in the open.* This is what Montcalm decides to do. It is a hasty decision and one which will prove disastrous for Quebec. Montcalm, however, does not know where Bougainville is and whether he can come to the rescue. Also, Montcalm feels his best chance lies in attacking Wolfe before the latter can get the rest of his troops in position. He cannot afford the risk of waiting.

At about 10:00 on September 13 the two armies meet on the Plains of Abraham. They are of about equal strength, each with perhaps forty-five hundred men, but the British soldiers are far better disciplined and more experienced.

As the French advance, the British hold their fire until the French are within 90 m . . . 70 m . . . 40 . . . At this point a pounding hail of bullets tears great holes in the ranks of the French. The French line breaks, then retreats.

The entire battle lasts less than fifteen minutes. When the smoke clears, Wolfe lies mortally wounded on the battlefield. Informed that his army has won, he quietly says "Now, God be praised, I will die in peace." Montcalm too is mortally wounded and dies in Quebec the next morning. Although skirmishing continues for a while the Battle of Quebec is in effect over.

It was a monumental event in the history of Canada. Although the French won later victories over British armies, the fall of Quebec signalled the end of the French empire in Canada.

After the Battle

The Treaty of Paris, signed in 1763, ended the war between England and France. As a result of the Treaty, France lost most of its possessions in North America. Only two tiny islands off the coast of Newfoundland, St. Pierre and Miquelon, remained in French hands. Can you find them on a map? They are still French possessions today.

Britain agreed that any French subjects who wished to leave Canada would be allowed to do so. Over two thousand Canadians accepted this offer. Many belonged to the aristocratic and merchant classes. When they left, New France was left without many of its leaders in government, business, and society. More

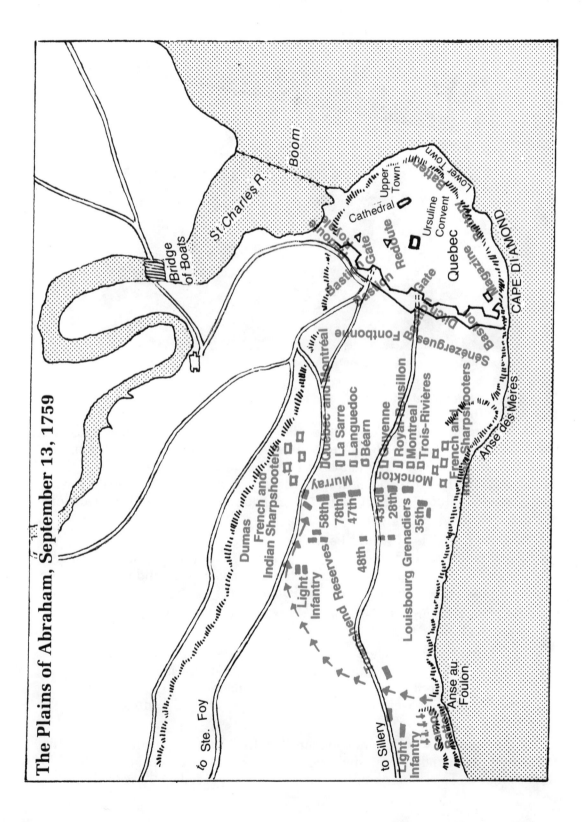

The Plains of Abraham, September 13, 1759

Montcalm wounded. He died in Quebec City the next day.

than ever, the *habitants* of New France looked to their farms for survival and to the Church for guidance.

In Britain there was much debate as to what policy should be adopted for the governing of Canada. Some felt that the French, as conquered subjects, should be made to follow English laws and customs. Others upheld the right of French Canadians to live according to their own customs. The debate was finally settled by the Quebec Act of 1774. Among its most important decisions were the following:

> *Government* There would be no elected assembly based on the English model. Canada would be governed by a Council appointed by England. The Council would be headed by a Governor and would be composed of both French and English members.

> *Religion* The French Canadians were allowed the right to retain the Roman Catholic faith.

> *Laws and Customs* The new Province would operate under two sets of laws. British law would be used in criminal cases, French law in civil cases. Civil cases usually deal with matters of property or personal rights. As well, the seigneurial system of landholding was retained.

These were very important decisions for the future of Canada. It meant that Canada now officially supported two very different societies, one French, the other English. The shape of modern Canada was moulded by these decisions.

Death of Wolfe. Is there anything about these two paintings that seems unrealistic?

As we have seen, the Battle of Quebec was not an easy victory for the British. If choices made at critical times by both sides had been different, could the results have been different? Can we guess at what Canada might be like today if France and not England had won?

Places to Know

Anse au Foulon   Lower Town   Upper Town
Beauport   Montmorency   Batiscan
Isle d'Orléans   Plains of Abraham   St. Pierre and Miquelon
Point Lévis

Things to Do: 1. Review the decisions you made in this chapter. How many good decisions did you make?

2. Who do you think was the better general, Wolfe or Montcalm? In trying to answer this, make a list of the decisions made by each man, and indicate which were good and which were mistakes.

3. Outline a general plan of attack

you might have drawn up if you had been placed in charge of the British forces. What would you have done differently in defense of the city if you had been in Montcalm's shoes? When answering this question try to be specific about small details, such as the number of men you have, where you would station them, the position of your artillery, and the movement of your forces.

3
The War of 1812

If you were asked the question, "What makes Canadians different from Americans?", how would you answer?

Here are some answers to this question suggested by other Canadian students:

—Americans are more money-hungry
—Canadians know more about the world
—Americans think Canada is always cold and full of snow
—Canadians have a more honest government
—Canadians respect the cultures of immigrants; Americans tolerate only one culture, their own
—Americans think they are superior to Canadians.

Most of these answers only scratch the surface. Some have very little real evidence to back them up. The real differences may be harder to pinpoint. Most Canadians and Americans have a common language. Many have similar roots in Europe, Asia, or Africa. We live on either side of a common border. Most Canadians and Americans see the same movies, watch the same television programs, read the same books and magazines, and listen to the same music. If you saw a man or woman walking down the street, could you tell whether that person was Canadian or American?

Because we live in the shadow of one of the strongest countries on earth it must often appear to others that we are only carbon copies of the United States. Yet it seems most Canadians feel that in some way they are different from Americans. We can discover many of the reasons for this feeling in the story of our past. The Loyalists who fled to Canada from the United States in the 1780s brought with them a loyalty toward Britain and a strong dislike for the new American republic. This feeling was strengthened by the only war ever fought between Canada and the United States, the War of 1812. This war, fought so long ago, helped to shape the Canadian identity. Although neither side really won the war, Canadians gained new pride in their young country. They began to think of themselves as different from either the British or the Americans.

The mistrust of the United States which carried over from this war would take many years to erase. As late as the 1920s, Canada's military strategy still included plans for the defense of our country in case of American attack.

As you read through this chapter, try to keep the following questions in mind:

1. What were the issues which started the war?
2. What were the aims of both sides in the war?
3. Which of these aims were achieved by the war's end?
4. Was the war necessary?
5. What events might have given Canadians new pride in themselves and their country?

The Background of the War

In 1812 Canada was still a young, developing country with a small, scattered population. The two provinces in which the war was mainly fought were very different. The population of Lower Canada, which made up two-thirds of the total, was mainly French Canadian. Most of Upper Canada's small population had come from the United States. Many were Loyalists who had fled to Canada after the American War of Independence. Many others, however, were Americans who had come to take advantage of the offer of free land in Canada. There was also some concern about the attitude of the French Canadians. Many still considered themselves a "conquered people" and resented Britain's control. In case of war, could Upper Canada count on their support?

In the United States many people still carried bitter memories of the Revolutionary War against Britain. Anti-British feelings were increased by two events which, at first glance, do not seem to have anything to do with Canada. Yet they would soon lead to war between Canada and the United States.

One event was the continuing series of wars between the western Indians and American settlers. As the settlers advanced further and further west, they had been buying or taking Indian lands at an increasing rate. In defence of their lands, the Indians often attacked the settlements. The last battle in this series was fought in the Indiana Territory at Tippecanoe. The Battle of Tippecanoe resulted in the defeat of the Indians. But their leader Tecumseh swore vengeance, and American settlers still had cause to fear. Many American settlers strongly believed that the British were encouraging the Indians to attack them. Why would these Americans feel this way?

The second event was the continuing war in Europe. Since 1793 the British and their allies had been locked in a struggle against Napoleon Bonaparte. During this war both Britain and France took actions which were strongly resented by other countries. England decided to blockade the coast of France. This meant using her powerful navy to block any shipping trade between France and foreign countries. Since the United States carried on a great deal of trade with France, this blockade was bound to hurt the American economy.

Britain also claimed the right to search American ships for English deserters. Cases of desertion were very common at this time, and many deserters served on American ships. Unfortunately, when the British recaptured suspected deserters they often carried off American sailors as well.

These incidents created more and more resentment of Britain. By 1812 many Americans were calling for a "second War of Independence" against the British.

The Outbreak of War

On June 1, 1812, the United States declared war on Great Britain. President Madison gave these reasons:

> British ships have been violating the American flag on the high
> seas, and carrying off persons sailing under it. Under the pretence of
> searching for British subjects, thousands of American citizens have
> been torn away from their country to risk their lives in the battles of
> their captors. Against these acts, the United States has pleaded in
> vain.
>
> British ships have also been violating the rights of our coasts.
> They interfere with our ships as they enter and leave port. They have
> even spilled American blood within our own territory.
>
> Under the pretence of a blockade, our trade has been robbed on
> the high seas, and our goods have been prevented from getting to
> their markets.
>
> It has become clear that the commerce of the United States is to be
> sacrificed not because of the war rights of Great Britain but because
> she desires a monopoly on this commerce for herself.
>
> Our attention is drawn to the renewal of warfare on the northwest-
> ern frontier by the Indians—a warfare which spares neither age nor
> sex. It is difficult to account for the activity which has been taking
> place between these tribes and British traders, without making a con-
> nection between Indian hostilities and British influence.
>
> These are the injuries and indignities which have been heaped
> upon our country. We see in short, a state of war on the side of Great
> Britain against the United States.

1. Which of the reasons for war stated by Madison are concerned with the war in Europe?

2. What effort does he say the U.S. has taken to ease the friction between itself and Britain?

3. What does he say is the true reason for the British blockade?

4. How does Madison link the Indian wars to the British presence in Canada?

5. Looking closely at Madison's statements,

   a) which sections of the U.S. do you
   suspect might be most in favour
   of war? Why?

b) what does Madison hope to
   achieve by the war?

6. Based on the above reasons, do
   you think the U.S. had good cause
   for going to war?

Let us search a little more deeply. Were President Madison's reasons the
true causes of the war? How was Canada involved? Were Americans right to ac-
cuse the British of stirring up the Indians? Some of the answers to these questions may be found in the statements which follow.

The first statement is part of a speech made by a Senator from the American
west, Henry Clay. Because of the friction between Britain and the United States,
many Americans were in favour of war. Those in the American government
who felt this way were called "War Hawks". They also felt that the best way to
strike at Britain was through Canada. Clay, one of the leading War Hawks,
made this speech in 1810:

> No man in this country wants peace more than I. But I prefer war,
> with all its horrors, to the silent rottenness of a humiliating peace.
> Britain has violated the personal rights of American freemen in the
> imprisonment of our seamen. She has murdered American seamen.
>
> Some say that nothing will be gained by war with Great Britain. In
> considering war, we should think not only of the benefits to ourselves
> but of the injury to be done to the enemy. The conquest of Canada is
> within our power. I believe that the militia of Kentucky alone could
> place Montreal and Upper Canada at our feet. Does Canada mean
> nothing to Britain? Is it nothing to the British king to have the last of
> his North American possessions removed from his control? Is it
> nothing to wipe out the torch which lights up Indian warfare?
>
> A certain amount of military desire is necessary for the protection
> of our country. If we surrender without a struggle, we will lose the
> respect of the world, and what is worse, of ourselves.

1. Why did Clay want war?
2. Compare this speech with Madison's. Do you think their aims were

the same?

3. What reasons does Clay give for an
   attack on Canada?

The second statement is by the respected Indian Chief, Tecumseh. It gives
an idea of the cause of friction between the Indians and the American settlers.
Most Indians believed that the land had been given by God to all Indians. They
did not believe that land should be sold to become the private property of any
one person. But some white land speculators made a practice of swindling the
Indians. They would sell alcohol to certain tribes. Once the Indians were under

the influence of the whisky, they were persuaded to sell their lands for almost nothing.

Two Indian tribes once sold more than one million hectares of land in this way. The other tribes in the area were enraged. Tecumseh presented their case:

> The Indians, once a happy race, have been made miserable by a people who are never happy, but always wanting more. To stop this evil it is necessary for all red men to unite in claiming a common equal right in the land, as it was in the beginning and should still be. For the land was never divided, but belongs to every one for the use of each person. This no one has the right to sell, even to each other, much less to strangers.
>
> The white people have no right to take the land, because the Indians had it first. It is theirs. They may sell it, but everyone must agree. A sale not agreed to by everyone is not valid. This recent sale is bad. It was made by a part only, not by everyone. All red men have equal rights to the unoccupied land.

1. *How does Tecumseh see land ownership? How is the Indian attitude to land different from the European's?*
2. *Under what conditions would he allow the sale of land to Europeans?*
3. *Why is he opposed to the most recent sale of land?*

The third statement, made by a famous American, Daniel Webster, expresses the feelings shared by many of his fellow countrymen:

> Too small a portion of public opinion was in favour of the war to justify it originally. An even smaller portion is in favour of the way in which it has been conducted. Public opinion is not with you in your Canada project. The acquisition of that country is not an object desired by the people. Some gentlemen say that they wish it only as a means for achieving other purposes. But a large portion of the people believe that the conquest of Canada is the real objective. This aim has even been stated by leaders in public. And if this is not the aim, it is hard to see the connection between your methods and your aims. You say you are at war for rights at sea and freedom of trade. But they see you lock up your trade and abandon the ocean. They see you invade an interior province of the enemy. They see you become involved in a bloody war with the Indians.

1. *Is Webster in favour of war or against? Why?*
2. *What does he say is the true aim of those who want the war? How does he support this charge?*

As a final piece of evidence, let us examine how the American government voted on the issue of war. After reading the war message by President Madison earlier in this chapter, you were asked to indicate which areas of the United States you believed might be in favour of war. This was to be done on the basis of the causes stated by Madison. These issues included:

1. Seizure of American ships and cargo by the British.
2. Seizure of American sailors by the British.
3. Harm to American trade by the British blockade.
4. Attacks on American settlers in the Northwest by Indians encouraged by the British.

Which American states would be most harmed by the seizure of shipping? Which states would most sailors come from? Which states were being harmed by the Indian wars? In trying to answer these questions, refer to the map on page 282.

Logically, these states should be the ones to vote for war. Compare your findings with the actual vote taken state by state by the American Congress:

Congressional Voting on the Declaration of War, by States

	House of Representaives		Senate	
	For	Against	For	Against
New Hampshire	3	2	1	1
Vermont	3	1	1	0
Massachusetts (Including Maine)	6	8	1	1
Rhode Island	0	2	0	2
Connecticut	0	7	0	2
New York	3	11	1	1
New Jersey	2	4	1	1
Delaware	0	1	0	2
Pennsylvania	16	2	2	0
Maryland	6	3	1	1
Virginia	14	5	2	0
North Carolina	6	3	2	0
South Carolina	6	0	2	0
Georgia	3	0	2	0
Ohio	1	0	0	1
Kentucky	5	0	1	1
Tennessee	3	0	2	0
Total	79	49	19	13

The United States in 1812

1. Compare the voting record with your answers. Which areas of the United States seem to be in favour of war? Which areas seem to be against? Considering Madison's statement, are you surprised?

2. Aside from the reasons Madison gives, what other reasons might the southern and western states have for war with Britain?

So the United States was set upon war against Britain. Because of America's weakness on the seas, everybody thought that Canada would be the target for attack. Luckily for Canada many Americans were opposed to the war, as we have seen. At Boston, flags flew at half-mast when the war was declared. Some eastern states refused to pay taxes meant for the war against Canada. Some Americans, like the wealthy businessman John Jacob Astor, even tipped off Canadian troops about American army movements during the war. This divided loyalty certainly helped to save Canada.

Meeting of Brock and Tecumseh, 1812.

Canada Prepares   Despite the dissension in enemy ranks, Canada's position was still desperate. At the beginning of the war few people even in Canada thought their troops would be able to resist the Americans. The British regular troops numbered only seven thousand. Less than two thousand were stationed in Upper Canada.

The British forces were led by General Isaac Brock, who was also the Lieutenant-Governor of Upper Canada. Brock had good reason to be worried. He was uncertain how the French Canadians would react in the coming war. He knew the French in Lower Canada had never resigned themselves to being forever under British rule. Would they now take this opportunity to join the Americans and strike back at their rulers?

In Upper Canada, how would the former American settlers decide? Would they fight against their former countrymen and relatives?

As Brock travelled through Upper Canada trying to stir up support he found this attitude among the people:

Fort George, U.C.
July 12th 1812

The militia which assembled here on account of war being declared by the United States have been improving daily in discipline. But so great was the clamour to return and attend to their farms that I found myself compelled to sanction [approve] a large proportion and I am not without my apprehension [fear] that the remainder will, in defiance of the law which can only impose a fine of twenty pounds, leave the service the moment the harvest commences—There can be no doubt that a large portion of the population in this neighbourhood are sincere in their professions to defend the country, but the greater part are either indifferent to what is passing, or so completely American as to rejoice in the prospects of a change of governments.

York
July 29, 1812

My situation is most critical, not from anything the enemy can do but from the disposition of the People—the population, believe me, is essentially bad—a full belief possesses them all that this province must succumb [fall]—Legislators, Magistrates, Militia Officers, all, have imbibed [accepted] the idea.

What a change an additional regiment would make in this part of the Province!! Most of the people have lost all confidence. I however speak loud and look big—

1. What do most people seem to think of the war?
2. What problems does Brock run into in trying to get men to enlist? What is the fine for desertion?
3. What does he feel would be required to revive spirits and encourage men to enlist? What does Brock do to encourage people?

There were some good signs. The Loyalists were solidly pro-British and anti-American. They could be relied upon to put a stiff fight. Another hopeful note was the presence of Tecumseh, who had brought his Indians across the border into Canada to help Brock fight the Americans.

The United States Prepares   At the outset of the war the Americans had the advantage of a much larger army, perhaps thirty-five thousand men, while Britain had a superior navy. What strategy would each side adopt?

1. *Take into account the geography of Canada, the location of its settled areas, the location of its forces, and the strengths and weaknesses of the two sides. What strategy would you plan for the conquest of Canada if you were an American general?*

2. *At the same time, consider Brock's position. His forces are greatly out-numbered. Canadian morale is very low. Should he await the American attack or act first?*

3. *Find the places and dates of the major battles on the following map. Which side struck first? Can you discover the American strategy from this map? If so, how does it compare with your own?*

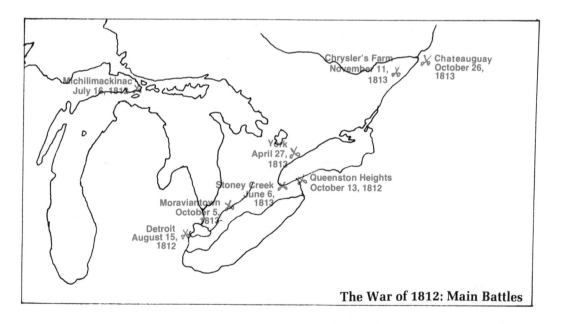

The War of 1812: Main Battles

Actually it is very difficult to discover an American plan of war, because they really didn't have one. Experts ever since have been saying that if the Americans had attacked Montreal, the war would have ended very quickly. This strategy would have cut off Upper Canada from Lower Canada and would have separated the British forces. If the Americans had done this, it would surely have meant the defeat of Canada. Canada today might be simply a part of the United States. This is why the War of 1812 is sometimes called the most important war in Canada's history. Again we see how individual decisions have been so important to Canadian history.

Perhaps the reason the Americans may not have had a strong plan of action from the beginning was their overconfidence. Many Americans agreed with Henry Clay when he said, "I believe that the militia of Kentucky alone could place Montreal and Upper Canada at our feet."

Others believed with General Hull that Canada could be won simply by sending an invitation to join the United States. Convinced of this policy, Hull sent the following proclamation to the inhabitants of Canada:

INHABITANTS OF CANADA,

. . . The army under my command has invaded your country. To peaceable inhabitants it brings neither danger nor difficulty. I come to find enemies, not to make them; I come to protect, not to injure you.

. . . You have felt Great Britain's tyranny; you have seen her injustice; but I offer you the invaluable blessings of civil, religious and political liberty—that liberty which has given us a greater measure of peace and security, of wealth and improvement, than ever fell to any other people.

. . . Remain in your homes. Do not raise your hands against your brothers. I do not ask for your assistance. I have a force which will break down all opposition. If you should take part in the coming war, you will be considered and treated as enemies.

. . . No white man found fighting by the side of an Indian will be taken prisoner—instant death will be his lot.

. . . The United States offers you peace, liberty, security. Your chance lies between these and war, slavery and destruction. Choose, then, but choose wisely.

1. *How did Hull appeal to Canadians to join his side?*
2. *Why was Hull hopeful that many Canadians would join his army?*
3. *What threats did the General make to those who would oppose him?*
4. *Did the Americans expect a long or short war? What indications are there of this feeling?*
5. *What might be your answer to the Proclamation if you were*
   a) Loyalist;
   b) an American settling in Canada?

Faced with Hull's invading army, Brock decided to issue a proclamation too. Before reading Brock's message, put yourself in his place and compose your own. Remember, in this message you are trying to rally the Canadian people, boost their morale, and give them reasons for remaining loyal to Britain. Now compare your message with Brock's.

The unprovoked declaration of War, by the United States of America against the United Kingdom has been followed by the actual invasion of this Province.

. . . Where is the Canadian Subject who can truly say to himself that his person, liberty or property has been injured by the Government? Where is to be found in any part of the world a growth so rapid in wealth and prosperity as this colony shows?

The consequence of a separation from Great Britain would be the loss of this great advantage. And what is offered you in exchange? To become a territory of the United States, and then you will be returned to the dominion of France. The return of Canada to the Empire of France was the reward stated for the aid given to the United States.

Are you prepared, Inhabitants of Canada, to become slaves to the Despot who rules the Nations of Europe with a rod of Iron [Napoleon]? If not, exert your energies, co-operate with the King's regular Forces to repel the invader.

288 Shaping the Canadian Character

1. *Which message do you think would have been more effective, yours or Brock's?*
2. *According to Brock, why should the Canadians remain loyal to Britain?*
3. *Compare Brock's proclamation with Hull's. Which argument would appear stronger to you if you were a Canadian who had not yet taken a stand on the war?*

The Fighting Begins

As the war began, Brock put his own strategy into effect. Usually, when an army is badly outnumbered and fighting on its own home ground, it will wait for the enemy to attack. But Brock was no ordinary leader. He realized that the one thing which would boost the sagging morale of the Canadian people was an early victory. Brock therefore decided to take the offensive.

His first move was to send an army against Michilimackinac, an American fort on Lake Michigan. The American commander, who had not even been told that the war had begun, surrendered immediately. This victory convinced the Indian tribes to the north to join the Canadian side.

Brock next won a major victory over the Americans at Detroit. He boldly marched his small force against General Hull's large army camped at Fort Detroit. On August 16, 1812, Hull surrendered the fort. Brock describes the results.

> I hasten to apprize Your Excellency of the Capture of this very important Post: 2500 troops have this day surrendered Prisoners of War, and about 25 pieces of Ordnance have been taken, without the sacrifice of a drop of British blood; I had not more than 700 troops including Militia, and about 400 Indians to accomplish this service.

On October 13, 1812, one of the most famous battles of the war was fought at Queenston Heights near Niagara Falls. An eyewitness gives this account:

> Before daylight on the morning of the 13th of October, a large division of General Van Rensellaer's army, . . . effected a landing at the lower end of the village of Queenston (opposite to Lewiston), and made an attack upon the position. . . .

> Major-General Brock, on receiving intelligence, immediately proceeded to that post, from Fort George, and arrived at the juncture when the handful of British regulars was compelled to retire for a time before an overwhelming force of the enemy. However, on the appearance of their gallant chief, the troops were seized with a fresh

animation, and were led on by that brave general to a renewed exertion to maintain the post; but at the moment of charging the enemy's position, within pistol-shot of the line, General Brock was killed by a musket ball, and with him the position was for a short time lost. Colonel Macdonnel, his provincial aide-de-camp, was mortally wounded about the same time, and died shortly afterwards of his wounds.

A reinforcement of the 41st Regiment, commanded by Captain Derenzy, with a few of the Lincoln Militia and a party of Indians, were immediately marched from Fort George to the succour of the troops at Queenston, under the direction of Major-General Sheaffe, who now assumed the command; and persons who were, by their situations in life and advanced age, exempt from serving in the militia, made common cause, seized their arms, and flew to the field of action as volunteers.

The conflict was again renewed. . . . The fight was maintained on both sides with a courage truly heroic. The British regulars and militia charged in rapid succession against a force in number far exceeding their own, until they succeeded in turning the left flank of their column, which rested on the summit of the hill. The event of the day no longer appeared doubtful.

Major-General Van Rensellaer, commanding the American army . . . re-crossed the Niagara river . . . but, to his utter astonishment, he found that at the very moment when their services were most required, the ardour of the engaged troops had entirely subsided. . . . Crowds of the United States Militia remained on the American bank of the river, to which they had not been marched in any order, but run as a mob; *not one of them would cross.* They had seen the wounded re-crossing; they had seen the Indians, *and were panic-struck.* . . .

Brigadier-General Wadsworth was therefore compelled, after a vigorous conflict had been maintained for some time on both sides, to surrender himself and all his officers, with 900 men, between three and four o'clock in the afternoon [15:00 and 16:00], to a force far inferior to his in numbers . . .

The loss of the British in this battle did not exceed 100 men, including killed, wounded, and missing; while that on the side of the Americans, including deserters, was not less than 2000; but amongst the killed, the British government and the country had to deplore the loss of Sir Isaac Brock, one whose memory will long live in the warmest affections of every British subject in Canada.

1. Was this account written by an American or a Canadian eyewitness? Give reasons for your answer.
2. From this account, can you tell who started the battle?
3. What happened to General Brock in this battle?
4. Why did the American troops under Van Rensellaer refuse to cross the river to help their fellow soldiers?
5. Which side had the largest army? Which side suffered the most losses?

The loss of Brock was a serious blow to Canadian hopes, but shortly after, another important Canadian victory revived morale. This was the victory at Chateauguay in Lower Canada. The question of whether French Canadians would remain loyal to Britain in this war was answered at Chateauguay. The hero of the battle was Major Charles de Salaberry. He describes the battle and the role of the French Canadians in a letter to his father.

My Dear Father:

The 26th has been a glorious day for me and those of my troops engaged.—the American Army commanded by General Hampton and another General has been repulsed by a little band, all Canadians—and yesterday that army commenced its retreat. . . . The enemy's force consisted of all his troops, about 7000 men and five pieces of cannon, 300 cavalry. The action lasted four hours, and it ended in the enemy being obliged to return to his former position five miles back, leaving many of his dead and wounded behind and a great number of his scattered men in the woods, also many drums, 150 firelock etc., etc., baggage etc.—The number of my men engaged did not exceed three hundred—the rest were in reserve in the lines I had constructed. Our killed and wounded are only twenty-four including officers. There were none but Canadiens amongst us. . . . I am proud to think that this defence on our part has at least prevented the American Army from penetrating to La Prairie—we are here situated about thirty-five miles from Montreal. This is certainly a most extraordinary affair. . . . I remain in haste, my dear Father, yours faithfully,

Charles de Salaberry

De Salaberry at Chateauguay, 1813.

1. *What do you think would have been the effects of these victories*
   a) *on the spirit of the Canadian soldiers?*
   b) *on the confidence of the Americans?*
2. *What does the battle of Chateauguay show about the attitude of the French Canadians in this war?*
3. *If you were a neutral American settler living in Upper Canada, how might your attitude toward the war be changed by these battles?*

Of course there were defeats for the Canadians as well. York, the capital of Upper Canada, was captured in August, 1813. Two months later at Moravian-town, near present-day Chatham, Ontario, the British suffered another loss. In this battle they also lost their great ally Tecumseh.

The disasters of war, whether large, or small and personal, often helped to build patriotism among the Canadian people. Read the following accounts of two incidents of the war:

Tecumseh at the Battle of the Thames, 1813.

... At the peep of day on the 27th. I descried from the Bedroom Window the whole Yankie Fleet 13 in number off the Light House ... the Enemy coming up in such Force, having Landed 4000 men, our whole strength did not amount to more than 450 ... at length General Sheaffe ordered the Powder Magazine to be blown up, His Majesty's Colours to be struck, and the Bugle to sound a general retreat—the enemy advanced and were wofully cut up by the Explosion, 250 killed upon the spot the numbers wounded not known ... The Town capitulated & His Majesty's Troops retreated to Kingston. ... The moment they [*the Americans*] got in they began to plunder and burn the public Buildings which they continued for four days ... The public Buildings burnt on this occasion were—The Governt. House, The Block House at the Garrison, The Naval Barracks. ...

As my mother and myself were sitting at breakfast, the dogs kept up a very unusual barking. I went to the door to discover the cause; when I looked up, I saw the hill-side and fields, as far as the eye could reach, covered with American soldiers. . . .

Two men stepped from the ranks . . . came into the room where we were standing and took coals from the hearth without speaking a word. My mother knew instinctively what they were going to do. She went and asked for the commanding officer. . . . She entreated him to spare her property and said she was a widow with a young family. He answered . . . that his orders were to burn, but that he would spare the house, which he did; and he said as a sort of justification for the burning, that the buildings were used as a barrack, and the mill furnished flour for British troops. Very soon we saw columns of dark smoke arise from every building, and of which at early morn had been a prosperous homestead, at noon there remained only smouldering ruins. . . . My father had been dead less than two years. Little remained of all his labours.

1. *Why were the government buildings in York burned?*
2. *The owner of the farm was Mrs. John Harris. Why did the Americans burn her farm? Why did they spare the house?*
3. *What would be your feelings toward Americans*
   a) *if you were a resident of York?*
   b) *if you were in Mrs. Harris' position?*

Some incidents of the war were both amusing and tragic. In 1814, a British fleet sailed toward the American capital of Washington. The defenders, caught by surprise, were easily defeated. Everything happened so quickly that in the President's mansion British soldiers found the dinner which President Madison and his wife Dolly had been forced to desert. In revenge for the burning of York, the British partly burned the mansion. Later, the Americans covered the mansion with a coat of white paint to hide the smoke damage. Since that day, it has been known as the White House.

Three weeks later an English fleet was bombing the fort at Baltimore, but could not bring down the American flag. One of the observers was Francis Scott Key. Key was so impressed with this stand that he wrote *The Star Spangled Banner*, the song which would become the American national anthem.

But the War of 1812, like all wars, caused great sadness, suffering, and bloodshed. One incident during the Battle at Queenston Heights shows the tragedy of war and the effect war has on those who take part:

In this regiment there were a father and three sons, American U.E. Loyalists, all of them crack shots. In a covering party one day the father and one of the sons were sentries on the same point. An American rifleman dropped a man to his left, but in so doing exposed himself, and almost as a matter of course, was instantly dropped in his turn by the unerring aim of the father. The . . . old man of course (for it was a ceremony seldom neglected) went up to rifle [rob] his victim. On examining his features he discovered that it was his own brother. . . . This would have horrified most men, but a Yankee has much of the stoic in him and is seldom deprived of his equanimity [calmness]. He took possession of his valuables, consisting of an old silver watch and a clasp knife, his rifle and appointments, coolly remarking that it, "served him right for fighting for the rebels, when all the rest of his family fought for King George."

1. *What does this incident show about the feelings of the Loyalists toward Americans?*

2. *Can you understand why the Loya-list father acted as he did? What does this story tell you about the effect of war on human behaviour?*

By 1814, both sides had grown weary of a war that it now appeared neither side would win. By late 1814, Britain and the United States agreed to end it.

The last battle of the war was a bizarre one. Early in 1815 the Americans under Andrew Jackson won a great victory at New Orleans against a large British force. After the rejoicing was over, it was learned that Britain and the United States had agreed to peace terms several weeks before. The news had arrived too late to prevent the battle.

The Results of the War

The Treaty of Ghent, signed December 24, 1814, brought the War of 1812 to an end. At this time, Britain seemed to have the upper hand, but the Americans refused to surrender any territory. Canada had hoped to pick up some land south of the Great Lakes, but with the Americans being firm in their attitude, Britain did not want to push the point. Canadians too were tired of the war and agreed to the results. In the end, the Treaty of Ghent left things almost exactly as they had been before the war.

Was the war necessary? Let us first examine the American point of view. Many Americans believed they had fought another War of Independence, to maintain their rights of trade, and their rights on the seas. Great Britain agreed to recognize these rights, so in this matter the Americans were successful. Of course they were not successful in capturing Canada.

For Canada it was a struggle for its very existence. In this respect, the war was a success. Did Canadians gain anything else? There were some economic gains. Although they were not involved in heavy fighting, the Maritime provinces benefited because of the increased shipping of war materials and other products during the war. The large sums of money spent by Britain to buy food and supplies, build ships, and restore buildings also meant new wealth for Upper Canada.

Some other gains could not be seen at the time of the war. During the years of conflict, the separate provinces of British North America had shown friendship and co-operation. This spirit would be one of the first steps toward a full union of these provinces, Confederation.

By far the most important effect of the war on Canadians, though, was in the discovery of a new sense of pride and nationalism. Here are some viewpoints from Canadians who lived in the period during and after the war:

> Madison and his group of British haters naturally supposed that as Upper Canada consisted of 70 000 inhabitants, our country would fall an easy prey to his ambition. But British and Canadian loyalty, patriotism and courage defeated their dark designs against the liberties of mankind. Even the patriotic and intellectual part of the American people denounced this causeless war against Great Britain. . . . And when the war was declared, our fathers knew their duty. The blood of our United Empire Loyalist forefathers warmed again in their bosoms, and pulsated in the hearts of their sons and grandsons, and in the hearts of hundreds of others who had adopted Canada, under the flag of British law and liberty, as their home. . . .

> The people of Canada are proud of the men, and of the deeds, and of the recollections of those days. They feel that the war of 1812 is an episode in the story of a young people, glorious in itself and full of promise. They believe that the infant which, in its very cradle, could strangle invasion, struggle and endure bravely . . . is capable of a nobler development, if God wills further trial.

> We do not wish to make our children quarrelsome or offensive, but we do wish them to be patriotic Canadians, full of loyalty to their flag, their Empire and their King. We wish them to understand what their predecessors did in order that they may have faith in themselves and in their country; and we intend that they shall learn the achievements of the past in order that they may have a true basis for their

own manhood and womanhood. . . . The noble deeds of our ancestors performed for high purposes are the surest sources for the development of the strong and true emotions that make human character vital.

We should teach other lessons from the War of 1812. We should fill each child's life with a splendid courage that can never be dismayed, by telling how a few determined settlers scattered widely over a new country successfully repelled invading armies coming from a country with a population of twentyfold larger. We should teach reverence not only for manhood but for womanhood by recounting the terrible hardships endured willingly by Canadian women generally, as well as by proudly relating the noble work done by individual women.

. . . I am a flag-waver, and I shall make every boy and girl whom I can ever influence a flag-waver who loves his flag and waves it because it represents freedom, and honour, and justice, and truth, and unity, and a glorious history, the most triumphantly progressive that has been achieved by any nation in the development of the world.

1. *What words and sentences in these speeches convey the speakers' pride and patriotism?*

2. *What lessons do they want Canadians to learn from the War of 1812?*

The War of 1812 had been called the war which both sides won. The Canadians, because of their success against great odds, and the bravery of their soldiers, considered the war a victory. These things, combined with the loyalty to Britain showed by the French Canadians, encouraged Canadians in feeling that they were different from Americans. The sense of a unique Canadian nationality and "personality" began with the War of 1812.

Places to Know

Queenston Heights   Lundy's Lane   Laura Secord's house
Brock's Monument   Fort George

All of these places, historic sites of the War of 1812, can be visited during one trip to the Niagara Peninsula.

Things to Do: 1. *Review:*
—*What do you think were the issues which started the war?*
—*What were the American aims in the war?*
—*What were the Canadian aims?*
—*Which of the above aims were achieved at the end of the war?*

2. *Debate the proposition: The War of 1812 was a needless war and should never have been fought.*

3. *Write a short story using the War of 1812 as a background. Your two leading characters could be two teenage brothers: one is United Empire Loyalist and fights for Canada; the other has remained in the United States and fights for the Americans. The two are on opposite sides in the Battle of Queenston Heights.*

4. *By the end of the war, many Canadians felt themselves to be different from Americans. Do you think there is a difference between Canadians and Americans today? If so, make a list of the differences you find.*

Brock's Monument at Queenston Heights.

4
The Rebellions of 1837

A popular figure in books and movies is the loner, the rebel who stands against society or against the people in power, the *ESTABLISHMENT*. Look at the section on Nellie McClung, page 363. Nellie McClung has recently become a popular subject for books and plays. Can you explain why this might have happened? Turning to a different kind of rebel, part of the popularity of such groups as the Beatles and the Rolling Stones is due to the impression they give of being against the Establishment. Do you remember the stir the Beatles caused when they introduced the long hair style?

One of the first Canadians who fought the Establishment was William Lyon Mackenzie. A fiery, Scottish-born newspaper editor, Mackenzie left his mark on Canada through his fight to win *RESPONSIBLE GOVERNMENT* for Canadians. Pitted against Mackenzie was the power of the political Establishment, then called the *FAMILY COMPACT*.

The concept of responsible government is a simple but very important aspect of Canada's government. It means that those in Parliament who are responsible for making the laws must be "responsible" to the people. In Canada, the Prime Minister and his Cabinet shape the laws. They are responsible to the people of Canada for these laws. Of course, in such a large country, the government cannot consult all the people directly. This is why we have elected representatives. By being "responsible" to our elected representatives in the House of Commons, the government is also responsible to the people. If the majority of our Members of Parliament vote against some proposed government legislation, the Prime Minister and his Cabinet must resign. This is the meaning of "responsible government".

In the 1830s a group of men called *REFORMERS* tried to win responsible government for Upper Canada. The leader of this group was William Lyon Mackenzie. The system of government then practised in Upper Canada can be seen in the chart on the next page.

At the head of the government was Sir Francis Bond Head, the Lieutenant-Governor of the province, sent by Britain. The Reformers accused Sir Francis of placing in the important positions of government people drawn from a small circle of his friends: wealthy men and Church of England officials. This small group was called the Family Compact.

Responsible Government

GOVERNOR

—appointed by Britain
—formed government policies
—called elections
—Executive and Legislative Councils
  responsible to him, not to the
  Elected Assembly

GOVERNOR-GENERAL

—nominated by Cabinet
—does not make policies

EXECUTIVE COUNCIL

—advised Governor
—carried out his policies
—appointed by Governor

LEGISLATIVE COUNCIL

—voted on legislation passed
  by Legislative Assembly
—appointed by Governor

SENATE

—votes on legislation
  passed by House
  of Commons
—appointed by
  Cabinet

PRIME MINISTER
and CABINET

—responsible to
  House of Commons
—introduce government
  legislation

LEGISLATIVE ASSEMBLY

—passed legislation
—elected by people

HOUSE OF COMMONS

—passes legislation
—elected by People

PEOPLE

1837

PEOPLE

TODAY

William Lyon Mackenzie.

Mackenzie became a leader of the Reformers. Through his newspaper, the *Colonial Advocate,* he attacked the Family Compact. One evening in June, 1826, some of his opponents broke into his printing shop on Front St., York (Toronto), smashed his printing press and tossed it into the harbour. The sympathy Mackenzie received from this incident made him a champion of the people. He was elected to the Assembly and continued his attack on the Family Compact from there.

Follow the bitter feud between Mackenzie and the Family Compact.

Mackenzie:

> The most extraordinary collection of sturdy beggars, parsons, priests, pensioners, army people, place-men, bank directors, and stock and land jobbers ever established to act as a paltry screen to a rotten government. They cost the country about £40,000 a year, and the good laws by which it might benefit, they tomahawk. They don't like to be called a *nuisance*.
>
> This family connexion rules Upper Canada according to its own good pleasure, and has no efficient check from this country to guard the people against its acts of tyranny and oppression.
>
> It includes the whole of the judges of the supreme, civil and criminal tribunal. . . .
>
> It includes half the Executive Council and provincial cabinet.
>
> It includes the Speaker and eight members of the Legislative Council.
>
> It includes the persons who have control of the Canada Land Company's monopoly. . . .
>
> This family compact surround the Lieutenant-Governor, and mould him like wax to their will; they fill every office with their relatives, dependants, and partisans; by them justices of the peace and officers of the militia are made and unmade. . . .

Sir Francis Bond Head:

> The "family compact" of Upper Canada is composed of those members of its society who, either by their abilities and character have been honoured by the confidence of the executive government, or who, by their industry and intelligence, have amassed wealth. The party, I own, is comparatively a small one; but to put the multitude at the top and the few at the bottom is a radical reversion of the pyramid of society which every reflecting man must foresee can end only by its downfall.

1. *What arguments does Mackenzie present against the Family Compact? What positions do its members hold in government?*
2. *How does Bond Head defend the Family Compact?*

Following a particularly bitter attack against the Family Compact, Mackenzie was expelled from the Assembly. When new elections were held, the undaunted Mackenzie ran again. Here are the results:

A political meeting at "The Corners" in 1837.

Forty sleighs came down into York and escorted their champion (Mackenzie) to the polls. It was generally believed that Colonel Washburn would stand up against Mackenzie, but he withdrew his name and gave his support to Mr. Street, who was introduced to the electors by Col. E. W. Thomson. . . . Mackenzie made a speech, and the names of the candidates were submitted. A forest of hands went up when Mackenzie's name was proposed. But one hand was raised when Mr. Street's name was presented. . . . At 1:20 o'clock [13:20] the polls opened. At 3 o'clock [15:00] Mackenzie had polled one hundred and nineteen votes and his opponent one. The latter then withdrew from the unequal contest.

1. *What does the vote show about Mackenzie's popularity?*

2. *What is the difference between the methods of voting then and today?*

Were Mackenzie's actions really aimed at winning responsible government, or was he, as his opponents accused, trying to separate Canada from Britain?

Mackenzie:

We have planted the Standard of Liberty in Canada, for the attainment of the following objects: . . . Civil and Religious Liberty . . .

The Abolition of Hereditary Honors . . .

A Legislature, composed of a Senate and Assembly chosen by the People.

An Executive, to be composed of a Governor and other officers elected by the public voice.

A Judiciary, to be chosen by the Governor and Senate, and composed of the most learned, honorable, and trustworthy, of our citizens . . .

A Free Trial by Jury . . .

The Vote by Ballot . . .

No man to be compelled to give military service . . .

Ample funds . . . to secure the blessings of education to every citizen. . . .

The Family Compact:

. . . The proximity of these provinces to the United States is one cause of our agitation and discontent . . . presenting an extensive frontier to the United States, new opinions about politics have been introduced from that great manufactory of such commodities; and many native Americans, settling among us, have doubtless imported with them a prejudice against G. Britain which, among the lower classes of the United States' citizens, has, ever since the revolution, descended from father to son. . . .

. . . In many parts of the province the teachers are Americans. For the sake of obtaining employment they have swallowed the oath of allegiance which agrees so ill with them that the rest of their lives is spent in attempts to disgorge it. These men are utterly ignorant of every thing English and could not if they tried instruct their pupils in any of the duties which the connection of the province with England casts upon them. The books they use are all American, filled with inflated accounts of American independence and the glorious wars with England.

1. *Which of Mackenzie's demands are concerned with responsible government? Do you think his demands are reasonable?*
2. *According to the Family Compact, what is the real source of discontent in Upper Canada? Is the same complaint made in Canada today? How?*

The government refused to consider any of Mackenzie's proposals. As the elections of 1836 approached, Bond Head campaigned against Mackenzie and the Reformers. This was a very unusual step for a man in the position of Lieutenant-Governor. Here is an example of an election poster:

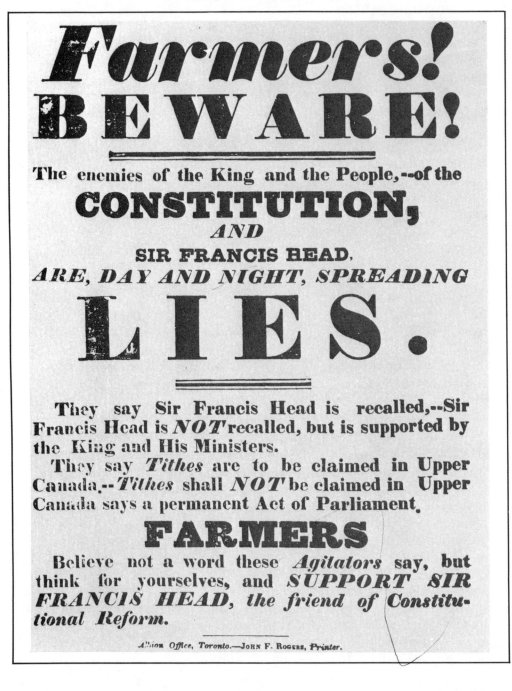

Farmers!
BEWARE!

The enemies of the King and the People,--of the

CONSTITUTION,
AND
SIR FRANCIS HEAD,
ARE, DAY AND NIGHT, SPREADING
LIES.

They say Sir Francis Head is recalled,--Sir Francis Head is *NOT* recalled, but is supported by the King and His Ministers.

They say *Tithes* are to be claimed in Upper Canada,--*Tithes* shall *NOT* be claimed in Upper Canada says a permanent Act of Parliament.

FARMERS

Believe not a word these *Agitators* say, but think for yourselves, and *SUPPORT SIR FRANCIS HEAD, the friend of Constitutional Reform.*

Albion Office, Toronto.--JOHN F. ROGERS, *Printer.*

As a result of such tactics, Mackenzie and most of the Reformers were defeated in the election. This meant that any chance of peaceful changes in government had almost disappeared. Mackenzie decided to take desperate measures. On November 27, 1837, he issued this handbill:

CANADIANS! Do you love freedom? I know you do. Do you have oppression? Who dare deny it? Do you wish perpetual peace, and a government founded upon the eternal heaven-born principle of the Lord Jesus Christ—a government bound to enforce the law to do to each other as you would be done by? Then buckle on your armour, and put down the villains who oppress and enslave our country. . . . One short hour will deliver our country from the oppressor; and freedom in religion, peace and tranquillity, equal laws and an improved country will be the prize. . . .

Up then, brave Canadians! Get ready your rifles, and make short work of it. . . .

1. *What is Mackenzie asking his followers to do?*

2. *What causes does Mackenzie tell the people they are fighting for?*

In Lower Canada, for similar reasons, fighting broke out between government forces and Reformers under Louis-Joseph Papineau. The uprisings of Mackenzie and Papineau are the first rebellions in Canada's history. The end came quickly for both movements. On December 7, 1837, Mackenzie's rebels gathered at Montgomery's Tavern, on Yonge St. Here are two eyewitness accounts of the "battle":

A Loyal Volunteer:

As the militia advanced, their opponents melted away. . . . I could see there two or three hundred men, now firing irregularly at the advancing loyalists; now swaying to and fro without any apparent design. . . . We had by this time arrived within cannon shot of the tavern itself. Two or three balls were seen to strike and pass through it. A crowd of men rushed from the doors, and scattered wildly in a northerly direction. Those on the hill wavered, receded under shelter of the undulating land, and then fled like their fellows. Their horsemen took the side-road westward, and were pursued, but not in time to prevent their escape. Had our right and left wings kept pace with the main body, the whole insurgent force must have been captured.

A Rebel Volunteer:

That night we marched down as far as McGill street and then fell back when we could have chased Sheriff Jarvis' men right into the city.

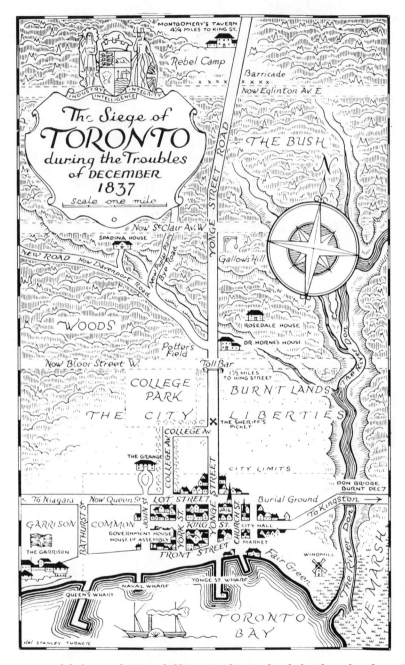

The Siege of TORONTO during the Troubles of DECEMBER 1837

Things would have been different if we had had a leader. Poor Mackenzie meant well, and was brave enough, but he was no soldier. If old Colonel Van Egmond had been there that night all the English in Toronto—and there were not many just then—could not have kept the city from us. But he wasn't there, and we missed our chance.

1. *Would you call this a real battle? Why?*   2. *What hindered the rebels, according to the two accounts?*

The "fighting" lasted less than one hour. Most of the rebels were pardoned immediately, except Mackenzie. He escaped to the United States, where he lived until his pardon a few years later. He then returned to Canada, where he died in 1861.

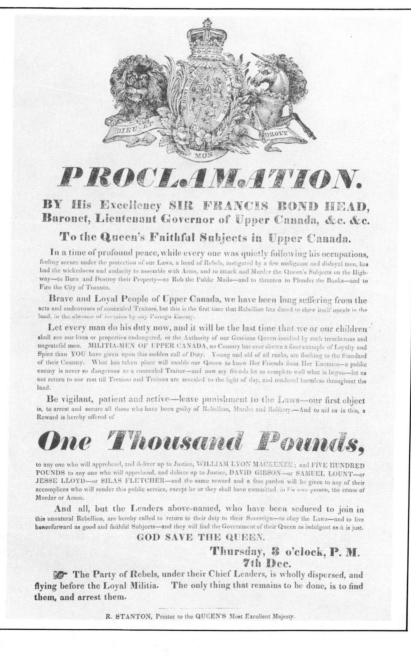

PROCLAMATION.

BY His Excellency SIR FRANCIS BOND HEAD,
Baronet, Lieutenant Governor of Upper Canada, &c. &c.

To the Queen's Faithful Subjects in Upper Canada.

In a time of profound peace, while every one was quietly following his occupations, feeling secure under the protection of our Laws, a band of Rebels, instigated by a few malignant and disloyal men, has had the wickedness and audacity to assemble with Arms, and to attack and Murder the Queen's Subjects on the Highway—to Burn and Destroy their Property—to Rob the Public Mails—and to threaten to Plunder the Banks—and to Fire the City of Toronto.

Brave and Loyal People of Upper Canada, we have been long suffering from the acts and endeavours of concealed Traitors, but this is the first time that Rebellion has dared to show itself openly in the land, in the absence of invasion by any Foreign Enemy.

Let every man do his duty now, and it will be the last time that we or our children shall see our lives or properties endangered, or the Authority of our Gracious Queen insulted by such treacherous and ungrateful men. MILITIA-MEN OF UPPER CANADA, no Country has ever shewn a finer example of Loyalty and Spirit than YOU have given upon this sudden call of Duty. Young and old of all ranks, are flocking to the Standard of their Country. What has taken place will enable our Queen to know Her Friends from Her Enemies—a public enemy is never so dangerous as a concealed Traitor—and now my friends let us complete well what is begun—let us not return to our rest till Treason and Traitors are revealed to the light of day, and rendered harmless throughout the land.

Be vigilant, patient and active—leave punishment to the Laws—our first object is, to arrest and secure all those who have been guilty of Rebellion, Murder and Robbery.—And to aid us in this, a Reward is hereby offered of

One Thousand Pounds,

to any one who will apprehend, and deliver up to Justice, WILLIAM LYON MACKENZE; and FIVE HUNDRED POUNDS to any one who will apprehend, and deliver up to Justice, DAVID GIBSON—or SAMUEL LOUNT—or JESSE LLOYD—or SILAS FLETCHER—and the same reward and a free pardon will be given to any of their accomplices who will render this public service, except he or they shall have committed, in his own person, the crime of Murder or Arson.

And all, but the Leaders above-named, who have been seduced to join in this unnatural Rebellion, are hereby called to return to their duty to their Sovereign—to obey the Laws—and to live henceforward as good and faithful Subjects—and they will find the Government of their Queen as indulgent as it is just.

GOD SAVE THE QUEEN.

Thursday, 3 o'clock, P. M.
7th Dec.

☞ The Party of Rebels, under their Chief Leaders, is wholly dispersed, and flying before the Loyal Militia. The only thing that remains to be done, is to find them, and arrest them.

R. STANTON, Printer to the QUEEN'S Most Excellent Majesty.

Mackenzie's rebellion was a dismal failure. But were his ideas also failures? Bond Head was recalled to England the very next year. In that same year the British government sent out Lord Durham to investigate the causes of the rebellion. His recommendation: responsible government for Canada. This recommendation became reality in 1849. Mackenzie, the failure as a rebel, had seen his goals fulfilled.

Word Study

Colonial Advocate   Family Compact   Lieutenant-Governor
Establishment   Legislative Assembly   Reformers
Executive Council   Legislative Council   Responsible Government

Things to Do   1. *Historians often debate the importance of the role of outstanding people in shaping history. Some say that great people create movements and events. Others argue that such events would have happened in any case: that seemingly "great individuals" are only products of their time; that these people happened to be at the right place at the right time. Which do you agree with? Can you think of individuals who have brought about great changes in the way people live?*

2. At the same time that William Lyon Mackenzie led his rebellion in Upper Canada, Louis-Joseph Papineau was leading a similar rebellion in Lower Canada. Find out more about rebellion in Lower Canada. Compare it with that in Upper Canada in terms of:
    —causes of the rebellions
    —personalities of the leaders
    —battles fought
    —results of the rebellions.

3. Do you agree with Mackenzie that force was necessary to change the existing order of things in 1837?

If you wished to bring about changes in our country, what channels would be open to you to make those changes in a peaceful way? How would you go about gaining support for your views?

4. In every generation, young people have fought against the accepted way of doing things. In the search to find their own identity, young people often create their own culture and their own heroes. In the past, the symbols of youth's "rebellion" against the Establishment have included rock music, long hair, and flower children.

What are the symbols of today's youth culture? Who are the heroes of today's young people?

5. Mackenzie rebelled against the political establishment. Do you think "rebellion" in today's youth culture has the same purpose?

5
Confederation

Bob Allen, twenty-six, works as a carpenter, building houses for a construction company. He likes his work, and he feels that his job is an important one. This morning on his way to work he is thinking carefully about a decision he may soon have to make. The union which represents Mr. Allen and his fellow workers has begun talks with the company over the terms of a new contract. The union will be asking for safer working conditions, a shorter work week, and higher pay.

Mr. Allen agrees with some of these demands. The cost of everything has gone up; his pay cheque cannot buy as much now as it did a year ago. Still, the union demand of a $2.00 an hour raise seems too high, even to him. It does not seem likely the company will agree to this. Mr. Allen wonders if the union will threaten a strike. He hopes not.

At work he expresses his doubts to his friend Harry Stein. "I can't help feeling our demands are too high," he says, "and yet, the company offer is just not enough." Stein is older, and he has been through many of these discussions before. He explains the bargaining process. "You see, Bob, the union doesn't really expect to receive all they ask for. On the other hand, the company will raise its offer. At some middle point, they will probably reach agreement. This is what we call a COMPROMISE solution."

"But why don't both sides simply state their true offers right from the start. Wouldn't this cut out a lot of bargaining?"

"That way, one side would win, and the side which gives in would lose," explained Stein. "No one wants to lose. The nice part of a compromise is that neither side gets everything they want, but neither side loses. Neither side is perfectly happy with the solution, but in one sense, both sides are winners. This is the meaning of compromise."

Most labour disputes in Canada are settled by this type of compromise solution. The strike weapon is used in a very small number of all labour disputes, about three per cent. In fact, compromise is familiar to Canadians in almost every walk of life. In your own activities, hardly a day goes by in which some form of compromise does not occur. On Saturday night, your parents want you home by 22:00. You would like to stay out until 24:00. Perhaps both sides can agree to a 23:00 curfew. On Sunday afternoon you like to watch hockey on television. Your sister would prefer a movie. Solution? You may watch hockey one Sunday, she will watch a movie the next. Perhaps you can think of other occasions both at home and at school in which you are forced to accept a compromise solution.

Canada's political history too is dotted by the principle of compromise. Often this has tended to make Canadian history seem dull and boring. After all, a problem settled by war and bloodshed seems far more exciting than one settled peacefully by negotiation and compromise. Yet war really settles very few problems, and creates many more of its own. The best hope for solutions lies in compromise, where each side may feel that it has gained by the results.

The creation of the Canadian nation, Confederation, was achieved by the process of compromise. South of the border, the United States was born out of the Revolutionary War of 1776. It was later kept together by a great Civil War. In contrast, Canada's unity and the growth of its independence were achieved by peaceful negotiation. The spirit of compromise has been an important factor in shaping the Canadian personality.

In this chapter we will study how Confederation, which is Canada's most important political event, was achieved. You will be asked to (a) examine the political problems facing Canada at this time; (b) suggest possible solutions to these problems; (c) discuss the solutions offered by the politicians; (d) decide which solution would be most acceptable to all concerned, in the best spirit of compromise. As you weigh the solutions, you will see that Confederation was only one of the solutions to the problems which faced Canada. Perhaps if you had been a leader of Canada at that time, your solution might have been totally different.

CONFEDERATION DAY
The Dominion of Canada

With the first dawn of this gladsome midsummer morn, we hail the birthday of a new nationality. A united British America, with its four millions of people, takes its place this day among the nations of the world. Stamped with a familiar name, which in the past has borne a record sufficiently honourable to entitle it to be perpetuated with a more comprehensive import, the DOMINION OF CANADA, on this First day of July, in the year of grace, eighteen hundred and sixty-seven, enters on a new career of national existence. Old things have passed away. The history of old Canada, with its contracted bounds, and limited divisions of Upper and Lower, East and West, has been completed, and this day a new volume is opened, New Brunswick and Nova Scotia uniting with Ontario and Quebec to make the history of a greater Canada, already extending from the ocean to the head waters of the great lakes, and destined ere long to embrace the larger half of this North American continent from the Atlantic to the Pacific.

In these words, the Toronto *Globe* hailed the creation of a new country. The union of the Provinces of British North America, Confederation, shaped the political future of Canada. Most Canadians, through their annual July 1 celebrations, recognize this fact. For them the idea of a united Canada is as natural as maple syrup on pancakes.

Many Canadians take Confederation for granted. Few, probably, are aware of how close the whole idea came to being rejected in 1867. Confederation was never a "sure thing". There was a great deal of opposition to it both before and after it became a fact. Even today there are groups opposing it. Yet imagine the consequences if Confederation had not been achieved: the provinces today might be units on their own, separate countries with perhaps a few social or economic ties. More likely, as small, weak units they would have been swallowed up by the United States. Confederation has allowed Canadians to remain independent. It has allowed them to retain their identity as a separate people.

The Background

In 1867, British North America consisted of six Provinces, widely separated from each other by natural barriers and poor communications. They knew little of each other and were united only by their loyalty to the British Crown. Their very survival as separate provinces was threatened in the decade before 1867. Each province had problems both inside and outside its borders. It seemed no province could solve these problems on its own.

The largest of the British North American colonies was the Province of Canada. The Act of Union of 1841 created this province by uniting Upper and Lower Canada (now Ontario and Quebec). Most of the population of Lower Canada was French, while that of Upper Canada was English. If this union was to succeed, it was clear that co-operation between English and French would be necessary.

The hoped-for co-operation was not to be. Differences between English and French surfaced many times after 1841. The main barriers to agreement and understanding were the cultural and religious differences of the two areas. These problems divided and weakened the government. Soon it was caught in a "deadlock". This meant that each side supported only its own interests and refused to compromise with the other side.

The partnership was not working. A new solution would have to be found. The Maritime provinces of Nova Scotia, New Brunswick, and Prince Edward Island were prosperous, although Newfoundland was not as well off. These provinces had a common geography and economic interests. To many, the idea of a Maritime union seemed to make more sense than the idea of a general Canadian union.

In British Columbia, the discovery of gold had attracted thousands of prospectors during the 1850s. After 1863 the gold fields were exhausted and the population began to decline. The colony on Vancouver Island suffered as a result. In 1866 the two colonies joined to form the Province of British Columbia. As it had little contact with the other Canadian provinces, British Columbia relied on Great Britain for help.

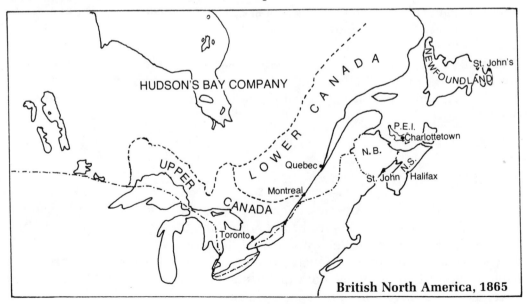

British North America, 1865

Cariboo Road to the gold fields of B.C.—miners going in, coach coming out guarded by armed men.

On the surface it seemed that neither the Maritimes nor British Columbia would have strong reasons for entering a union of the Provinces of British North America. By 1867, several factors outside their borders caused the provinces to rethink their position. The greatest of these was the threat from the United States.

The American Threat Americans had been fighting a bloody Civil War. The issue was whether the nation would remain united or separate into two countries. By 1865, the Northern States had defeated the Southern States, and the United States of America remained one country.

The war and its result created concern in Canada. During the war, relations between Britain and the North had become very tense. Many Northerners believed that the British supported the South. There was considerable anti-British and anti-Canadian feeling among Northerners. Would the victorious North now use its large army against the British Provinces in revenge? Many in Canada thought so.

A number of United States politicians and newspapers had also been urging the takeover of Canada. Many Americans at this time believed in "Manifest Destiny". They believed that it was the destiny of the United States to take over all of North America. This feeling is expressed in the following statement by an American politician:

> So I look upon Prince Rupert's Land and Canada, and see how an ingenious people are occupied with bridging rivers and making railroads and telegraphs, to develop, organize, create and preserve the great British provinces of the north, by the Great Lakes, the St. Lawrence and around the shores of Hudson's Bay, and I am able to say, "It is very well you are building excellent states to be hereafter admitted to the American Union".

"IT'S ONLY A QUESTION OF TIME."
OLD FOGYISM MAY HOLD HER BACK FOR A WHILE, BUT SHE IS BOUND TO COME TO US.

In 1867 the United States bought Alaska from the Russians. At the same time, Americans were eyeing the empty plains of the Northwest. They hoped to make this area part of the United States. If this were allowed to happen, British Columbia would be completely surrounded by American territory. If British America hoped to hold both British Columbia and the Northwest, it would have to act quickly.

In the first half of the nineteenth century, large numbers of Irish migrated to the U.S. At the time, England controlled all of Ireland. Many Irish people who resented this British control moved to the U.S. Once there, they continued to hold a grudge against England. A few decided to strike at England by attacking Canada. These people were called *Fenians*. Although the U.S. government claimed to have no interest in the Fenians, many Canadians felt the U.S. was secretly supporting them.

This picture shows a Fenian attack on Canada. What do the letters IRA on the flag stand for? How might the Fenian raids provide an argument for Confederation?

Economic Problems Another main concern in British North America was the new trade problems facing the provinces. As members of the British Empire, the Canadian provinces had long enjoyed certain privileges in their trade relations with Great Britain. British North America could count on Great Britain giving its products preferred treatment. The same products from other countries were subject to heavy *TARIFFS*, or taxes and so they had to be sold for a higher price. As long as Britain carried on this policy, British North America had a sure and steady market.

In 1846, however, Britain removed these special privileges. Canadian prod-

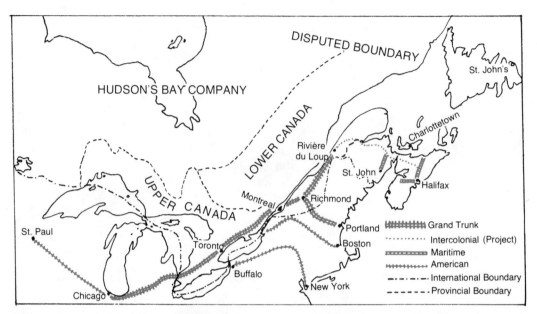

This map of British North America in 1865 shows the main railway routes in Canada and the U.S. Northeast. If a Canadian businessman were shipping goods by rail, would he find it easier to trade with the Maritimes or with the U.S.? What was needed to improve trade between Canada and the Maritimes? How would better trade aid the Confederation movement?

ucts now had to compete with those from other countries. Trade between Canada and Great Britain decreased. Canada turned to the United States as a possible trading partner. The problem was that the United States had placed a tariff wall around its own markets.

What is a tariff? A tariff is a tax placed by a country on foreign goods coming into its country. This policy has many advantages. Let us suppose that imported Japanese radios could sell for $25.00 in Canada. If locally made Canadian radios of the same quality sold for $35.00, the public would naturally buy the less expensive Japanese radios. This would hurt the Canadian radio business and create unemployment. The Canadian government can counter this by placing a $10.00 tariff on Japanese radios. This would push up the price of Japanese radios and make Canadian radios competitive. In turn this would help the radio industry, and create employment. Of course, there are also disadvantages. As we can see, the public has to pay higher prices for certain products. Also the Japanese might strike back by placing tariffs on some of our products entering Japan. This would then hurt Canadian sales to that country.

In balance, do you think tariffs are useful or harmful?

In 1854 the United States and the British North American provinces agreed to a *RECIPROCITY* Treaty. A "reciprocal" agreement is one in which both sides receive benefits. This treaty of 1854 allowed both sides to import certain products free of tariffs. These products included various foods, lumber, and furs. The Reciprocity Treaty produced increased trade and economic benefits for the Canadian provinces.

The tension created by the Civil War brought an end to the Reciprocity agreement in 1866. Unless some solution was found to their economic problems, the Canadian provinces would face a hard time. The solution was made more difficult by the fact that the Provinces had put up trade barriers against each other.

What solutions were available for all the problems which faced Canada? By 1867, Great Britain did not want to go on pouring money and troops into the defence of Canada. It hoped Canada would find a way to protect its own interests. To this end Britain favoured the proposal of some Canadian politicians. This was a union of all the provinces of British North America—Confederation.

Why was Confederation the answer? Here are the answers of some Canadian statesmen. Do you agree with their arguments?

George Cartier on the American threat:

> The question reduces itself to this—we must either have a Confederation of British North America or be absorbed by the American union. Some are of the opinion that it is not necessary to form such a confederation to prevent our absorption by the neighbouring republic, but they are mistaken. . . . The English provinces, separated as they are at present, cannot alone defend themselves. . . . When we are united, the enemy will know that if he attacks any province, either Prince Edward Island or Canada, he will have to deal with the combined forces of the Empire.

Alexander Galt on the trade barriers between the Provinces:

> . . . I go heartily for the union, because it will throw down the barriers of trade and give us the control of a market of four millions of people. What one thing has contributed so much to the wondrous material progress of the United States as the free passage of their products from one State to another? . . . I am in favour of a union of the provinces . . . because it will make us the third maritime state of the world.

On September 1, 1864, the leading politicians from all the provinces gathered at Charlottetown, P.E.I. Here the first proposals for Confederation were discussed. Two months later they met again at Quebec. After several more months of debate, these "Fathers of Confederation" worked out the basic plan for union.

The delegates still had to convince the citizens of their own provinces that Confederation was in their best interest. There would be three more years of meetings and discussions. At the end of these meetings the basic nature of Confederation was agreed upon.

Sir George Etienne Cartier. Cartier was French Canada's leading pro-Confederation spokesman.

The "Fathers of Confederation" at the Charlottetown Conference. Examine the picture closely. How many of these famous statesmen do you recognize?

What is Confederation?

The Nature of the Union   As a citizen of Canada, you consider yourself a Canadian. Yet you may also refer to yourself as Albertan, or *Québécois*, or Nova Scotian, or Ontarian. Indeed, in many parts of Canada there still exists among the people a feeling of local pride and fierce loyalty to one's province.

An American travelling through the Maritimes made this observation of Nova Scotians:

> Nova Scotia regards itself as more or less a country in its own right, much closer to maritime New England than to the prosperous Scottish business world of Montreal. The Nova Scotians are likely to refer to the rest of the now rather misnamed "Dominion" as "Canada" or "Upper Canada". I am told that there is even on the island of Cape Breton a kind of Cape Breton nationalism which makes a distinction between its own inhabitants and the rest of the population of Nova Scotia.

Was this written in 1867? Actually it was written in 1964, almost a century after Confederation!

Canadians in every part of the country can still feel such local loyalty because of the decision made by the Fathers of Confederation.

When the union of the Provinces of British North America was proposed, the delegates at Charlottetown were faced by the question: what sort of union shall we have? They had several examples to draw from, including Great Britain and the United States. Which system was best suited to Canada?

The Choices

1. LEGISLATIVE UNION In this type of government the provinces would agree to give up all powers to one government. This would make for a unified country. There would be no provincial governments, so there would be no conflicts between one government and another.

On the other hand, the qualities which made one part of the country different from another would tend to disappear. The same language and laws would apply to all parts of the country. This is the system practised in Great Britain.

2. FEDERAL UNION In this type of union the provinces would keep most of the important powers, while the central government would get some of the less important ones. This would allow each region of the country to develop in its own way.

On the other hand, the central government would be weak. It might not have the power to prevent quarrels between the provinces or to enforce decisions affecting the whole country. The United States was a Federal Union before 1860.

3. *CONFEDERATION* In this type of government, the provinces would remain individual units. They would have their own government to look after local matters. The provinces would agree to give to a central government certain powers which affected the country as a whole. This would allow certain areas to keep their individual customs, language, and even laws. They would be allowed to develop differently than other parts of the country. The central or federal government would have greater powers than the provinces.

On the other hand, the national government might not have the power needed to make decisions for the good of the whole country. Conflict might also develop between the provincial governments and the national government. The country might not be as unified as under a legislative union.

The following diagrams may help you see more clearly the differences between the three systems. In each diagram, two provinces, A and B, with capitals X and Y, are uniting to form one country, C, with the capital at Z. In a Federation the capital Z is more powerful than the provincial capitals, and is higher in the diagram. In a Confederation the provincial capitals are more powerful and so they are higher in the diagram.

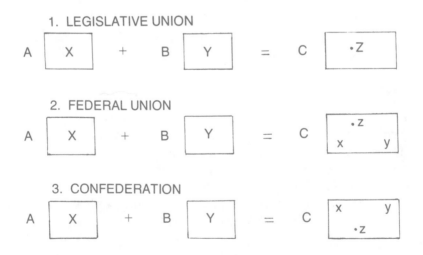

Do you remember the discussion of the term "compromise" at the beginning of this chapter? Compromise was to be a key to the decisions made by the delegates from the provinces. It meant that each province might have to give up its individual choice, for the sake of the national interest.

John A. Macdonald.

One of those who faced this problem was the man destined to be our first Prime Minister, John A. Macdonald:

> Now, as regards the comparative advantages of a Legislative and a Federal Union, I have never hesitated to state my own opinions. I have again and again stated in the House, that, if practicable, I thought a Legislative Union would be preferable. I have always contended that if we could agree to have one government and one parliament, legislating for the whole of these peoples, it would be the best, the cheapest, the most vigorous, and the strongest system of government we could adopt.

Macdonald's personal choice was for a Legislative Union. He realized, however, that this system would never be accepted by the other delegates. It failed to take into account the unique quality of British North America. What factors would the statesmen have to consider in making their decision? Why were the following important in their thinking:

—The geography of British North America
—The cultural makeup of the population
—The religious differences of the population
—The cultural and economic differences of the different regions?

Which of the three choices we have looked at would best recognize these important factors? Which would be the best "compromise" choice?

If you had been faced with this choice in 1864, how would you have decided? The decision was a difficult one for the founders as well. Let us weigh the problems facing the delegates at the Quebec Conference.

The Experience of History   As loyal British subjects, the delegates naturally wished to borrow as much as possible from the British experience. The provincial governments were already based on the British example. In this respect, the delegates naturally would lean to the British system.

However, Canada was different from Britain in several ways. The provinces were widely separated, unlike the British communities, and they had already developed different customs. In this respect, Canada was more like the United States.

Into the balance was thrown the recent horrors of the Civil War in the United States. Canadian statesmen could see the results of a Federal Union where the individual states were very strong and the central government weak. The threat of individual states breaking away had always been present, and in 1861 at last led to war.

The Canadian Experience   The experience of other countries was a factor in the final decision, but it was the Canadian experience which made the difference. Unlike Britain and the United States, Canada was made up of two founding peoples, English and French. Any system set up in Canada must take into account the differences in language, religion, laws, and customs of the two peoples. Neither French nor English would ever accept a system which might deprive them of their rights. Which system would best safeguard these rights?

The French Canadian choice is outlined in the following statements by French Canadian leaders:

Dorion:

> If a legislative union of the British North American Provinces is attempted there will be such an agitation in this portion of the province as was never witnessed before. . . .

Langevin:

> What we desire and wish, is to defend the general interests of a great country and of a powerful nation, by means of a central power. On the other hand, we do not wish to do away with our different manners, customs and laws; on the contrary, those are what we are most desirous of protecting, in the most complete manner by means of a Confederation. Under the new system we will have no more reason than at present to lose our character as French or English, under the pretext that we should all have the same general interest; and our interests in relation to race, religion and nationality will remain as they are at the present time.

Cartier:

> No other scheme presented itself but the Federation system*. . . . Some parties—through the press and by other modes—pretended that it was impossible to carry out Federation, on account of the differences of races and religions. Those who took this view of the question were in error. It was just the reverse. It was precisely on account of the variety of races, local interests, etc., that the Federation system ought to be resorted to, and would be found to work well.

> *In 1864, the delegates spoke of "federalism". Today that system is called Confederation. Over the years, the two terms have exchanged meanings.

1. *Which system of Government do the French leaders prefer? Why?*
2. *What advantages do they suggest will be present for the whole country under such a system?*

The delegates from the Maritimes also had strong views on this subject:

> The delegates from Prince Edward Island were almost without exception hostile to the original purpose of Legislative Union which the Conference was assembled to consider, but appeared not disinclined to the adoption of a Federal Union with Canada, provided their separate institutions were maintained as now existing.
> There was as great a disinclination on the part of the various Maritime Provinces to lose their individuality as separate political organizations, as we observed in the case of Lower Canada herself. Therefore we were forced to the conclusion that we must either abandon the idea of Union altogether, or desire a system of union in which the separate provincial organizations would be in some degree preserved. So that those who were . . . in favour of a Legislative Union, were obliged to modify their views and accept the project of a Federal Union as the only scheme practicable.

1. *What system is favoured by the Maritime delegates? Why?*
2. *In what respects is the Maritime choice similar to that of French*

Canada?

3. *Under the circumstances, what is the best "compromise" solution available?*

In view of these strong feelings from both Lower Canada and the Maritimes, it appeared that only one system would be acceptable to all—Federalism. How would Canadians deal with the dangers which had resulted in a Civil War in the U.S.? John A. Macdonald offered a solution; today, we call this system "Confederation":

> . . . In framing the constitution, care should be taken to avoid the mistakes and weaknesses of the United States' system. . . . We must reverse this process by establishing a strong central Government. . . .
>
> . . . our attempt was to form a government upon federal principles, which would give to the General Government the strength of a legislative and administrative union, while at the same time it preserved . . . liberty of action for the different sections. . . . In doing so we had the advantage of the experience of the United States . . . They declared by their Constitution that each state was a sovereignty in itself. . . . Here we have adopted a different system. We have strengthened the General Government. We have given the General Legislature all the great subjects of legislation. . . . We have thus avoided that great source of weakness which was the cause of the disruption of the United States.

1. *According to Macdonald, what were the weaknesses of the American system?*
2. *How would his solution avoid*

these weaknesses? Compare Macdonald's solution with your original choice. Are they similar?

This was in effect the agreement arrived at in the British North America Act, which is Canada's constitution. It provides for the sharing of the powers of government between the provincial and the central governments. Here are some examples of the division of these powers:

Some Powers of the Federal Government

—Unemployment insurance
—Taxation in any form
—Postal service
—Naval and military service

—Currency and coinage
—Indians and reservations
—Immigration
—Criminal law

Some Powers of Provincial Governments

—Sale of public lands
—Hospitals
—Education

—Direct taxation
—Property and civil rights

An important clause was also included. The Federal government had the power "to make laws for the Peace, Order and good Government of Canada", in those areas not assigned to the provinces.

1. Which of the above powers do you think are more important, the Provincial or the Federal? Why?
2. Do you think they would have been regarded in the same way in 1867? Which do you think have risen in importance since 1867?
3. What do you think is meant by the "Peace, Order and good Government" clause? Why do you think it was included?

The meeting of Canada's first Parliament under Confederation, Ottawa, 1867.

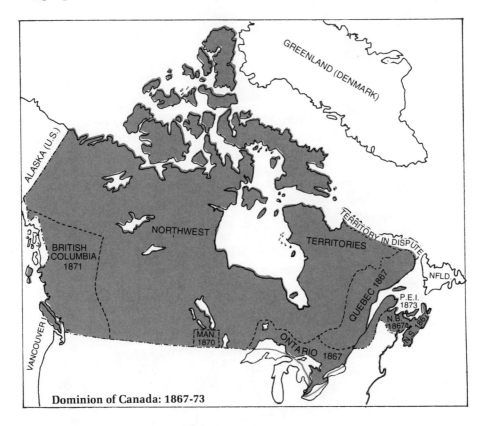

Dominion of Canada: 1867-73

Confederation Achieved

When the debates were over and it was time for decision, it was found that Confederation had hearty support in Upper Canada. It was passed by a narrower margin in Lower Canada, the French Canadian vote being twenty-seven in favour, twenty-one against. Nova Scotia and New Brunswick were also in favour. At last, on March 31, 1867, the British Parliament passed the British North America Act. This act united the two provinces of Canada, now called Ontario and Quebec, as well as Nova Scotia and New Brunswick into one country, the Dominion of Canada. Prince Edward Island, however, held out until 1873. British Columbia would not join until it was guaranteed a railway connection to the east. This province became part of Canada in 1871. The other province, Newfoundland, remained a British colony, and became Canada's tenth province only in 1949.

Thomas D'Arcy McGee gave Canadians this famous vision of Confederation:

> I look to the future of my adopted country with hope, though not
> without anxiety. I see in the not remote distance one great nationality,

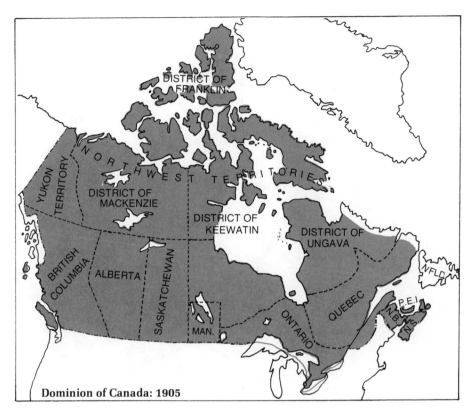

Dominion of Canada: 1905

bound, like the shield of Achilles, by the blue rim of Ocean. I see it quartered into many communities, each disposing of its internal affairs, but all bound together by free institutions, free intercourse and free commerce. I see within the round of that shield that peaks of the Western Mountains and the crests of the Eastern waves, the winding Assiniboine, the five-fold lakes, the St. Lawrence, the Ottawa, the Saguenay, the St. John, and the basin of Minas. By all these flowing waters in all the valleys they fertilise, in all the cities they visit in their courses, I see a generation of industrious, contented, moral men, free in name and in fact—men capable of maintaining, in peace and in war, a constitution worthy of such a country!

Word Study

tariff
Act of Union
constitution
Quebec Conference
Charlottetown Conference

Confederation
Legislative Union
Federal Union
Grand Trunk
deadlock

compromise
Reciprocity
British North America
Maritime Union
Manifest Destiny

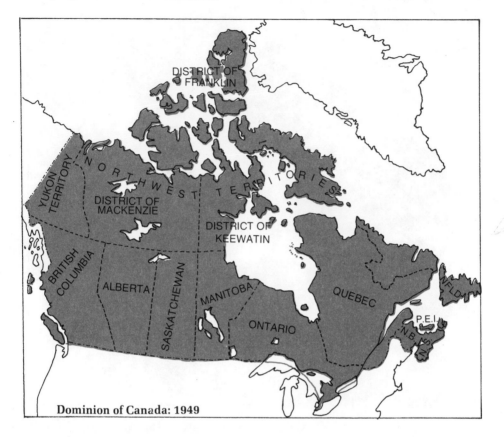

Dominion of Canada: 1949

Things to Do 1. Review the chief causes of the union of the provinces of British North America? Which do you think was the most important?

2. List the chief arguments presented by French Canadians against Confederation. Debate the proposition: Confederation has made French Canadians a minority within Canada and has damaged French Canadian culture.

3. If the founding Fathers of Confederation had adopted a Legislative Union instead of a Federal Union in 1867, how would Canada be a different country today?

4. Using other history books and the encyclopedia, write a short biography of each of the following: George Brown; George Cartier; John A. Macdonald; A. T. Galt; Charles Tupper. Which man do you think did the most to achieve Confederation?

5. Write a short paper on the condition the Canadian provinces would be in today if Confederation had never been achieved.

6. Compare the powers of the Federal and provincial governments as set out in the B.N.A. Act. Which do you think has more responsibility?

7. What sources of tax money are available to the Federal Government? What sources are available to the provincial governments?

6
The Riel Rebellions

It is July 20, 1885. The setting is a small, hot courtroom in the town of Regina, Northwest Territories. A stocky, bearded man sits in the prisoner's dock as the charge is read. The prisoner "did maliciously and traitorously attempt . . . by force and arms to subvert and destroy the Constitution and Government of this realm". The trial of Louis Riel, the most famous trial in the history of Canada, is about to begin.

The trial of Louis Riel was the end of fifteen years of unrest and rebellion in the West. These rebellions were the first and only time Canadians fought against other Canadians. It was the first time a Canadian government had to raise an army on its own soil, to fight its own cause, without the help of Britain. How had events come to such a state? Who was to blame?

The Background of the Rebellion

In 1869, less than two years after Confederation, the Hudson's Bay Company sold its possessions in the Northwest to Canada. The Company was giving Canada control, not only of a vast region, but of the people in it as well. This included a number of Indian nations such as the Cree and the Blackfoot. It also included the white settlers of the Red River colony and ten thousand *METIS* scattered throughout the territory. Who were the Métis? An observer describes them in this way:

> The active opponents of the incoming Government are all of what is termed the "French halfbreed" population. Their total number is about five thousand, of whom between six and eight hundred appear to be fighting men. In these numbers I include only the local population of the settlement at Red River,—but scattered up and down the territory of Rupert's Land there are great numbers of the same class, regarding the gross number of whom I possess no means of forming an idea.

> The whole nation has its origin between the traders and servants, European and Canadian, of the Hudson's Bay Company, and the Indian women whom they have married. Born at the different trading posts in every part of the country, the children of these people have settled at Red River, and, while still largely supporting themselves by

Métis buffalo hunters.

the buffalo hunts and other roving modes of life, have brought certain limited portions of land in the colony under rude cultivation.

As a class, they are quiet and civil when not excited, but when roused are quite destitute of self control. Their honesty and trustworthiness are well known, their hospitality, more especially to each other, is great according to their means. . . .

They claim to be a nation, already, along with the English half-breeds, whom they claim as their brethren, in possession of this country, and entitled, under the Act of Confederation, to a voice similar to that conceded to the other Provinces respecting their entrance into the Confederation. They have always claimed a commanding interest in the country, and are now indignant at the Hudson's Bay Company for not having more effectually protected their assumed rights at the period of the transfer to Canada.

The English half-breeds have altogether abstained from taking any part in the demonstrations now being made. They, however, will not actively oppose them, and profess no sentiments of loyalty whatever to the Canadian authorities.

1. Where did the Métis come from?
2. Where did they live?
3. Write a list of the adjectives used to describe the Métis.
4. How did the Métis make their living?
5. What did they think of the sale of the Northwest to Canada? What did the English Métis think of their coming union with Canada?

Part Indian, part European, the Métis did not consider themselves members of either group. A proud people, they thought of themselves as a separate nation. For years they had lived independent lives, their economy based on the annual summer buffalo hunts. By 1869, however, most of the buffalo were gone. The migrating herds had been destroyed in senseless slaughters in the United States. Many of the Métis began to settle down, establish roots, and build farms in the Red River area. What did this group have to fear from Canada? The first concern of the Métis was: would the government of Canada respect the Métis rights to their land, their French language, and their Roman Catholic religion?

Prime Minister John A. Macdonald might have calmed their fears. However, he failed to inform the Métis of Canada's true intentions. The suspicious Métis set up their own government to look after their rights. One of the leaders of this government was Louis Riel.

In the summer of 1869 Louis Riel was only twenty-four. His father was a Métis and his mother was the daughter of the first white woman in the West. Riel was well educated. He had studied religion and law in Montreal. He was a good student, and also proud and hot-tempered. When he returned to the West his education made him a natural leader of the Métis. His men blocked the entry of Canadian officials into the Red River territory. Riel claimed they had no right to be there.

These actions angered a number of the Canadians at Red River, including John Schultz and Thomas Scott. They led a revolt against Riel's Provisional Government. The revolt failed and Scott was captured. He and Riel quarrelled constantly. Finally the Provisional Government tried and executed him. Why was Scott executed?

An Observer:

> Scott had so exasperated his guards that they threatened to shoot him themselves. This they would almost certainly have done.

Scott:

> I believe they are bad enough to shoot me, but I can hardly think they dare do it.

Riel:

> Scott, at the head of his troops, attempted to seize the President of the Government by surrounding a house where the President was often to be found.
> ... the English settlers and Canadians had laughed at and despised the French Half-breeds, believing that they would not dare to take the life of anyone, and that, under these circumstances, it would be impossible to have peace and establish order in the country; an example must therefore be made.
> Scott was executed because his execution was necessary to maintain order.
> We must make Canada respect us.

1. *Do you think the execution of Scott was justified?*
2. *What do you think were the real motives behind the execution?*

Executing Scott was Riel's greatest mistake. Before this, many people including some English sympathized with his cause. Even Macdonald admitted that many of Riel's aims had been reasonable.

But the execution created great uproar. Prime Minister Macdonald was forced to send troops to put down what was called the "Métis rebellion" and capture Riel. Riel, afraid for his life, escaped to the United States. The following year, 1871, the Red River settlement entered Confederation as part of a new province, Manitoba. Riel was actually elected as a Member of Parliament from that province, but with a price on his head, he was never able to serve.

The Rebellion of 1885

In time most of the Métis, fearing the advance of settlement from the East, sold their lands for almost nothing to land speculators. They travelled far to the west and took up farmlands in the valley of the South Saskatchewan River, near Duck Lake. Here they hoped to be free to follow their way of life. They would soon be disappointed again.

The Government Position   The Canadian Government's position on the West was influenced by one large factor: the need to build a railway to the Pacific. The Government put all its energy into this project, ignoring the problems of the Native People of the West. By 1882, the Indians and Métis of Saskatchewan were voicing the same complaints heard at Red River in 1869. They wanted assurances of the title to their lands. The Indians were especially bitter because the Canadian government did not appear to be keeping its treaty obligations. With the coming of the railroad there would be a new influx of white settlers. Again the Indian way of life would be threatened. To Prime Minister John A. Macdonald, however, the problems of settlement and of the Native Peoples of the West were second in importance to the railway. In fact, Macdonald did not take the complaints of the Indians and Métis seriously. His attitude toward these people is revealed by many of his statements.

On the Indian Chiefs Big Bear and Piapot:

> Indian loafers

On the complaints of the Indians and the Métis:

> If you waited for a half-breed or an Indian to become contented you may wait till the millenium.

On giving the Métis *SCRIP*, or paper title to their land:

> They will either drink it or waste it or sell it.

On the possibility of a rebellion in the West:

> I do not believe there is the slightest danger from the half-breeds unless they should be joined by the Indians. . . . our information goes to show that the Indians are quite quiet and there is no danger their joining with the half-breeds.

1. *What is there in Macdonald's statements to indicate his lack of understanding of the Métis and Indian position?*

Macdonald's government was indeed in a difficult position. In 1869 at Red

River they had not intended to take away the land from the Métis. It was a mistake on Macdonald's part not to inform the Métis that their rights would be respected. He had delayed, putting things off until the last moment, and then it was too late. The same thing was now happening again in Saskatchewan. It was because of this common human weakness of delaying the inevitable that John A. was known to his friends as "Old Tomorrow".

Macdonald states his view of the problem:

> If they desire to be considered as Indians there are most liberal reserves that they could go to with the others; but if they desired to be considered white men they would get 160 acres [64 ha] of land as homesteads. But they are not satisfied with that; they want to get land scrip of equal quantity—I think upwards of 200 acres [80 ha]—and then get as a matter of course their homesteads as well.

There was the further problem that many Métis had sold their original titles at Red River very cheaply to land speculators. Would the same thing occur in Saskatchewan?

Macdonald noted:

> ... The half-breed had his own lot, he was not cultivating the land that he had. Giving him his land and giving him more land was giving him nothing. The nomadic half-breed, who had been brought up to hunt, having had merely his shanty to repair to in the dead season, when there was no game—what advantage was it to him to give him 160 or 240 acres [80 or 96 ha] more? It was of no use to him whatever, but it would have been of great use to the speculators who were working on him and telling him that he was suffering. Oh! How awful he was suffering, ruined, destroyed, starving, because he did not get 240 acres somewhere else, or the scrip for it, that he might sell it for $50! No, Sir; the whole thing is a farce.

1. *What did Macdonald have to consider, in deciding whether the Métis were entitled to land?*
2. *What did Macdonald fear would* *happen, if he agreed to Métis land claims in Saskatchewan? What solutions would you have suggested for these problems?*

By 1884 the Métis in Saskatchewan felt threatened again by the powerful East. What were they to do? The answer: bring back Louis Riel.

Riel agreed to return. Again came the Métis demands for recognition of their land and their rights. Again silence from the government. This time the result was a true rebellion. In 1885, at Duck Lake, Frog Lake, Frenchmen's Butte, Cut Knife Hill, Fish Creek and Batoche, the Métis and their Indian allies fought detachments of North West Mounted Police and Canadian soldiers.

The Métis and Indians, under the leadership of Gabriel Dumont, Big Bear, and Poundmaker, fought well. But they fought against overwhelming odds. Along with superior manpower, the Canadian army also had the advantages of cannon and Gatling guns.

The 12th and 35th Regiments on their way to fight the Métis in Saskatchewan, 1885, under the command of General Middleton.

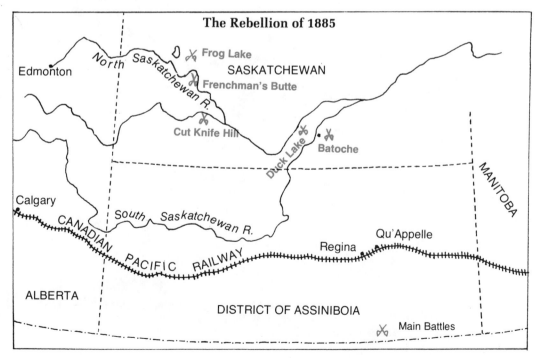

The Rebellion of 1885

Poundmaker, chief of the Crees.

The Battle of Fish Creek. The Métis are hidden at the bottom of the hill. As the Canadian soldiers show themselves at the top, they become easy targets.

Moreover, Louis Riel had begun to act strangely. He began to call himself a prophet. He believed he would set up a new Church in the West with himself as Pope. During the fighting, Riel often walked around in the open holding up a crucifix. He became an actual hindrance. Once he prevented Dumont from ambushing and destroying a Mounted Police force. Later, Dumont wrote sadly: "I had confidence in his faith and his prayers and that God would listen to him."

The end of the Northwest Rebellion came quickly. Riel himself was captured with most of the leaders of the rebellion.

The capture of Batoche.

As his trial began in July, 1885, Riel's lawyers wanted to offer a plea of insanity. Riel rejected this saying "I cannot abandon my dignity." He knew that to plead insanity would betray the Métis cause, making it seem insane also. Was Riel in fact insane? Medical witnesses at the trial were divided on this question.

Dr. Daniel Clark, superintendent of the Asylum for the Insane at Toronto:

> . . . I spoke to some of the half-breeds who were in all his fights, and they said positively that Riel was apparently rational enough until the Duck Lake fight, and that after the excitement of that fight he

seemed to have changed entirely and become a religious fanatic; he organized no opposition, did no fighting, but was looked upon as inspired—running about with a crucifix and calling upon the Trinity for aid. . . . On the question of the previous history of Riel. . . . There was evidence in existence of his having been committed legally to an asylum in Washington, also of his having been committed legally to Longue Pointe, Montreal, . . . I would consider him insane, but that I was not prepared to say so from my short examination.

Dr. James M. Wallace:

Q. Have you formed an opinion of his mental responsibility, of his sanity or insanity?
A. I have so far as my time and opportunities enabled me to do so.
Q. What is that opinion?
A. I have not discovered any insanity about him, no indication of insanity.
Q. What would you say then in view of the evidence and your examination? Is he of sound mind or is he not?
A. I think he is of sound mind.
Q. And capable of distinguishing right from wrong?
A. I think so.

The politicians could not agree either.

Edward Blake:

Unquestionably he had been insane. . . . What is undisputed and indisputable is that the man was insane from 1876 to 1878, and that the symptoms had recurred in the year 1885. . . .

Wilfrid Laurier:

Sir, I am not of those who look upon Louis Riel as a hero. Nature had endowed him with many brilliant qualities, but nature denied him that supreme quality without which all other qualities, however brilliant, are of no avail. Nature denied him a well-balanced mind.

The Jury:

He seemed to us no more insane than any of the lawyers and they were the ablest men in Canada. He was even more interesting than some of them.

Riel:

> ... I know that through the grace of God I am the founder of Manitoba; I know that though I have no open road for my influence, I have big influence concentrated, as a big amount of vapour in an engine. I believe by what I suffered for 15 years, by what I have done for Manitoba and the people of the North-West that my words are worth something ...
>
> It is said that I had myself acknowledged as a prophet by the Half-breeds. The Half-breeds have some intelligence. . . . It is not to be supposed that the Half-breeds acknowledge me as a prophet if they had not seen that I could see something into the future. . . .
>
> I am glad that the Crown have proved that I am the leader of the Half-breeds in the North-West. I will perhaps be one day acknowledged as more than a leader of the Half-breeds, and if I am I will have an opportunity of being acknowledged as a leader of good in this great country. . . .
>
> ... If it is any satisfaction to the doctor to know what kind of insanity I have, if they are going to call my pretensions insanity, I say, humbly, through the grace of God I believe I am the prophet of the New World. . . .

1. *From his actions in 1869 and 1885, do you think Riel was insane?*
2. *If you had sat on the jury would you have found Riel innocent or guilty of treason?*

The jury found Riel sane and guilty, but recommended mercy. The judge, however, sentenced Riel to hang. English Protestant Ontario cheered loudly. French Catholic Quebec protested equally loudly. Macdonald, who held Riel's fate in his hands, said, "Riel shall hang though every dog in Quebec bark in his favour." And so on November 16, 1885, Riel was hanged. His last words were, "I ask forgiveness of all men. I forgive all my enemies."

The execution created a deep split between English and French Canada. It would take a long time to heal.

Recently the government of Pierre Elliot Trudeau has removed the stain from Riel's name. He is no longer considered a traitor to Canada. In 1968 Trudeau made this statement:

> Riel and his followers were protesting against the Government's indifference to their problems and its refusal to consult them on matters of their vital interest. Questions of minority rights have deep roots in our history. . . . We must never forget that, in the long run, a democracy is judged by the way the majority treats the minority. Louis Riel's battle is not yet won.

Would the Northwest Rebellions have happened without Riel? Was Riel a hero or a traitor? What do you think?

Word Study

Gatling Gun   Old Tomorrow   Scrip
Métis   Provisional Government   Treason

Things to Do 1. Manitoba joined Confederation in 1871. Louis Riel believed himself to be the "Father of Manitoba". Do you think the stand taken by Riel and the Métis in 1870 helped to speed the entry of Manitoba into Confederation?

2. By 1870 the old Métis way of life appeared doomed. The great migrating buffalo herds upon which the Métis depended returned from the United States in smaller numbers each summer. At the same time more and more settlers pushed west. Faced with these problems, what could the Métis do to establish a new way of life?

3. Along with Louis Riel, three other outstanding figures led the Rebellion of 1885. They were Gabriel Dumont, a Métis, and Indian Chiefs Big Bear and Poundmaker. Write a short biography of each of these men. Try to discover why they supported the Rebellion, and their part in it.

4. What part did prejudice between French and English play in the government's attitude towards the claims of the Indians and Métis in the West? Was prejudice a factor in Riel's trial and execution? How did the death of Riel affect future relations between English and French?

7
The Conscription Crisis

On May 4, 1968, the American Gary Mason entered Canada at the Niagara Falls border. Mason was only nineteen and he did not know when he would be able to return to the United States. He was a draft dodger. He had come to Canada to escape military service in Viet Nam.

Mason was only one of thousands of such young men who refused to serve their country in war. As a result they would have to suffer the penalty for breaking the law of their country: imprisonment or banishment.

They had many reasons for their decision. Mason refused to fight because he felt the Viet Nam war was wrong. He believed America should not become involved in the wars of another country, killing and being killed. Others objected for different reasons. Some were devout Christians who believed their religion prevented them from being soldiers. They believed that the commandment "Thou shalt not kill" applied in all cases, even war. Still others objected to the war because it was taking them away from their families, their jobs, or their education.

At stake was this issue: does a country have the right to force its citizens to fight in a war against their will? Canadians too have faced this question. They faced it for the first time during World War I, and the answers threatened to split the country in two.

The Background of the Crisis

In August 1914, one of the great wars of history, World War I, began. When Great Britain and her allies France and Russia went to war against Germany and Austria, Canada too became involved. Although Confederation had made Canada a separate country in 1867, Canada was still part of the British Empire. In fact, Canada did not even declare war. When Britain declared war on Germany on August 4, 1914, Canada was at war automatically.

At the beginning of the war Canada had a very small force, since the Canadian army was based on voluntary service. However, by October of 1914 thirty-three thousand Canadian soldiers landed in Britain for training. Soon they were fighting in the front lines in France.

What was the Canadian reaction to joining in a European war?

Canadian soldiers fighting in the trenches and in the skies over France. As you can see, conditions in the trenches were bleak and miserable. The life of a flier certainly seemed glamorous by comparison. Yet the average life span of a flier in 1917 was six weeks.

Prime Minister Borden:

> If it is conceded that there is an emergency, are we not fighting in France and Flanders for the defence of Canada? . . . Where is Canada's first line of defence. . . . It is in the North Sea, where the Empire's Navy holds back Germany's power, and in the trenches where the Canadians with the other Allied armies are slowly but surely freeing the soil of France and of Belgium from the insulting tread of the invader. If that is not our first line of defence, where is it? Who then will say that the Canadian Expeditionary Force is not fighting for the defence of Canada?

Liberal leader Wilfrid Laurier:

> Today the allied nations are fighting for freedom against oppression, for democracy . . . for civilization. . . . If my words can be heard beyond the walls of this House in the province from which I come, among the men whose blood flows in my own veins, I should like them to remember that in taking their place to-day in the ranks of the Canadian army to fight for the cause of the allied nations, a double honour rests upon them.

Publisher Henri Bourassa (1914):

> It is Canada's national duty to contribute according to her resources and by fitting means of action, to the triumph and especially to the endurance of the combined efforts of France and England. . . . I have not written and will not write one line, one word, to condemn the sending of Canadian troops to Europe.

1. What is the attitude of each speaker towards Canada's participation in the war?

2. To whom is Laurier addressing his remarks?

Over the course of the next four years Canada made a great contribution in manpower to the war effort. Out of a small population of eight million, Canadians enlisted in the following numbers:

1914	59 144
1915	158 859
1916	176 919
1917	63 611

Although enlistment was high, so were the casualties. Thousands of Canadians were being killed or wounded in the front lines. Of equally great concern, it appeared that by the end of 1916, enlistment was beginning to drop. In

As enlistments began to decline by 1917, more and more posters like this one appeared. What is the significance of the names on the flag? To what emotions is this poster appealing?

January it was over twenty-nine thousand. In August 1917 enlistment had dropped to three thousand. If things did not improve, soon there would not be enough fresh troops to replace the dead and wounded. It was at this point that the bitterness of ethnic conflicts appeared.

French vs. English

By 1916 English Canada began to feel that French Canada was not doing its share in the war effort. A Member of Parliament from Ontario presented these findings:

> When this war broke out I said: At last Canada will be a united country; nothing can keep Canada from doing her full duty to the Empire in this great war. Fancy my chagrin, fancy my surprise, when I read the figures that show what our neighboring province is doing in recruiting. . . .
>
> What are the figures in regard to recruiting in this country? Allow me to place upon Hansard the figures by Provinces. These figures show the enlistments up to December 31, 1916:
>
> | | |
> |---|---|
> | Ontario | 157 908 |
> | Quebec | 41 729 |
> | Maritime provinces | 34 802 |
> | Manitoba and Saskatchewan | 77 254 |
> | Alberta | 34 517 |
> | British Columbia | 37 575 |
>
> When we take into consideration the population of each of these various districts or divisions, as represented by the last census, that of 1911, we find that the enlistments per thousand of population are as follows:
>
> | | |
> |---|---|
> | Ontario | 63 |
> | Quebec | 20 |
> | Maritime provinces | 38 |
> | Manitoba and Saskatchewan | 81 |
> | Alberta | 92 |
> | British Columbia | 104 |

1. *Which province contributed most, based on population? Which province contributed least?*

   As more criticism of Quebec's war effort followed, Henri Bourassa, publisher of the newspaper *Le Devoir*, became the spokesman for the position of French Canada. Bourassa accounted for the uneven enlistment across the country in this way:

> The newcomers from the British Isles have enlisted in much larger proportion than English-speaking Canadians born in this country, while these have enlisted, more than the French Canadians. The western Provinces have given more recruits than Ontario, and On-

tario more than Quebec. In each Province the floating population of the cities, the students, the labourers and clerks, either unemployed or threatened with dismissal, have supplied more soldiers than the farmers. . . . It proves that military service is more repugnant to the rural than the urban population.

There is among the French Canadians a larger proportion of farmers, fathers of large families, than among any other ethnical element in Canada. Above all, the French Canadians are the only group exclusively Canadian in its whole and by each of the individuals of which it is composed. . . . Their sympathies naturally go to France against Germany; but they do not think they have an obligation to fight for France. . . . English Canada, not counting the "blokes", contains a considerable proportion of people still in the first period of national incubation. . . . a fair number have not yet decided whether their allegiance is to Canada or to the Empire, whether the United Kingdom or the Canadian Confederacy is their country.

As to the newcomers from the United Kingdom, they are not Canadian in any sense. England or Scotland is their sole fatherland. . . .

In short, French-speaking Canadians enlist in much smaller number than the newcomers from England because they are more Canadian. French Canadians enlist less than English Canadians because they are exclusively Canadian.

1. *What reasons does Bourassa give for Quebec's lower enlistment?*
2. *What is the French Canadian attitude towards France? How does this differ from the English Canadian attachment to Britain?*
3. *In what way did recent immigration patterns have a bearing on the enlistment figures for English Canada?*
4. *Explain Bourassa's last statement.*

By the spring of 1917, the military authorities warned that the manpower situation was serious. Borden had to take action. Only one solution seemed possible to him: compulsory military service—*CONSCRIPTION!*

On June 11, 1917, Borden introduced the Military Service Act in Parliament. The debate raged for weeks. On one side was Borden. On the other, leading the anti-conscription forces, was Bourassa. In the middle was Wilfrid Laurier, leader of the Liberal party, who was concerned about the welfare of the whole country. Laurier had been in favour of Canada's war effort, but he too was against conscription. He said, "The law of the land declares that no man in Canada shall be subjected to compulsory military service except to repel invasion or for the defence of Canada."

Was Canada in fact in danger?

Borden:

> Canada's first line of defence is in the North Sea and in the trenches. If this war continues for two more years who shall say that we may not see German aircraft in Canada? German submarines crossed the Atlantic nearly a year ago.

Bourassa:

> The territory of Canada is not exposed to the attacks of any of the belligerent nations. An independent Canada would be to-day in absolute safety. The dangers to which her trade may be exposed result from the fact that she is a British possession. . . . It is therefore the duty of Britain to defend Canada, and not the duty of Canada to defend Britain.

The argument continued.

Borden:

> I desire to point out that this enactment is based upon the principle . . . that while the state owes to its citizens certain duties, the citizen also owes corresponding duties to the state. To the citizen the state assures protection and security of his person and property, the enforcement of law and orderly government. To the state, each citizen owes a duty of service, and the highest duty of all is the obligation to assist in defending the rights, the institutions and the liberties of his country. . . . There never has been and there never will be, an occasion when that duty could be . . . more urgent . . . than at the present time.

Bourassa:

> We are opposed to further enlistments for the war in Europe, whether by conscription or otherwise, for the following reasons:
> 1. Canada has already made a military display, in men and money proportionately superior to that of any nation engaged in the war;
> 2. any further weakening of the manpower of the country would seriously handicap agricultural production and other essential industries;
> 3. an increase in the war budget of Canada spells national bankruptcy;
> 4. it threatens the economic life of the nation and, eventually, its political independence;
> 5. conscription means national disunion and strife, and would thereby hurt the cause of the Allies to a much greater extent than the addition of a few thousand soldiers to their fighting forces could bring them help and comfort.

Canada's wartime Prime Minister, Robert Borden. What
was his position on Conscription?

1. *Do you think that Canada was in danger in 1917?*
2. *Examine closely Borden's arguments in favour of conscription. Do you think any country has the right to force conscription on its citizens? Defend your answer.*
3. *What are Bourassa's main arguments against conscription? Which ones do you feel are valid?*

The conscription bill finally passed the House of Commons. The vote was divided almost entirely along ethnic lines. English Canada voted in favour, French Canada voted against it. It appeared to the country that Quebec alone stood against conscription. For his stand against conscription Bourassa became a hated man outside Quebec. He was being called "objectionable, offensive, exasperating, arch traitor, rebel". Bourassa would not budge. He was proud of being a Canadian, and felt his position was in the best interest of all Canada.

A famous wartime election poster. Which side do you think the cartoon is supporting? Why?

Borden decided to test the popularity of the conscription bill in a general election. He invited members of all political parties to join him in forming a Union party. Some Liberals broke with Laurier and joined Borden.

Shortly before the election, Borden introduced two new measures. One gave the right to vote to women who had husbands and relatives in the army. This was the first time Canadian women were allowed to vote. The second measure took away the vote from people who had emigrated from enemy countries and had become Canadian citizens after 1902. Also forbidden to vote were those who objected to the war on religious or moral grounds.

The election of 1917 produced these results:

Province	Number of Seats in the House of Commons		Popular Vote	
	Liberal	Union	Liberal	Union
P.E.I.	2	2	12 224	10 450
Nova Scotia	4	12	48 831	40 985
New Brunswick	4	7	32 397	35 871
Quebec	62	3	240 504	61 808
Ontario	8	74	263 300	419 928
Manitoba	1	14	26 073	83 469
Sask.	0	16	30 829	68 424
Alberta	1	11	48 865	60 399
B.C.	0	13	40 050	59 944
Yukon	0	1	776	666
Total	82	153	744 849	841 944

When the soldiers' vote was counted it showed 215 849 votes in favour of Borden, and 18 522 opposed.

1. *What effect would the pre-election measures have had on the election? Do you think these actions were fair?*
2. *Was Quebec the only province to vote against Borden and conscription?*
3. *Why do you think the soldiers' vote was so heavily in favour of Borden?*

Was conscription successful? Over twenty-seven thousand Canadians became draft dodgers, sixty per cent of them from outside Quebec. Yet Borden was able to get enough recruits to bolster the Canadian army. The debate still goes on over whether conscription was a military success. Certainly from the standpoint of French-English relations it created bitterness, division, and resentment. It has been called Canada's greatest crisis.

Today Henri Bourassa is remembered as a great Canadian nationalist. What do you think?

Word Study

Allies	Draft dodgers	Trenches
Conscription	Military Service Act	Union Party

Things to Do 1. *When World War I broke out, Canada was automatically at war because of its ties with Britain. In 1939 World War II was declared. This time Canada made its own decision as to whether it would join. Between the wars, Canada matured as a nation. As a project, trace the development of Canada's independence between the wars.*

2. *Debate the proposition: "No country should have the right to force its citizens to fight a war they do not feel is their cause."*

3. *Canadian soldiers distinguished themselves on many occasions during World War I. Among the famous battles in which Canadians fought were Ypres, Mons, and Vimy Ridge. Gather information on these battles and write a summary of the part played by Canadians in the fighting.*

4. *Would you have enlisted voluntarily in the Canadian army in World War I*

(a) *if you had been a young French Canadian living in Quebec?*

(b) *if you had been a young English Canadian living in Ontario?*

8
Profiles of Canadian Women

1975 was declared International Women's Year by the United Nations. This is a sign that countries around the world are beginning to recognize women's demands for equality. In Canada, women have been fighting for equal rights and job opportunities for many years. In 1918, they received the right to vote and soon began to sit as members of Parliament. In 1957 Ellen Fairclough became our first woman Cabinet Minister. Canada has never had a woman Prime Minister, but this too may change in the near future.

The struggle for equal rights before the law and equal job opportunities is taking place on many fronts. Women in Canada today hold jobs which at one time were thought to be for men only. More and more women are seeking careers as doctors, lawyers, airplane pilots, and construction workers. There are women officers in the Royal Canadian Mounted Police.

Throughout our history, women have contributed to shaping a strong Canadian society. In this chapter we will study the achievements of some Canadian women in different centuries.

Madeleine de Verchères

In seventeenth-century New France, women and men worked together in building a new land. In a harsh environment, they shared the tasks of clearing the land, tilling the soil, building homes and raising large families. Sometimes, as in the story you are about to read, they had to fight together for their homes and lives.

The *Seigneur de Verchères* was the owner of a large farm on the banks of the St. Lawrence River, about twenty miles east of Montreal. In October 1692, the *Seigneur* was doing military service in faraway Quebec City, while his wife was in Montreal. In charge of the family property was his daughter, fourteen-year-old Marie Madeleine.

One day, Madeleine was inspecting the property along the river. Some of the *habitants* were at work in the fields. Suddenly a shot rang out. In horror, Madeleine watched as a party of forty Iroquois fell upon the unsuspecting workers. Several warriors began to chase Madeleine herself.

In Madeleine's words, this is what followed:

I ran for the fort, commending myself to the Holy Virgin. The Iroquois who chased after me, seeing that they could not catch me alive before I reached the gate, stopped and fired at me. The bullets whistled about my ears, and made the time seem very long. As soon as I was near enough to be heard, I cried out, *To arms! to arms!* hoping that somebody would come out and help me; but it was of no use. The two soldiers in the fort were so scared that they had hidden in the blockhouse. At the gate, I found two women crying for their husbands, who had just been killed. I made them go in, and then shut the gate. I next thought what I could do to save myself and the few people with me. I went to inspect the fort, and found that several palisades had fallen down, and left openings by which the enemy could easily get in. I ordered them to be set up again, and helped to carry them myself. When the breaches were stopped, I went to the blockhouse where the ammunition is kept, and here I found the two soldiers, one hiding in a corner, and the other with a lighted match in his hand. "What are you going to do with that match?" I asked. He answered, "Light the powder, and blow us all up." "You are a miserable coward," said I, "go out of this place." I spoke so resolutely that he obeyed. I then threw off my bonnet; and after putting on a hat, and taking a gun, I said to my two brothers: 'Let us fight to the death. We are fighting for our country and our religion. Remember that our father has taught you that gentlemen are born to shed their blood for the service of God and the King." . . .

I assembled all my troops, that is to say, six persons, and spoke to them thus: "God has saved us to-day from the hands of our enemies, but we must take care not to fall into their snares to-night. As for me, I want you to see that I am not afraid. I will take charge of the fort with an old man of eighty and another who never fired a gun; and you . . . will go to the blockhouse with the women and children, because that is the strongest place; and, if I am taken, don't surrender, even if I am cut to pieces and burned before your eyes." . . .

I may say with truth that I did not eat or sleep for twice twenty-four hours. I did not go once into my father's house, but kept always on the bastion, or went to the blockhouse, to see how the people there were behaving. I always kept a cheerful and smiling face, and encouraged my little company with the hope of speedy succor.

Day after day, Madeleine and her small group continued to hold off the Iroquois force. Everyone shared in the effort. The women loaded the guns while the men and young boys fired from every corner of the fort. This trick fooled the Iroquois into thinking the fort was full of troops.

Madeleine closing the gate. (The Iroquois attack on Fort Verchères.)

On the eighth night of the siege, relief finally came:

> We were a week in constant alarm, with the enemy always about us. At last Monsieur de la Monnerie, a lieutenant sent by Monsieur de Callières, arrived in the night with forty men. . . . As soon as I saw Monsieur de la Monnerie, I saluted him, and said, "Monsieur, I surrender my arms to you." He answered gallantly, "Mademoiselle, they are in good hands."

In the history of Canada Madeleine de Verchères certainly stands out as a figure of courage. Of course, today it would be difficult to find teenage heroines in her soldier mould. Yet she is not the only Canadian girl to achieve great things. Today's heroines most often come from the world of sports or entertainment. Some of the most famous in recent years include Marilyn Bell, Nancy Greene, Karen Magnussen, Cindy Nicholas, and Anne Murray. Do you know for what achievements each of these women gained her fame? Can you think of other famous Canadian heroines?

Catherine Parr Traill

Pioneer life in Canada's backwoods has often been described in a very romantic way. To many of us it seems very exciting to live in the woods, to rely on one's own skill for survival. Our reactions are probably the results of weekend camping and fishing trips, or short vacations at the cottage.

In truth, pioneer life in Canada in the 1800s was a very difficult life. It was full of hard work, discomfort, and personal disaster. The only real triumph was survival. This sort of life was even more difficult for those people who had been used to a more comfortable life in the cities. It took a great deal of courage to leave a life of leisure in England for an uncertain future in the forests of Canada.

One such "gentle pioneer" was Catherine Parr Traill. She not only succeeded as a pioneer, but actually found time to write about it. Much of what we know about the role of women in pioneer Upper Canada comes from books such as her *The Backwoods of Canada*.

Catherine Parr Strickland Traill was born in 1802, the fifth daughter of Thomas Strickland, a successful London businessman. Catherine had five sisters and three brothers. Of these, five became writers as well. Susanna, Catherine's youngest sister, shared her experiences in pioneer Canada. She too wrote about them in a famous book titled *Roughing It in the Bush*.

When Catherine was only sixteen, her father died. His business had failed and most of the family fortune was gone. Over the next ten years, Catherine busied herself with her writing career. In the meantime her younger brother Samuel took up a new life as a settler in Upper Canada.

In 1832 Catherine Strickland married Thomas Traill, a member of a well known English family. He planned to make their new home in Canada. They seemed an unlikely pair to take up pioneer life in the Canadian woods. Yet Thomas Traill had travelled much of the world and was a man of wide experience. Catherine Traill made up for her lack of experience by her great enthusiasm, energy, and determination.

In *The Backwoods of Canada* Mrs. Traill describes her experiences pioneering in early Upper Canada. Her description begins with an account of the ocean voyage. Depending on weather conditions, such trips could take anywhere from thirty to seventy-five days.

> Though we have been little more than a week on board, I am getting weary of the voyage. I can only compare the monotony of it to being weather-bound in some country inn. . . .
>
> I have endured the horrors of *mal de mer*, and except when the weather is fine I sit on a bench on the deck, wrapped in my cloak, and sew, or pace the deck with my husband. . . . I really do pity men who are not actively employed: women have always their needle as a resource against the overwhelming weariness of an idle life; but where a man is confined to a small space, such as the deck and cabin of a trading vessel, with nothing to see, nothing to hear, nothing to do, and nothing to read, he is really a very pitiable creature. Every space is utilized in a ship. The bench on which the bed of cloaks is spread for me covers the hen coop. Poor prisoners to be killed and cooked as needed!

The Traill homestead was near Lakefield, a community on the Otonabee River north of Peterborough. To reach their land, the Traills travelled by steamer, canoe, buckboard, and foot. Mrs. Traill describes her first experience plodding through the Canadian woods:

> Just as we were emerging from the gloom of the wood we found our progress impeded by a *creek*, as the boy called it, over which he told us we must pass by a log-bridge before we could get to the town. Now, the log bridge was composed of one log, or rather a fallen tree, thrown across the stream, rendered very slippery by the heavy dew that had risen from the swamp. . . . I had the ill luck to fall in up to my knees in the water, my head turning quite giddy as I came to the last step or two; thus was I wet as well as weary.

Even worse was the trip on Canadian roads by horse and wagon:

> Our progress was but slow on account of the roughness of the road, which is beset with innumerable obstacles in the shape of loose

blocks of limestone, with which the lands on the banks of the river and lakes abound; to say nothing of fallen trees, big roots, mud-holes, and corduroy bridges over which you go jolt, jolt, jolt, till every bone in your body feels as if it were being dislocated. An experienced bush-traveller avoids many hard thumps by rising up or clinging to the sides of his rough vehicle.

As the day was particularly fine, I often quitted the waggon and walked on with my husband for a mile or so.

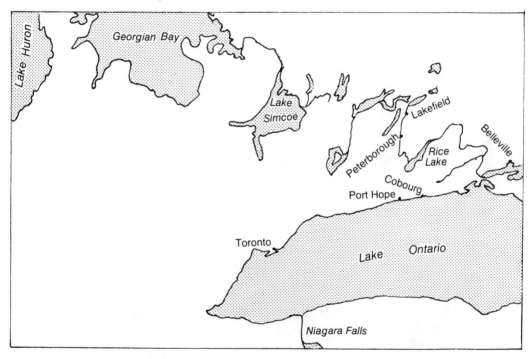

At last the Traills reached their destination. By a stroke of luck, their homestead was located beside that of Catherine's brother Samuel. With his pioneering experience, Samuel was able to help the newcomers overcome the problems of the first few months.

The first requirement was a house. For this, a "bee" was organized. Mrs. Traill describes this Canadian practice:

... We are, however, to call the "bee," and provide every thing necessary for the entertainment of our worthy *hive*. Now you know that a "bee," in American language, or rather phraseology, signifies those friendly meetings of neighbours who assemble at your summons to raise the walls of your house, shanty, barn, or any other building: this is termed a "raising bee." Then there are the logging-bees, husking-bees, chopping-bees, and quilting-bees. The nature of the work to be done gives the name to the bee. In the more populous and long-settled districts this practice is much discontinued, but it is highly useful, and almost indispensable to new settlers in the remote townships, where the price of labour is proportionately high, and workmen difficult to be procured. . . .

The log cabin they built must have been very disappointing to someone like Catherine Traill, who had been raised in a fine mansion in England. She had mixed reactions to the first Canadian log cabins she saw:

> . . . The interior of this rude dwelling presented no very inviting aspect. The walls were of rough, unhewn logs, filled between the chinks with moss and irregular wedges of wood to keep out the wind and rain. The unplastered roof displayed the rafters, covered with moss and lichens, green, yellow, and grey; above which might be seen the shingles, dyed to a fine mahogany-red by the smoke which refused to ascend the wide clay and stone chimney, to curl gracefully about the roof. . . .

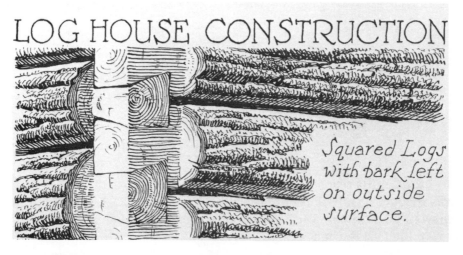

Nothing can be more comfortless than some of these shanties, reeking with smoke and dirt, the common receptacle for children, pigs, and fowls. But I have given you the dark side of the picture; I am happy to say all the shanties on the squatters' ground were not like these: on the contrary, by far the larger proportion were inhabited by tidy folks, and had one, or even two small windows, and a clay chimney regularly built up through the roof; some were even roughly floored, and possessed similar comforts with the small log-houses. . . .

In the construction of their own cabin the Traills ran into several problems. First, they found the wood used in the building was wet and "unseasoned".

> The next misfortune that happened was that the mixture of clay and lime that was to plaster the inside and outside of the house between the chinks of the logs was one night frozen to stone. Just as the work was about half completed, the frost suddenly setting in, put a stop to our proceeding for some time, as the frozen plaster yielded neither to fire nor to hot water, the latter freezing before it had any effect on the mass, and rather making bad worse. Then the workman that was hewing the inside walls to smooth them wounded himself with the broad axe, and was unable to resume his work for some time.

Fortunately the Traills had enough money to carry them through their first year, when they were clearing the land. They could not have grown enough crops to feed themselves.

Like other pioneers they found land-clearing a slow process. The Traills hired Irish labourers to clear some of their land at the cost of thirty-five dollars a hectare. Everything except the stumps was to be cleared. It would take another ten years for the stumps to decay. Progress was slow:

> We shall have about three acres [about one hectare] ready for spring crops, provided we get a good burning of that which is already chopped near the site of the house—this will be sown with oats, pumpkins, Indian corn, and potatoes: the other ten acres [four hectares] will be ready for putting in a crop of wheat. So you see it will be a long time before we reap a harvest. We could not even get in spring-wheat early enough to come to perfection this year.
>
> We shall try to get two cows in the spring, as they are little expense during the spring, summer, and autumn; and by the winter we shall have pumpkins and oat-straw for them.

Mrs. Traill's first experience with a Canadian winter brought this reaction:

> ... The 1st of March was the coldest day and night I ever experienced in my life; the mercury was down to twenty-five degrees [$-4°C$] in the house; abroad it was much lower. The sensation of cold early in the morning was very painful, producing an involuntary shuddering, and an almost convulsive feeling in the chest. Our breaths were congealed in hoar-frost on the sheets and blankets. Every thing we touched of metal seemed to freeze our fingers.

Yet she did manage to find some form of amusement even in the isolation of the woods. Her brother Samuel introduced her to one of Canada's favourite winter pastimes—sleighing:

> Soon after this I made another excursion on the ice, but it was not in quite so sound a state. We nevertheless walked on for about three-quarters of a mile [about one kilometre]. We were overtaken on our return by S—— with a handsleigh, which is a sort of barrow, such as porters use, without sides, and instead of a wheel, is fixed on wooden runners, which you can drag over the snow and ice with the greatest ease, if ever so heavily laden. S—— insisted that he would draw me home over the ice like a Lapland lady on a sledge. I was soon seated in state, and in another minute felt myself impelled forward with a velocity that nearly took away my breath. By the time we reached the shore I was in a glow from head to foot. . . .

The coming of spring brought the warm weather. It also brought a rather unpleasant surprise:

> . . . The insects are already beginning to be troublesome, particularly the black flies—a wicked-looking fly, with black body and white legs and wings; you do not feel their bite for a few minutes, but are made aware of it by a stream of blood flowing from the wound; after a few hours the part swells and becomes extremely painful.
> These "*beasties*" chiefly delight in biting the sides of the throat, ears, and sides of the cheek, and with me the swelling continues for many days. The mosquitoes are also very annoying. I care more for the noise they make even than their sting. To keep them out of the house we light little heaps of damp chips, the smoke of which drives them away; but this remedy is not entirely effectual, and is of itself rather an annoyance.

During the summer, the first of the nine Traill children was born. Catherine Traill was unable to help much with the farmwork that summer, but she busied herself cultivating a garden. She also learned to make bread, butter, porridge from Indian corn, and preserves. She developed a skill for spinning wool, dyeing yarn, knitting and sewing, as well as looking after her pigs, hens and ducks.

Canadian wildlife continued to interest her. She tried to identify new species of flowers, birds, and animals. Very concerned that the spread of settlement might destroy the beauties of nature, she was determined to preserve this inheritance for herself and her children.

Catherine Traill certainly had come a long way in one year from her comfortable life in England. She noted that pioneer life produced a different attitude to social class. In England, the difference between upper and lower classes

Catherine Parr Traill as an old woman.

was still very noticeable. As members of the upper class, the Traills could not forget their upbringing altogether. They still conducted themselves as members of the "gentleman class". Yet in the Canadian woods these class differences were starting to break down. Mrs. Traill notes:

> Our society is mostly military or naval; so that we meet on equal grounds, and are, of course, well acquainted with the rules of good breeding and polite life; too much so to allow any deviation from those laws that good taste, good sense, and good feeling have established among persons of our class.
>
> Yet here it is considered by no means derogatory to the wife of an officer or gentleman to assist in the work of the house, or to perform its entire duties, if occasion requires it; to understand the mystery of soap, candle, and sugar-making; to make bread, butter, and cheese, or even to milk her own cows, to knit and spin, and prepare the wool for the loom. In these matters we bush-ladies have a wholesome disregard of what Mr and Mrs So-and-so think or say. We pride ourselves on conforming to circumstances. . . .

The Traills spent seven years in their backwoods home. During this time they suffered through serious diseases, bad weather, and poor crops. Yet they did manage to survive. Finally they sold their farm and moved to a house near Peterborough. In 1846 they moved again to the Rice Lake area, a region which Catherine Traill especially loved. In 1858 Thomas Traill died.

Catherine Traill received a grant of money from the government in England, for she was by now a famous writer. Her books *The Backwoods of Canada, Canadian Crusoes,* and *The Female Emigrant's Guide,* as well as her nature writings, were well known in England. With this money she bought a house back in Lakefield, near her brother Samuel. She lived here the rest of her life, continuing her writings, and honoured by all as one of the last of the early pioneers of Upper Canada. She died in 1899 at the age of ninety-seven.

Catherine Traill faced the trials of pioneer life as other Canadian women had. Through it all she continued to express faith and confidence in her new land. Her spirit is summed up in one sentence from *The Backwoods of Canada*: "Canada is the land of hope; here everything is new; everything is going forward."

Nellie McClung

Are women "persons"? You might think the question silly. How could anyone possibly think that women were not "persons", just as men are? (In lawyer's language a "person" is someone who has all the rights guaranteed by the law, such as voting, or owning property). It might surprise you to learn that it was not until 1929 that women in Canada became "persons" before the law. Before this time the law stated that women "are not persons in matters relating to rights and privileges."

One of the women who helped change this law and push forward the cause of women in Canada was Nellie McClung. Nellie McClung was one of the most remarkable women in Canadian history. Over her long career "Mrs. Western Canada", as she was called, served as teacher, politician, author, wife, mother, and leader in the early Canadian women's movement.

Nellie McClung was born in Chatsworth, Ontario, in 1873, the youngest of six children of John and Letitia Mooney. When she was seven, the family moved to a homestead in Manitoba. They travelled by boat and train to St. Boniface. From here to their new home near Wawanesa they would have to travel by wagon. The distance was over three hundred kilometres over muddy, swampy roads. Fifteen kilometres a day was a good distance, and seven-year-old Nellie walked every metre of it.

The Mooney family spent the first winter in a one-room log cabin with a grass roof. The temperature inside the home often dropped to well below freezing. Prairie life was hard, and the women worked as hard as the men in farming the land. In their "spare time" it was the women who fed, clothed, and cared for the men and children. It is not surprising that many Prairie women died of overwork at early ages.

The children too were kept busy. There were very few schools, and even these were usually too far away for most children. Nellie McClung herself did not go to school until she was ten. Before this she could not read. Girls had a particularly hard life in those times. They were told not to have opinions contrary to those of men. They were not allowed to go out unless they were accompanied by a father or brother. They could not compete in sports against the boys because they had to keep their legs covered. Hockey, for example, was forbidden to Nellie because her parents were afraid her red bloomers might drop.

Nellie McClung was determined to become a teacher. At the age of sixteen she set off for Winnipeg and Teachers' College. Her first teaching job in Manitou, when she was only seventeen, paid her forty dollars a month. While teaching in Manitou she met Robert Wesley McClung, and six years later they were married. Wes McClung encouraged his wife in her ambitions, especially her desire to write. He did not share the accepted male opinion that a woman's role should only be that of housewife and mother.

Mrs. Nellie McClung.

The first of their four children was born in 1897. After this Mrs. McClung devoted much of her time to trying to right what she considered were the evils in society. In her mind, one of the worst social evils was drunkenness. In the West there were few forms of entertainment available. Drinking was the most common form of escape from the loneliness and drudgery of daily life. Women and children were most often the innocent victims of this frontier problem.

Nellie McClung was determined to help them. She joined the Women's Christian Temperance Union, a group dedicated to abolishing the sale and use of alcohol. Working for a common goal with other women, she discovered her talent for public speaking, and a new career.

Her efforts were not always successful. Once she was trying to demonstrate the dangers of alcohol to a class of schoolchildren. In her experiment she brought out two glasses, one filled with water, the other with whisky. Into each glass she dropped a dew worm. Of course the worm in the water survived, while the one in the whisky curled up and died. In triumph, Mrs. McClung asked the children what lesson they had learned. One little boy thought for a moment, then replied, "We learn that if we drink lots of whisky we'll never have worms."

At the same time she became a successful writer. Her first novel, *Sowing Seeds in Danny*, published in 1908, sold over one hundred thousand copies. It was the first of nine successful books, and it brought her both money and fame. This success did not prevent her from remembering the plight of women less fortunate than she. Her next efforts were aimed at bringing political rights to Canadian women.

Nellie McClung helped found the Political Equality League. The aim of the League was to obtain the vote for women and to improve working conditions for women in factories. These efforts brought Nellie McClung and the League into conflict with the government of Manitoba. The Premier of Manitoba, Sir Redmond Roblin, believed politics was no place for women. He was fond of saying that politics was often a hard, dirty business, and that Canadian women were too pure and noble to be involved in it. He told Mrs. McClung that, "Nice women don't want the vote."

Her reply was to give her a reputation as a hard fighter for women's rights. She told Roblin, "By nice women you probably mean selfish women, who have no more thought for the underpaid, overworked women than a pussycat in a sunny window has for the starving kitten in the street. Now in that sense I am not a nice woman, for I do care."

The efforts of the League were finally rewarded. In 1916 Manitoba became the first province in Canada to grant women the vote. Alberta and Saskatchewan followed in the same year. The other provinces were slower to follow their example:

British Columbia	1917
Ontario	1917
Nova Scotia	1918
New Brunswick	1919
Prince Edward Island	1922
Quebec	1940
Federal Government	1918

Now that women had the right to vote, Nellie McClung believed they should run for office. She felt that women could make a great contribution to Canada's political life. She stated, "Women have cleaned up things since time began, and if women ever get into politics there will be a cleaning out of pigeonholes and forgotten corners on which the dust of years has fallen."

By 1921, the McClungs had moved to Alberta. Mrs. McClung ran in the provincial election of that year and was elected. She held her seat in the Alberta legislature for five years. During this time she fought for laws in support of medical care for children, mothers' allowance, and property rights for women. She also favoured birth control and family planning.

In 1928, Nellie McClung and some of her friends had a new battle to win. They had discovered that under British law women were not legally "persons". The group fought this law all the way to the Supreme Court of Canada. Surprisingly, Canada's highest court upheld the law that women were indeed not "persons". The determined women took their case all the way to the Privy Council in England. In 1929, the Council finally decided to reverse the law, and at last agreed that women were after all "persons".

Nellie McClung continued to write, lecture and travel in her efforts to improve social conditions not only for women, but for people all over Canada. She died in 1951 at the age of seventy-eight. Her husband Wes wrote, "She has fought a good fight and kept the faith."

Dr. James Barry: Canada's First Woman Doctor

In Canada today women are finding more and more doors to different professions being opened to them. The entry of women in what were at one time strictly male professions, such as law and medicine, is now commonplace. For example, there are almost four thousand women doctors serving in Canada today. A milestone was reached when, in June 1974, Dr. Bette Stephenson became the first woman president of the Canadian Medical Association.

This acceptance was not easily won. Only one hundred years ago men were shocked when women tried to enter universities. This was bad enough, but the desire of women to become doctors? Ridiculous! Women had no need for higher education. Their role was to care for their families. Besides, the Victorian period considered the human body disgusting. Its study was an improper thing for young ladies.

It was not until 1879 that women were first admitted to Toronto School of Medicine. When Queen's University in Kingston, Ontario, admitted women to its School of Medicine, the male students went on strike. The problem was finally solved in 1883 when women were given their own medical school.

Yet there was a woman doctor who practised medicine in Canada long before this. She managed to accomplish this feat by using the only way open to her—she disguised herself as a man! Her name was James Miranda Barry. Little is known of James Barry's early life. She was born in England, probably the daughter of a certain Mrs. Bulkeley. She came under the protection of an uncle, James Barry. The uncle was a firm believer in higher education and in women's rights. One person the young girl met at this time was a General Miranda, who had a large library of medical books. It was he who interested her in medicine.

The uncle died before his niece had a chance to go to university. His death, however, provided the young girl with a perfect alias. She adopted the name James Miranda Barry, disguised herself as a man, and was admitted to Edinburgh University. Later she studied medicine in London. How did she manage to get away with this pretence?

Her own appearance helped her. She was described as a small, fragile person, about one and a half metres tall. She had small hands and a long, masculine nose. She kept her reddish hair short, so there was little to betray her secret.

Dr. Barry joined the Army Medical Department and rose quickly through the ranks. She was appointed Colonial Medical Inspector to South Africa. In this job she did much to try to improve conditions in jails, mental asylums, and leper colonies. Dr. Barry had a fiery temper and did not always get along well with her superiors. At the same time some of her co-workers made note of her unusual personality. One recalled his first sight of Barry:

> I beheld a beardless lad apparently my own age, with an unmistakably Scotch type of countenance—reddish hair, high cheek bones. There was a certain effeminacy in his manner, which he seemed always striving to overcome.

Barry's constant quarrels with her superiors often caused her trouble. She was transferred to a series of postings, from Mauritius in Africa, to Jamaica, St Helena, Trinidad, Malta, Corfu, and the Crimea in Russia. In each of these places she did an outstanding job and was considered one of the best doctors in the army. She continued to receive many honours and promotions.

At last, in her sixties, she was sent to Canada as Inspector-General of Hospitals. In Canada Dr. Barry continued to carry out helpful reforms. Dr. Barry was a vegetarian herself, but she realized that the soldiers needed a balanced diet. She worked hard at improving the quality of food they were receiving. She also improved conditions in the soldiers' barracks. Before this time married soldiers and their wives all slept in the same barracks with unmarried soldiers. Dr. Barry fought hard to provide private rooms for each family. While Dr. Barry argued with her superiors, she must have been very popular with the ordinary Canadian soldiers.

In 1859 Dr. Barry became ill and returned to England. She was very much afraid of serious disease, for there was danger that her secret would be discovered. Once before when she had been very ill a doctor had discovered the truth. However, he promised to keep silence, and her secret was not revealed.

Dr. Barry was sixty-five now, and her recovery was slow. She asked to be sent back to Canada but her request was refused. She died six days later. When she died, her secret was at last revealed. At first many people refused to believe that Dr. Barry had actually been a woman. How could a woman have been ad-

Dr. Barry's grave in Kensal Green Cemetery. London, (England).

mitted to a university? How could she have become a doctor? How could a woman possibly do as fine a job as Dr. Barry had done? How could she have kept her secret for so many years?

The surprise and shock at Dr. Barry's secret was due to the Victorian period's prejudice against women. People simply could not believe that women could do the jobs men did. Today this attitude is changing. Women do not have to disguise themselves as men any longer in order to have a career. This progress is due in great measure to the courage and sacrifice of pioneer women such as Dr. James Miranda Barry.

Karen Kain

Great stars in the entertainment field have always held a special place in the hearts of Canadians. Whether they are movie stars, athletes, ballerinas, or singers, they are usually greatly admired, especially by young people. Unfortunately, many Canadian entertainers in the past had to leave Canada in order to gain recognition. When they became famous in other countries they found themselves accepted as stars by Canadians.

In the field of entertainment, Canadian women seem to have been far more successful than men. Mary Pickford, who left her native Toronto at the age of ten, became the greatest female star of the silent film era. She was often billed as "the world's most popular woman". Barbara Ann Scott and Karen Magnussen in skating, Ann Heggtveit and Nancy Greene in skiing, and Elaine Tanner in swimming have won gold medals for Canada in world championships. Marilyn Bell won world-wide fame for her courageous swim across Lake Ontario in 1953. In the music field today, Canada's most popular and famous singer is also a woman, Anne Murray.

Perhaps the most difficult of all fields of entertainment in which to achieve fame is ballet. Ballet has been a popular form of entertainment in other parts of the world for centuries. In Canada the popularity of ballet is much more recent. For this reason most of the famous ballet dancers come from other countries, especially the United States and Europe. In the past, Canadian ballerinas who wished to become famous had to go abroad to gain recognition.

Today there is a young ballerina who is achieving world-wide fame while remaining in Canada. Her name is Karen Kain.

Have you ever seen a ballet performance? Many young people who have never seen ballet seem to feel for some reason that it is "sissy". Actually ballet dancing requires great physical strength and athletic ability. There is more energy required to dance ballet than to play most sports, including football, hockey, and tennis. Indeed great ballet dancers are among the most athletic performers in the world.

Karen Kain with members of the corps de ballet in the National Ballet of Canada production of *Solitaire*, choreographed by Kenneth MacMillan.

Modern ballet takes two main forms. The most popular form, *BALLET D'ACTION*, is dancing which tells a story. It has a plot and characters like any drama. The dancers, however, do not use the spoken word. Everything is expressed through music, dancing, and gestures. *ABSTRACT BALLET* is dancing which expresses an idea or mood. In this form of ballet there is no plot and there are no characters. It is as though the dancers were "expressing poetry" by the music and the dancing.

One of the very finest ballet dancers in the world is Karen Kain. Miss Kain was born in Hamilton, Ontario, in 1952. Her mother came from a Manitoba farm and her father was born in Winnipeg. In 1959 her parents took her to see her first ballet performance. From that time, the child knew she wanted to be a ballerina. At first her parents resisted. They knew the road was difficult, and the chances for success small. But Karen was determined. She took her first lesson at the age of nine. Two years later she entered the National Ballet School. In 1969 she joined the National Ballet of Canada and soon became one of its leading dancers.

Immediately she began to receive recognition. In June 1973 Karen Kain and Frank Augustyn were chosen to represent Canada at an International Ballet Competition in Moscow. The pair won first prize in the duet category and Karen Kain tied for a silver medal in the women's division. It was a great achievement. International recognition soon followed. One American critic called her "one of the most talented ballerinas in the Western World . . . a very special dancer." Another asked, "Who is her equal?"

Despite her fame, Karen Kain must continue to work hard. Dancers in the National Ballet must rehearse and drill eight hours a day, five days a week. Once, when the Company was stranded in the Maritimes by an overnight snowstorm, they held class on the deck of the ferry to Prince Edward Island.

For Miss Kain, there are sometimes dangers of another sort when she is dancing. She is very nearsighted. This creates problems when dancing because, as she notes, "I can't see and sometimes my partner is just a blur on the other side of the stage. I can't wear contact lenses, and I can hardly wear glasses on stage." Once, as she leaped gracefully through the air, she almost missed her partner altogether. Fortunately he caught her before she landed in the orchestra.

The great amount of work and dedication necessary for success has also meant sacrifices. She would like to skate and ski, "but they are too dangerous— I might hurt myself and I can't take that risk." She also likes to cook, but is afraid of putting on weight. "I'm about 112 pounds and I eat like a horse and I'm always hungry," she says. "But apart from my appearance I have to remember my partners. They have to lift me all the time without it appearing any effort at all."

Canadians can take pride in the fame won by Karen Kain. Until recently it would not have been possible for a ballet dancer to remain in Canada and reach stardom. Today when Karen Kain dances in other countries, it is as a member of the National Ballet of Canada. Her success may encourage performers in all fields to stay and work in Canada. In this way they may succeed in gaining respect for both themselves and their country.

Agnes MacPhail, first woman elected to the House of Commons (1921).

Jeanne Sauvé (Liberal) Minister of Science and Technology (appointed 1972) and Minister of Communications (appointed 1975) in the Federal Government.

Grace Hartman, elected National President of the Canadian Union of Public Employees in 1975. This union is one of the largest in the country.

Dr. Bette Stephenson, first woman president of the Canadian Medical Association (1974-75), appointed Minister of Labour for Ontario in 1975.

Grace MacInnis, New Democratic M.P. for Vancouver-Kingsway, first elected in 1965.

Flora MacDonald, Conservative M.P. for Kingston and the Islands, elected 1972.

Word Study

Suffragette
Women's Liberation
Ballerina

Women's Christian
Temperance Union

Abstract Ballet
Ballet d'Action

Things to Do 1. *Debate these propositions. a) "Woman's place is in the home." b) "There are certain jobs in Canada which should not be open to women."*

2. *With the help of your teacher and librarian, find information on the Suffragette movement at the turn of the century. What were the Suffragette's basic demands? How many of them have been met?*

3. *One group fighting for women's rights put out a "Housewife's Bill of Rights". Among its demands are:*
   —A six-day work week
   —Paid vacations
   —Better working conditions
   —Free child-care centres.
Do you agree with these proposals?

4. *Canadian women seem to have reached stardom in the entertainment world more often than men. Can you suggest reasons for this?*

5. *Take a survey in your class. How many girls plan to have a career after they finish school? What careers seem to be the most popular among the girls? How many girls have chosen careers which in the past were considered "for men only"?*

6. *Among the jobs housewives must perform are the following:*

—cook
—dishwasher
—laundress
—seamstress
—practical nurse
—gardener
—housekeeper.

If these and other tasks were paid for on a professional level, a housewife would earn $257 per week, or about $13 400 per year. Do you think housewives should be paid?

7. *In this chapter we have had a glimpse of a few outstanding Canadian women. There have been many outstanding women in Canadian history. The list includes:*

—Marie de l'Incarnation
—Jeanne Mance
—Pauline Johnson
—Emily Carr
—Emily Stowe
—Ellen Fairclough
—Madame Vanier
—Mazo de la Roche
—Teresa Stratas
—Marilyn Bell
—Elizabeth Arden
—Lois Marshall

In what fields did each of these women gain fame? Write a brief biography of one of them.

Index

TIME LINE

50 000 B.C. ———— "Indians" arrive in North America.

Indians settle near Scarborough, — 7 000 B.C.
Ontario.

A.D. 1000 ———— Norse explorers discover Newfoundland and Labrador.

Columbus re-discovers America ———— 1492
for Europe.

1534 ———— Jacques Cartier makes his first voyage to Canada.

Champlain founds a French ———— 1608
colony at Quebec City.

1617 ———— The family of Louis Hébert becomes the first official settlers in New France.

Rupert's Land is granted by ———— 1670
Charles II of England to the
Hudson's Bay Company.

1692 ———— Madeleine de Verchères makes her courageous stand against the Iroquois.

The British build a naval base ———— 1749
at Halifax.

1759 ———— Wolfe defeats Montcalm on the Plains of Abraham.

The Treaty of Paris gives New ———— 1763
France to Britain.

1774 ———— The Quebec Act assures French Canadians of their basic rights and institutions.

The outbreak of the American ———— 1776
Revolution.

1783 ———— The end of the American Revolution is followed by a wave of Loyalist migrations to Canada.

Alexander Mackenzie reaches ———— 1793
the Pacific Ocean.

1811 ———— Selkirk establishes the Red River Settlement in Manitoba.

Canada and Britain go to war ———— 1812
against the United States.

1837 ———— Mackenzie and Papineau lead rebellions in Upper and Lower Canada.

The Act of Union joins Upper ———— 1841
and Lower Canada under
a common government.

1861-1865 ———— The United States fights a bitter Civil War.

Canadian Confederation. ———— 1867